Good *and* Evil
in the Garden
of Democracy

Good *and* Evil
in the Garden
of Democracy

RODNEY WALLACE KENNEDY

CASCADE *Books* • Eugene, Oregon

GOOD AND EVIL IN THE GARDEN OF DEMOCRACY

Copyright © 2023 Rodney Wallace Kennedy. All rights reserved. Except for brief quotations in critical publications or reviews, no part of this book may be reproduced in any manner without prior written permission from the publisher. Write: Permissions, Wipf and Stock Publishers, 199 W. 8th Ave., Suite 3, Eugene, OR 97401.

Cascade Books
An Imprint of Wipf and Stock Publishers
199 W. 8th Ave., Suite 3
Eugene, OR 97401

www.wipfandstock.com

PAPERBACK ISBN: 978-1-6667-1297-1
HARDCOVER ISBN: 978-1-6667-1298-8
EBOOK ISBN: 978-1-6667-1299-5

Cataloguing-in-Publication data:

Names: Kennedy, Rodney Wallace, author.

Title: Good and Evil in the Garden of Democracy / Rodney Wallace Kennedy.

Description: Eugene, OR: Cascade Books, 2023 | Includes bibliographical references and index.

Identifiers: ISBN 978-1-6667-1297-1 (paperback) | ISBN 978-1-6667-1298-8 (hardcover) | ISBN 978 1-6667-1299-5 (ebook)

Subjects: LCSH: Christianity and culture—United States—History—21st century. | Trump, Donald, 1946-—Language. | Democracy. | Rhetoric—Political aspects—United States.

Classification: BR526 .K55 2023 (print) | BR526 (ebook)

APRIL 11, 2023 6:04 PM

To Vin, Kirkland, Melissa, Jennifer, Jeffrey, Camron, Emily, Katie, Isaiah, Cleary, and Soren.

Children and grandchildren who deserve a world of goodness.

Contents

Preface | ix

Acknowledgments | xv

Introduction | 3

Chapter 1
Good and Evil Rhetoric in Proverbs and Plato | 26

Chapter 2
Biblical Good and Evil:
   A Picture of the Evil One from the Psalms | 105

Chapter 3
Rhetorical Evil:
   Trump's Evil in Starkest Terms–"Hitler's 'Battle'" | 119

Chapter 4
The Rhetorical Good: Vaclav Havel | 152

Chapter 5
Singing for Democracy | 178

Conclusion | 202

Bibliography | 211

Preface

I CANNOT THINK OF A time when I have been more upset and heartbroken than on January 6, 2021. Drinking even more coffee than usual (some of it with Bailey's), pacing the room, my eyes remained glued to the television as I watched and listened to President Trump incite his followers to march on the Capitol. What he said went beyond the pale of sedition in my mind, but to his followers he was simply repeating the fact that the election had been unfairly stolen from him. What happened can only be described as something between a coup and an insurrection. Trauma and shock made understanding impossible. When Trump finally gave in to demands from his allies to issue a statement, he gave one of his usual noncommittal statements. It was barely different from his "good people on both sides" statement after Charlottesville. The Donald, employing his favorite low-grade rhetorical trope, paralipsis, offered with one hand and took back with the other. "The Donald giveth and the Donald taketh away." His mystical stereotyping, his syrupy sentimentality, spoke of loving the domestic terrorists rummaging through the capitol building. In a video, Trump spoke of them as special people. He called them "great patriots" and explained their criminal actions as "these are the things and events that happen when a sacred landslide victory is so unceremoniously and viciously stripped away from great patriots who have been badly and unfairly treated for so long. Go home in love and peace. Remember this day forever!"[1] Perhaps there has never been a more captious president as he unleashed a rabble on the Capitol and on democracy.

Historian David Blight makes the case clear: "Our democracy allows a twice-impeached, criminally inclined ex-president, who publicly fomented an attempted coup against his own government, and still

---

1. Miller and Colvin, "'Remember this day forever!'"

operates as a gangster leader of his political party, to peacefully reside in our midst while under investigation for his misdeeds. We believe in rule of law, and therefore await verdicts of our judicial system and legislative inquiry." Impatient at the slowness of Lady Justice, I have taken up Blight's other suggestions: "Some of us pick up our pens and do what we can."[2]

January 6 tore the scab off an already deeply wounded democracy. As I sat with my eyes glued to CNN on that fateful day, I felt the wheels can come off the vehicle of democracy. Words from G. K. Chesterton seemed to fit the unfolding tragedy of democracy. "To fall into any one of the fads that offer alternatives to [democracy from authoritarianism to fascism to communism to theocracy]" would have been "obvious and tame. But to have avoided them all has been one whirling adventure; and in my vision the heavenly chariot flies thundering through the ages, the dull political heresies sprawling and prostrate, the wild truth reeling but erect."[3] I confess that on January 6, with a moody president oscillating between doing nothing and blaming the whole sordid affair on Speaker of the House Nancy Pelosi, I thought the "heavenly chariot" had crashed and burned. Then I realized that January 6 was merely sequel to the next two years. The prequel, which we should have seen coming, has been explained by Blight: "Yet Trumpism unleashed on 6 January, and every day before and since over a five-year period, a crusade to slowly poison the American democratic experiment with a movement to overturn decades of pluralism, increased racial and gender equality, and scientific knowledge. To what end? Establishing a hopeless white utopia for the rich and the aggrieved."[4] Never have the words of Vaclav Havel been more prophetic: "In this way, lies, violence, and hate become an indissoluble trinity. Each needs the others. Half-truth hates because it is afraid and, because it is afraid, employs violence."[5]

I should explain my motivation for writing yet another book about Donald Trump. I am a dissident of the Age of Trump. Stanley Hauerwas, in the preface to *Working with Words*, says, "The world probably does not need another book by me."[6] Those words made me ponder whether the world needs another book about Donald Trump. My answer, as this work

---

2. Blight, "Trump Has Birthed a New 'Lost Cause' Myth."
3. Chesterton, *Orthodoxy*, Kindle ed.
4. Chesterton, *Orthodoxy*, Kindle ed.
5. Havel, *Power of the Powerless*, 211.
6. Hauerwas, *Working with Words*, ix.

makes obvious, was yes. My reasons for writing about Trump are many. Trump is still a danger, a menace to democracy. "I think our democracy is in trouble," US District Judge Reggie Walton said, "because, unfortunately, we have charlatans like our former president who doesn't, in my view, really care about democracy and only about power."[7] I am convinced that Trump remains an important subject for evaluation because he has created a certain spirit in our political environment, and I believe it is toxic. Most of all, I write because I am a dissident, a dissident in the description offered by Vaclav Havel: "You do not become a 'dissident' just because you decide one day to take up this most unusual career. You are thrown into it by your personal sense of responsibility, combined with a complex set of external circumstances. You are cast out of the existing structures and placed in a position of conflict with them. It begins as an attempt to do your work well and ends with being branded an enemy of society."[8]

My claiming of the title of *dissident* offers me no status or power. I am just another dissident you find on every street corner, but I am convinced that this is good and necessary work. My hope is that I am not part of a small and isolated minority who think differently from everyone else. I confess to the longing that I speak aloud, write about, and reflect upon, what many others think. This has to do with the attempt to counter the notion that Trump simply says out loud, in his offensive and insulting ways, what his followers are thinking. Thus, I write as an anti-Trump dissident.

The term *dissident* doesn't usually occur in democratic societies, but we live in strange times. Since Democrats have been branded as "demons and devils," it appears to be within the realm of reason to refute this charge by claiming the title of *dissident*. A dissident may be defined as a person who has decided to live within the truth instead of the toxic environment of lies that prop up the Age of Trump. The original horizon of my attention was biblical and theological in nature. I gravitated toward a rhetorical study of ethos before my commitment reached beyond the narrow context of my immediate disciplines and my work became political in nature. While I don't think of myself as a direct political force, I am being political. My attempt is to be political in the sense that John Howard Yoder promotes in *The Politics of Jesus*.

---

7. Davis, "Judge Calls Donald Trump a 'Charlatan.'"
8. Havel, *Power of the Powerless*, 63.

My overall goal is to show the politics of Trump to be aligned with the ancient politics of the world identified by St. Paul as that of the "rulers, against the authorities, against the cosmic powers of this present darkness, against the spiritual forces of evil in the heavenly places."[9] Trump stands in the line of an infamous parade that extends from Pharaoh, Pilate, Herod, Caesar, Hitler, Putin, and an assortment of dictators and fascists. He is a cipher on the political stage. If you have seen one Donald Trump, you have seen them all.

A dissident, according to Havel, is usually a person who leans towards intellectual pursuits, "writing" people, "people for whom the written word is primary—and often the only—political medium they command."[10] From personal experience, I know that there is an invisible line you cross without becoming aware of it—beyond which I was treated as an "enemy" by the evangelical church that introduced me to faith in Jesus. The personal attacks I have received from, for example, the legion of creationists in the orbit of Ken Ham, has included the church I pastor, the seminary where I teach, and the seminary at which I studied. There is clearly nothing I can do about this except embrace the term of *dissident* as being of less emotional furor than the names I am now called by those who hate my work.

I am a dissident but that is not my profession. A dissident might be considered a person whose profession is grumbling about the state of things. In fact, as a dissident I am simply a Baptist pastor, a homiletics instructor at a Baptist seminary, a writer for Baptist Global News, *Word & Way*, and www.rightingamerica.net. My dissent is of the order of doing what I feel I must, and this puts me in the crosshairs of many evangelicals and many Republicans. At no point have I decided to be a professional malcontent. In fact, I was surprised to learn that my writing and preaching was considered dangerous or radical. I didn't discover I was a dissident until long after I had become one. So being a dissident is not my profession; it is my existential attitude. I am one of many who try to live within the truth, one of millions who want to but cannot. What I do should not be considered courageous, but simple honesty, from my perspective.

For five years Trump had been undermining democracy with a rhetoric of demolition and dissension. Historian David Blight asks,

---

9. Eph 6:12.
10. Havel, *Power of the Powerless*, 57.

PREFACE

"American democracy is in peril and nearly everyone paying attention is trying to find the best way to say so. Should we in the intellectual classes position our warnings in satire, in jeremiads, in social scientific data, in historical analogy, in philosophical wisdom we glean from so many who have instructed us about the violence and authoritarianism of the 20th century? Or should we just scream after our holiday naps?"[11] Blight makes clear that this is a battle between good and evil in a democracy confused about the meaning of good and evil. Why do I keep writing about Donald Trump? As Winston Churchill said of Hitler: "This is only the first sip, the first foretaste of a bitter cup which will be proferred to us year by year unless by a supreme recovery of moral health and martial vigour, we arise again and take our stand for freedom as in the olden time."[12] I am convinced that Trump is an evil person, on the order of, at least rhetorically, Hitler, and intent on the destruction of democracy. I am no Winston Churchill, and I'm not saying Donald Trump is Adolf Hitler, but I am drawing comparisons to the rhetoric in opposition to Hitler. Early on, Churchill's voice was a solitary one. He was criticized, castigated, ignored, and considered out of his mind as he consistently warned against the growing power of Hitler. On a lesser scale, perhaps, I assume the same rhetorical stance as Winston Churchill. I believe that the warnings about the dangers of Donald Trump are not only necessary for our future safety but are required by all the standards of truth-telling and honesty in our nation.

While the rest of the world ignored Churchill's prophetic warnings, they seemed to be like the people Søren Kierkegaard wrote about in relation to the Bible: "There is always something one has to look into first of all, and it always seems to know one has first of all to have the doctrine in perfect form before one can begin to live—that is say, one never begins."[13] Churchill, writing in a similar vein, responded to the First Lord of the Admiralty's assertion that everything was proceeding satisfactorily.

> We are always "reviewing the position." Everything, he assured us, is entirely fluid. I am sure that that is true. Anyone can see what the position is. The Government simply cannot make up their minds, or they cannot get the Prime Minister to make up his mind. *So they go on in strange paradox, decided only to be undecided, resolved to be irresolute, adamant for drift, solid for*

---

11. Blight, "Trump Has Birthed a New 'Lost Cause' Myth."
12. Churchill, "We Take Our Stand for Freedom."
13. Kierkegaard, *Journal*, 150.

fluidity, all powerful to be impotent. So we go on preparing for months and years—precious, perhaps vital to the greatness of Britain—for the locusts to eat. They will say to me, "A Minister of Supply is not necessary, for all is going well." I deny it. "The position is satisfactory." It is not true. "All is proceeding according to plan." We know what that means.[14]

The same nonchalant approach seems to allow Trump to continue his demolition of democracy. People say he's just being Donald. People say that he means well but he's just telling it like it is. Even when his supporters know he is lying, they seem impressed that he can lie and get away with it and not have his political career destroyed.

I don't find any of those excuses plausible. "In politics, being deceived is no excuse," Churchill said. "I have been mocked and censured as a scaremonger and even a warmonger, by those whose complacency and inertia have brought us all nearer to war and war nearer to us all. But I have the comfort of knowing I have spoken the truth and done my duty. Indeed, I am more proud of the long series of speeches which I have made on defense and foreign policy in the last four years than of anything I have ever been able to do, in all my forty years of public life."[15]

While I expect the opprobrium that this writing will elicit, I am fully prepared to accept all the consequences. I don't belong to a church that can excommunicate me. I am unmoved by the critics among the evangelicals, having previously done battle with the minions of Ken Ham of the Creation Museum. This is a matter of evil and good that requires attention biblically and rhetorically. I am not worried that my book will be controversial. Like Flannery O'Connor, what disturbs me is that the book may not be controversial enough. No doubt calling a person evil opens the door to all sorts of scurrilous charges of self-righteousness, hypocrisy, and meanness. I accept these charges and inconsistencies for the greater good of overcoming evil in one of its most chameleonic forms—Donald J. Trump.

---

14. Churchill, *Blood, Toil, Tears, and Sweat*, 121. Quoted in Wittenberg, "Churchill Appraises Hitler," 59 (emphasis mine).

15. Churchill, cited in Gilbert, *Churchill*, 539.

Acknowledgments

THIS BOOK IS THE sequel to *The Immaculate Mistake*. It is the result of five years of work and the contributions and encouragement of many. I would like to thank William Trollinger, history professor at the University of Dayton, for encouraging my writing for the last fifteen years. William Vance Trollinger Jr. has graciously allowed my essays into print at www.rightingamerica.net. Together with his wife, Susan L. Trollinger, English professor at the University of Dayton, I have felt the joy of their encouragement, their willingness to read my sermon manuscripts every week and edit my essays. Bill has written the prefaces for two of my other books. "Faithful friends are a sturdy shelter: whoever finds one has found a treasure" (Sirach 6:14). The Trollingers are a treasure to me.

Thanks also to two of my mentors, Andrew M. King and Kenneth Zagacki. These rhetorical scholars served on my dissertation committee at Louisiana State University and have remained involved in my writing across more than thirty years.

I also want to thank the editor of Baptist Global News, Mark Wingfield, and the editors at *Word&Way*, Jeremy Fuzy, Brian Kaylor, and Beau Underwood, for finding space for my essays every month. My life has been opened to new horizons by the generosity of these remarkable people who edit my work and make it better than I could.

My greatest debt of gratitude is owed to Rodney Clapp, Cascade editor, the most generous, the toughest, the sharpest-eyed reader I know. He has shepherded three of my books from manuscript to publication with unrelenting patience. He has answered the most unbelievable questions and helped me in ways that go far beyond any editor's job description. Each time I send him an email, "Dear Rodney," I feel as if I'm writing to myself.

"And when the orator instead of putting an ass in the place of a horse, puts good for evil, being himself as ignorant of their true nature as the city on which he imposes is ignorant; and having studied the notions of the multitude, persuades them to do evil instead of good,—what will be the harvest which rhetoric will be like to gather after the sowing of that fruit?"

PHAEDRUS, "ANYTHING BUT GOOD."[1]

"Sometimes there is a way that seems to be right, but in the end it is the way to death. Scoundrels concoct evil, and their speech is like a scorching fire. A perverse person spreads strife, and a whisperer separates close friends. The violent entice their neighbors, and lead them in a way that is not good. One who winks the eyes plans perverse things; one who compresses the lips brings evil to pass."

PROVERBS 16:25–30 NRSV

---

1. Plato, *Phaedrus*, 23.

Introduction

WHAT WOULD IT HAVE been like to live in the time of the judges as described in the Hebrew Bible? In the book of Judges, the people went through a seemingly unending series of political upheavals in a pattern of evil and good. God was not pleased with the turmoil, division, and dishonest and disgusting behavior. The reason for the dysfunctional politics: "all the people did what was right in their own eyes."[2] The image fits our politics: people doing as they please, telling lies and calling it truth, unwilling to compromise, condemned to rage and outrage. Philosopher Rupert Read suggests that people don't care that politicians lie. Being able to get away with lying and not being finished by it is "a sign of strength. If that is the reason why then . . . we are quite close to a neo-fascist situation here. Where there is in public a kind of active despising of truth—of the 'naïve' habit of truth-seeking and truth-telling."[3]

Judges depicts evil and good clashing continuously, on an endless loop, when the criteria for good is "what is right in their own eyes." The unfolding tragedy shatters all norms, expectations, decorum, rules, traditions. Here we have an embodied metaphor for our own struggle with evil and good: "what was right in their own eyes." The physical trope—the eyes—deals with seeing and vision. A person with 20/20 vision sees clearly; it's the gold standard for good eyesight. Michelle Holling and Dreama Moon apply this trope to intellectual acuity, or sharpness of thought or vision.[4] The events of the past seven years have given us two starkly different, competing visions. The two visions are biblical in nature and scope. There are two ways, and only two ways:

2. Judg 17:6 and 21:5.
3. Read, "What Is New in Our Time," 84.
4. Holling and Moon, "20/20 in 2020?," 435.

evil and good. "We have had it made clear to us: the world is broken into two parts. The way of evil and the way of good divide between themselves the sum-total of reality."[5]

When the vision of Scripture clashes with the defining trope of our politics—"they did what was right in their own eyes"—we are on the threshold of two competing visions for America. Michelle Holling and Dreama Moon label the competitors as "America" and "Amerikkka." This "points to the nation's vision as distorted by cataracts (a clouding of the eye's lens) that decrease its visual acuity and reconciliation with its past, hampering advancement of a national vision."[6] America has "eye" ("I") trouble. A gradual progression of vision loss may result in total blindness. "The Centers for Disease Control categorize vision loss as a 'public health problem' because it afflicts many people, compromises quality of life, inflicts financial costs, and is feared by many."[7] We suffer also from myopic vision. Suffering from nearsightedness, we have lost historical consciousness about the meanings of rights, freedoms, and democratic participation contained in our founding documents. Now, a portion of the population uses the Constitution only to promote a narrow vision of rights that apply only to a certain kind of people. At a time when the nation needs to address our flawed history, a myopic vision has distorted our history, cried out for writing off our national sins of racism, segregation, and sexism. This myopia causes some Americans to imagine a time of pristine perfection in America's past that never existed, but which they now claim to see with chilling certainty. As a result, they have concocted a future that restores this imagined "white Amerkkkia." Lacking imagination and creativity, small-minded, short-term agents of outrage scream about "wokeness," "Critical Race Theory," and America founded as a Christian nation. The result: a nation repeating its worst evils, a gathering of the Confederate ghosts of the Lost Cause. A powerful and haunting visual image of this lost cause was the January 6 rioter in the US Capitol waving a Confederate flag.

As Joseph Anthony Wittreich wrote, "History may not repeat itself but it does rhyme."[8]

---

5. Chouraqui, "Introduction," 6.
6. Holling and Moon, "20/20 in 2020?," 436.
7. Center for Disease Control and Prevention, "Vision Loss."
8. Wittreich, Wikiquote.

INTRODUCTION

Holling and Moon, using 20/20 as ophthalmological trope, suggest that the ability to see clearly extends beyond physical eyesight. "We want to apply this notion to intellectual acuity or sharpness of thought or vision."[9] This comes close to the prayer of St. Paul that "the eyes of our hearts may be enlightened."[10] The Hebrew word for heart, *lev*, and the Greek word for heart, *cardia*, refer to imagination. The church prays, "Lift up your imaginations." In a nation with vision problems, we need a restored imagination.

Our nation's vision is blurred. There are people deliberately engaged in reducing our ability to clearly see the systemic issues we face. Using the rhetoric of deception, demonization, and blame, they duck and dodge and "rope-a-dope" like Ali to avoid the rational blows that hit them again and again. We are a long way from the national vision bequeathed to us by previous generations of Americans. Systemic racism, social-economic-health inequities, and anti-blackness bear similarities to the public health problem of vision loss. "When one's physical vision is lacking acuity, it can be corrected; can the same be said for the nation's vision?"[11]

I believe that Trump's actions and rhetoric have damaged democracy by blurring our national vision. He has crossed the line between good and evil into clear and discernible evil. Words matter, especially the words of an American president. Trump's antagonism toward immigrants, persons of color, and women are evil. Hate groups hear the president's words as support for the causes of hate. "In Trump, white supremacists see one of their own."[12]

In losing vision, Americans have lost our manners. Taking the risk of sounding like Emily Post, in a post-truth world I sound the alarm that a democracy without manners cannot long survive. Political rhetoric has moved from serious deliberation, discussion, and wisdom to tweets, quips, insults, boasts, and profanity. A pack of howling "humbugs" govern with public displays of outrage, each one attempting to out-outrage the other. As Will Campbell once said in a debate about capital punishment, "It's tacky." When there was some confusion in the audience about the meaning of "tacky," Campbell responded, "Tacky means ugly, no style, no class. I do believe America as a nation has too much class, too much

---

9. Holling and Moon, "20/20 in 2020?," 435.
10. Eph 1:18.
11. Holling and Moon, "20/20 in 2020?," 435.
12. Coates, "First White President."

character, and too much style to go on sinking to such crudities. So for the sake of our own soul, let's just cut it out."[13] That may not sound like much of a condemnation, but we have become a tacky people ripping the tacks from the roof of democracy. The redoubts of the party of tweets, quips, and retorts are petty, lacking substance, and without foundation. Perhaps we have lost the humility of previous American leaders. Can you imagine Marjorie Taylor Greene, Matt Gaeta, John Kennedy, Marsha Blackburn, or Tom Cotton ever saying, "Better men (or women) than I were at hand for this mighty task, and I owe to you and to them every resource of mind and of strength that I possess to make your deed today a good one for our country and for our party"?[14] Those words were spoken by Adlai Stevenson, in 1952, in his acceptance speech as the Democratic candidate for president.

Stevenson sounds like an ancient echo, from a faraway land, that only lives now in dreams of those who value tradition, decorum, and manners. He may as well be from Peter Pan's Neverland. Yet his words still possess the ring of truth. "You have disagreed and argued without calling each other liars and thieves, without despoiling our best traditions—you have not spoiled our best traditions in any naked struggles for power."[15] He claimed the moral high ground when he said,

> I hope and pray that we Democrats, win or lose, can campaign not as a crusade to exterminate the opposing party, as our opponents seem to prefer, but as a great opportunity to educate and elevate a people whose destiny is leadership, not alone of a rich and prosperous, contented country, as in the past, but of a world in ferment. . . . And, my friends even more important than winning the election is governing the nation. That is the test of a political party, the acid, final test. When the tumult and the shouting die, when the bands are gone and the lights are dimmed, there is the stark reality of responsibility in an hour of history haunted with those gaunt, grim specters of strife, dissension, and materialism at home and ruthless, inscrutable, and hostile power abroad.[16]

Words reveal attitudes, character, and philosophy. The words now escaping from the mouths of vain, imperialistic politicians have escaped

13. Campbell, *Soul Among Lions*, 11.
14. Stevenson, "Let's Talk Sense to the American People."
15. Cited in Baker, "'Let's Talk Sense to the American People.'"
16. Cited in Baker, "'Let's Talk Sense to the American People.'"

from the Good Manners Prison. When rhetoric gets out of hand and becomes a weapon, when disgust, rancor, and anger win the votes, democracy develops heart trouble with multiple blocked veins, and ends up in intensive care. Trump's visual rhetoric, for example, offers a demeaning, disgusting, and hurtful menu of anger, blame, and insults. His fatuous, captious arguments defile the spirit of democracy. I find political arguments, by and large, to be incredibly fatuous. The captious persons responsible for producing these bits and pieces of overstatement, emotional overkill, and at times, astounding lies are undermining the pillars of our democracy. Their foolish, puerile, infantile, vacuous, and often witless attacks produce smoke, fog, and a smell offensive to all the senses. As presumptuous as these creatures are, their audacious and reckless attempts to sway the voting public seems to have more success than failure. I am contemptuous of facile and evasive arguments that offend our native intelligence and seek somehow to disencumber us of our ability to reason and to think critically. They seem possessed of a salutary scorn for any view of the intelligence and understanding of ordinary people. Aside from losing the 2020 election, condign punishment seems remote even if Trump has committed criminal acts.

What kind of president refers to women as "pigs" and "dogs"? Robert Farley fact-checked Trump's comments about women. Trump did call women "pigs," "dogs," "disgusting," and "animals." Trump played down these remarks by insisting "it's fun; it's kidding" and that the country has a problem with "being politically correct."[17] After Trump repeatedly insulted the "Squad"—four women members of Congress, Democratic Representatives Ilhan Omar, Alexandria Ocasio-Cortez, Rashida Tlaib, and Ayanna Pressley—a North Carolina gun shop put up a billboard with pictures of the four congresswomen and the words, "The Four Horsemen Are Idiots. Signed, the Deplorables. Cherokee Gun Shop."[18] Eye trouble signals that we also are developing heart trouble when the disgusting passes for humor. This "humor" has always been a tool of white supremacy, racism, and sexism in our national past.

President Trump's rhetoric is emotionally charged and repetitive, establishing a outpouring of macro-aggression pouring out of his mouth. Trump's anti-immigrant rhetoric damages democracy. Trump's racist rhetoric threatens democracy. Trump's misogynist rhetoric demeans

---

17. Farley, "Fact Check."
18. Edwards, "NC Gun Shop Billboard Targeting 'The Squad.'"

democracy. Trump's attack rhetoric increases the attitude of violence.[19] Everyone else is crazy, stupid, or a loser. Trump praises himself constantly. There was a time when our politicians were brilliantly epigrammatic; now they are reduced to being quipsters. Unless the voters realize that the quipsters are maladroit operators engaging in hot air and humbuggery, we will continue to be assailed by weaponized rhetoric.

Trump's rhetoric suggests that he is a "clear and present danger"[20] to democracy. Edward Brewer and Chrys Egan examined President Trump's rhetoric and reached this conclusion: "We contend that Trump generates a level of dangerous Presidential communication not publicly expressed by previous Presidents that arguably could be considered to overstep the limits of free expression set forth by the courts."[21] Twitter did decide that Trump's tweets constituted a danger to democratic deliberation. Crossing the line into incitement to criminal activity is no laughing matter. The evil that Trump produces is an evil directed at democracy. It is a perverted rhetoric. Instead of building community, consensus, and cooperation, Trump is dividing the nation.[22] Hate speech is protected by the constitution, but who will protect those who are the targets of hate speech?[23]

Understanding good and evil in democracy has become a challenge. The common ground about what constitutes good, and evil, has eroded faster than the land mass on the Louisiana Gulf Coast. Good has become what is good in the eyes of the beholder. There are people who call "evil" "good" and people who call everyone that disagrees with them "evil." Perhaps our best alternative is to visualize good and evil. That's the primary visual metaphor of *Good and Evil in the Garden of Democracy*. I am going to show you pictures of evil and pictures of good. Consider this an eye examination as you attempt to identify the letters on the eye chart. The pictures of evil are a series of rhetorical artifacts from the Hebrew Bible books of Proverbs and Psalms. There are artifacts from philosophy (Plato), history (Hitler), and politics. Then there are pictures of what constitutes the good from Vaclav Havel, Walt Whitman, and the African American prophetic tradition, with songs from the Song of Solomon re-inscribed as a love song to democracy. I place these pictures on the wall

19. Katyal and Schmidt, "Trump Is Threatening to Subvert the Constitution."
20. Brewer and Egan, "Clear and Present Danger," 44.
21. Brewer and Egan, "Clear and Present Danger," 44.
22. Brewer, *Religious Rhetoric*.
23. Calvert, "Hate Speech and Its Harms," 4.

like a detective's evidence board in the hope that you will connect the dots.

American historian David Blight has said that the time has come for us to scream, to sing, and fight for democracy. Borrowing his three-point sermon, this is a work of screaming, singing, and fighting. Showing pictures, offering visual rhetoric, seems to be the best way to hold up democracy as the best form of government in a world increasingly attracted to demagoguery, fascism, and authoritarianism. My purpose is to defend democracy as our greatest hope, our most prevailing vision. In the spirit of Franklin Roosevelt, I show you democracy as the highest expression of democratic government characterized by a specific kind of citizenship—the good citizen. Roosevelt said at University of Notre Dame on December 9, 1935: "We will never permit, if we can help it, the light to grow dim."[24]

Democratic display needs to be more symbolically demonstrated as accountability rather than spectacle. Part of the bewildering spectacle of the Trump years is how lack of accountability secured him the support and loyalty of millions. People liked that he could do as he pleased and not be done in by any of it.

I show you democracy in hope. An archetypal picture of a vision of goodness serves as the exemplification of all the other tropes offered in this work: Franklin D. Roosevelt. Roosevelt, for example, insisted that the nation put malevolence in the past. Blame can be firmly fixed, but punishment is not required. We need to see a "social point of view." We need reform not revolution; agonism not antagonism. "It is our task to perfect," Roosevelt said, "to improve, to alter, when necessary, but in all cases to go forward."[25] "These dark days will be worth all they cost us," he said in his First Inaugural, "if they teach us that our true destiny is not to be ministered unto but to minister to ourselves and our fellow men."[26]

Roosevelt's vision was a national government fashioned on the principles of the social gospel—the politics of Jesus. He seamlessly mixed democracy and religion. His supporters believed that his programs were deeply rooted in the compassion of Christianity. Roosevelt provides the template for the picture of goodness. Sounding like a preacher, he said, "Clearer every day is the one great lesson of history—the lesson taught by

---

24. Roosevelt, "Address at Notre Dame University," 495–96.

25. Roosevelt, "Annual Message to the Congress," 3:8. Quoted in Stuckey, "FDR, the Rhetoric of Vision," 131.

26. Roosevelt, "Inaugural Address," 14–15.

the Master of Galilee—that the only road to a happier and better civilization is the road to unity—the road called the 'Highway of Fellowship.'"[27] In his Second Inaugural, he said, "I paint it for you in hope—because the Nation, seeing and understanding the injustice in it, proposes to paint it out."[28] On this visual foundation, I argue that vision, understanding, empathy, wisdom, knowledge, and national unity point the way toward a future for a vital democracy.

Believing that Roosevelt was right to choose vision as the site of the struggle for democracy, I fight for your "eyes"—for the proper mode of seeing evil and good as the condition for victory in the political struggle. Clear-sightedness has to replace our clouded vision. Tennessee Williams stated well the vision problem in the words of Tom Wingfield, narrator in *The Glass Menagerie*, who refers to "that quaint period, the thirties, when the huge middle class of America was matriculating in a school for the blind. Their eyes had failed them or they had failed their eyes, and so they were having their fingers pressed forcibly down on the fiery Braille alphabet of a dissolving economy."[29] Now, it seems we are having our fingers pressed down on the fiery Braille alphabet of a disappearing democracy.

For Roosevelt, illusions, deceptions, and lies were all elements that created darkness. The chapters in this book on the evil displayed in Proverbs and Psalms expand this vision. Chouraqui remarks, "Two ways that are unequal and mutually hostile [light and dark], but that co-exist in time and space where they define the frontier of a war; and upon this line is inscribed all the catastrophic events of history."[30]

Roosevelt was determined to enlarge the vision of the people to a synoptic nation of unity. In contrast, Trump is determined to keep a myopic vision—with all attention centered on him and what he thinks and what he wants and what he likes. Our national myopia threatens to be so severe as to have a vision so short-sighted that it can't see past one news cycle. Democracy requires a vision of the nation as a whole rather than the vision of a single political party desperate to have control. We must look beyond our tortured partisanship. Biographer James MacGregor Burns said of Roosevelt, "He took the role of national father, of bipartisan

---

27. Roosevelt, "Address at Denton, Maryland," 7:513. Quoted in Stuckey, "FDR, the Rhetoric of Vision," 132.
28. Roosevelt, "Second Inaugural," 5:5.
29. Williams, *Glass Menagerie*, 5.
30. Chouraqui, "Introduction," 7.

leader, of President of all the people."³¹ Trump has adopted the role of bad boy, good father—a Janus-faced masculine right-wing populism that hides behind an ostentatious masculine posturing that has the virtue of being relatively malleable.³² The result is "a Janus-faced masculinity of outsiders-yet-insiders, bad-boys-yet-good-fathers."³³

The evil that now darkens our national vision can be best defined as a tragedy. Rather than use the word *tyrant* to suggest that all the evil exists in a single person, I use a literary term, *tragedy*, to suggest that the evil lies not only in a person but also in all of us. "When power is centralized at the top, the state hangs on the fragile emotions of privileged men and bad government amplifies routine individual moral failings—like deceit, revenge, and ambition—into social catastrophe, the suffering of helpless citizens, death, and the downfall of dynasties. Every empire fails, America will too. We might be watching it without knowing it."³⁴

Shakespearean tragedy suggests a way of seeing evil in proper context. All of Shakespeare's political rulers were medieval kings living in modern worlds. Donald Trump, with his privileged background, massive wealth, petulant personality, and penchant for making knee-jerk decisions based on his emotions of the day, has thrown us back into medieval politics. "Shakespeare called it 'tragedy'—the stark social inequality, self-important leaders of privilege, rampant corruption, and hypocrisy in government, fear, anger, resentment, hostility, incivility, warring factions—and then some random event ignites this political powder keg, leading to widespread violence, pain, suffering, death, and the downfall of nations. Let's hope [Shakespeare] was wrong."³⁵

The house of democracy always struggles between the dynamic of evil and good, like the man saying to his priest in Leviticus, "There seems to me to be some sort of disease in my house" (Lev 14:35). My previous work *The Immaculate Mistake* detailed the rhetorical perversion of President Donald Trump. After the events of January 6, I realized that the arguments of *The Immaculate Mistake* needed to be extended. Criticism of the ex-president no longer sufficed. There appeared to be a strong

---

31. Burns, *Definitive FDR*, 312.
32. Eksil and Wood, "Right-Wing Populism as Gendered Performance."
33. Eksil and Wood, "Right-Wing Populism as Gendered Performance," 733.
34. Wilson, *Shakespeare and Trump*, 12.
35. Wilson, *Shakespeare and Trump*, 15.

case for Donald Trump as the incarnation of political and religious evil. Setting out the arguments for the case unfolds in *Good and Evil in the Garden of Democracy*. My fundamental contention: Evil attempts to sever democracy from its roots. Ronald Reagan, in a 1984 television ad, famously claimed that it was "morning again in America."[36] Donald Trump's fearful, dark, angry rhetoric caused darkness to descend like the rule of Scar in *The Lion King*. There's rawness, vitriol, outrage, and so much fear. In Trump's America people should be afraid—of immigrants, terrorists, minorities, scientists, historians, academics of all stripes. And angry, real angry at ideas: wokeness, Critical Race Theory, national health care, *Roe vs. Wade*, voting rights, unions, taxes, radical left-wing liberals.

Trump painted a picture more like midnight in America than morning. Here are the archetypal metaphors of our human existence: light and dark. Genesis opens with "the earth was a formless void and darkness covered the face of the deep."[37] Then, God's first act of creation offers a foil to darkness: "'Let there be light; and there was light. And God saw that the light was good; and God separated the light from the darkness. God called the light Day, and the darkness he called Night."[38]

The ancient cosmic contest between good and evil begins. All entities will now decide to serve either the good or come under the power of evil. Then the later appearance of humanity intensifies the contest. Ironically, the battle ensues in a garden. The word *garden* in my title depicts the mythological garden of Eden and its ongoing recurrences in history. Borrowing from Kenneth Burke's powerful essay, "The First Three Chapters of Genesis,"[39] the light and dark of humanity in its original and fallen forms provide the backdrop. Language, according to Burke, is the bridge between sacred and secular realms of action. The language of politicians can be studied to help us grasp the quandaries of human governance.[40]

In 1982, Ronald Reagan confidently proclaimed, "Around the world today, the democratic revolution is gathering new strength." He claimed "democracy is not a fragile flower."[41] Now, forty years later, democracy withers on the vine, wilting under pressures produced by right-wing

36. Reagan, "Morning in America."
37. Gen 1:2. (NRSV).
38. Gen 1:3.
39. Burke, *Rhetoric of Religion*.
40. Duncan, "Sociological Model of Social Interaction."
41. Reagan, "Address to Members of the British Parliament."

tyrants. Optimism has turned to pessimism. On January 6, at 4:06 PM then president-elect Joe Biden said, "At this hour, our democracy is under unprecedented assault."[42]

Evangelicals recreate a fictional past that never existed—a state of innocence suggested by the garden of Eden. The parallel effort shows up in the attempt claim a Christian origin for the USA. I want to complicate the theological implications of the past being present, not in the sense of being repeated, but in the sense of reoccurring in different guises, by appealing to theologian James McClendon's notion of the "Baptist vision."[43] McClendon used a motto to explicate what he meant by Baptist vision: "The church now is the primitive church and the church on judgment day."[44] The fall has present-tense, ongoing historic significance here and now. Rhetorically, the "fall" is a tropological garden.

In other words, there have been other falls in other ages and other places. A rhetoric instigates a "fall." This exotic, seductive demolition rhetoric is smooth, twisted, enticing. It is the rhetoric of the serpent, the loose woman, the mischief maker, and of every evil rhetor in history. We are on the precipice of a fall now—a political fall—because it is midnight in the garden of democracy. As Coleridge put it, "A Fall of some sort or other—the creation, as it were, of the non-absolute—is the fundamental postulate of the moral history of man. Without this hypothesis, man is unintelligible; with it, every phenomenon is explicable. The mystery itself is too profound for human thought."[45]

The serpent acts as the antagonist. "Now the serpent was more subtil than any beast of the field which the LORD God had made."[46] The *New Revised Standard Version* says the serpent was "more crafty." Here we meet shades of Plato's insistence that there is a kind of rhetoric that is not a true art, but merely of the same genus as cooking.[47] The wise woman of Proverbs wasn't fooled: "Like the glaze covering an earthen vessel are smooth lips with an evil heart".[48] Evil lurks in smooth, easygoing, subtle,

---

42. Wagner et al., "Congress Finalizes Biden's Win."
43. McClendon, *Ethics*, 8.
44. McClendon, *Ethics*, 32.
45. Burke, *Rhetoric of Religion*, 174.
46. Gen 3:1 KJV.
47. Plato, *Gorgias*, 64.
48. Prov 26:23.

political rhetoric that has been surreptitiously weaponized. The symbol of this evil genius is a serpent—a talking snake.

The serpent is described as a "beast"[49] or a "wild animal."[50] Daniel will later speak of the "beast kings"[51] as the enemies of the good. The beast kings would rule our lives with the iron fists of evil. These terrifying beast kings came to life as a slick-talking snake in the garden. The snake—neither devil nor Satan—speaks. The cosmic war begins with rhetoric. Never trust an interrogator who has no declarative sentences of affirmation. The snake said to the woman, "Did God say, 'You shall not eat from any tree in the garden?' You will not die; for God knows that when you eat of it your eyes will be opened, and you will be like God, knowing good and evil."[52] One question unleashed hostility, resentment, destruction on all humanity. One question created a spirit of mistrust in the minds of people, a mistrust that had no basis but became and remains so real in its devastating effects. The story of the serpent and Eve illustrates what a spirit of mistrust and suspicion can do. Mistrust is allowed to gain traction, and disintegration and alienation are sure to follow.

Playing the role of the "talking snake," Trump convinced people to mistrust all our democratic norms, values, and institutions. He increased political polarization, fomented a distorted populism, and created an explosion of misinformation and lies. Philosopher Onora O'Neill argues that our society suffers from a crisis of trust.[53] She is not speaking of garden-variety cynicism that causes us to approach politics with suspicion. No, the malady goes much deeper because it changes how we view all of life. Suspicion and mistrust become epistemological anchors and we feel that the great institutions of our society are not working for us. The evil depicted here presents an evil rhetoric—evil because of the damage it does to democracy, to human flourishing.

While rhetorical scholars have decisively labeled Trump a demagogue,[54] the implication of this negative label fails to go far enough. As Eric Zorn puts it, "I see him as a populist demagogue."[55] Trump, no

49. Gen 3:1 KJV.
50. Gen 3:1 NRSV.
51. Dan 7:17.
52. Gen 3:1–5.
53. O'Neill, *Question of Trust*.
54. Mercieca, *Demagogue for President*; Steudeman, "Demagoguery and the Donald's Duplicitous Victimhood."
55. Zorn, "Donald Trump?"

doubt, is a duplicitous demagogue, but he is far more dangerous than previous demagogues like Huey Long, George Wallace, and Father Coughlin. Jennifer Mercieca is surely right when she asserts that Trump is a genius at weaponizing rhetoric. "I think that Trump's rhetoric is bad for American democracy."[56] January 6, 2021, forced American eyes to see with piercing clarity the danger of weaponized rhetoric.

The serpent remains ubiquitous in our history. The serpent reappears in Israel's history in various configurations. The serpent crops up in Proverbs as the loose woman and the mischief maker—the seductive, captious teacher of a facile, fake rhetoric of destruction. The serpent, through the work of the psalter, is unveiled as the ultimate doer of evil. Even more disturbing and relevant to the Trump/evangelical alliance is the strange narrative of the poisonous serpents God sent to punish the Israelites for their murmuring in Numbers 21. The story takes an even odder twist when God commands Moses to make a serpent of bronze and put it on a pole so that anyone who looks on the serpent will live. That should have been the end of the story, but for reasons never revealed, the Jews kept the bronze snake on a stick. Idolatry is subtle enough that centuries later the snake shows up in God's house. Here is biblical metaphorical power at its height, suggesting that the snake on a stick in the house of God is the Trump/evangelical alliance.

The snake shows up on a flag at the insurrection by Trump supporters. The bright yellow "JESUS SAVES" and "JESUS 2020" flags waved high in the midst of the rabble invading the Capitol on January 6. Even their flags were a cacophony of mixed images. Jesus was waving next to a flag with a snake and the battle flag of the Confederate States of America. How odd of Jesus to be among snakes and rebels.

Trump spewed suspicion and mistrust for so long that it finally erupted in an attack on the government. Having previously attacked the anchor institutions of democracy—press, education/science, and the courts—nothing was left but to destroy democracy itself. Attacking the pillars of the temple of democracy threatens to bring down the temple—recall Samson. Whatever labels apply to this insurrection in the future, the association of the name of Jesus with it begs for a dissent. Jesus is never a captive to death, to poisonous snakes.

When God "raised up" Israel from Egyptian slavery and the people headed to the promised land, they complained about the cost of their

---

56. Mercieca, *Demagogue for President*, Kindle edition, loc. 83.

new freedom. "Was it because there were no graves in Egypt that you have taken us away to die in the wilderness? What have you done to us, bringing us out of Egypt?"[57] God, tired of the "murmuring" of the people, sent poisonous snakes to punish them. The people begged Moses to get rid of the snakes. Moses must have prayed for God to remove the snakes. Instead of removing the snakes, God told Moses to make a replica of a poisonous serpent and set it on a pole. Anyone bitten by a serpent could look on the snake on a stick and they would live.

The Israelites carried the snake with them to the promised land, like Rachel taking her father's household gods with her.[58] The house that was to be the house of prayer for all nations had a snake on a stick in it. If you hang around snakes long enough, you will make offerings to them and give loyalty to them. You will even give the snake a name: Nehushtan.

In 2 Kings 18, we learn that Hezekiah enacted several executive orders: "He removed the high places, broke down the pillars, and cut down the sacred pole. He broke in pieces the bronze serpent that Moses had made, for until those days the people of Israel had made offerings to it; it was called Nehushtan."[59] In 2015, evangelical Christians, convinced that our nation was experiencing a plague of "poisonous serpents"—a.k.a. liberals and the like—asked God to send them a savior. They gave all their support and loyalty to Donald Trump, who turned out to be a snake. Evangelicals, having prepared the way for the coming of Trump, now made an idol of him. Trump, the talking snake, armed with poisonous tweets, became a fetish for evangelicals. And the poisoned darts of Twitter spread around the world. "From 2009 to 2012, Facebook and Twitter passed out roughly 1 billion dart guns globally. Chris Wetherell, one of the engineers who created the Retweet button for Twitter, says he now regrets it. 'We might have just handed a 4-year-old a loaded weapon.'"[60] We've been shooting one another ever since.[61] Like the ancient Israelites who kept the bronzed serpent and later ensconced it in their temple, the evangelicals placed Trump at the center of their loyalty.

57. Exod 14:11.
58. Gen 31:19–35.
59. 2 Kgs 18:4.
60. Haidt and Rose-Stockwell, "Dark Psychology of Social Networks."
61. Haidt and Rose-Stockwell, "Why the Past 10 Years of American Life Have Been Uniquely Stupid."

On the morning of January 6, with General Giuliani bellowing the order of "trial by combat,"[62] and the talking snake, President Trump, suggesting insurrection, it was "onward Christian soldiers marching as to war." The scene reminded me of fifteenth-century Catholic churches being ransacked in England. I suggest that the attempt to destroy the Capitol on January 6 has historical precedent. Historians have taught us that at the dawn of the fifteenth century the people of England longed for a simple, Bible-based religion free of all the Catholic frippery, idolatry, indulgences, priestcraft, penance, and purgatory. In 2021, the people longed for a second term for Donald Trump so they could be free from all the liberal heresies like socialism, environmentalism, science, and history.

The story of England was that the monks and nuns were fat, rich, and lazy. Then good King Henry VIII cleaned all that up. He reformed the church and made it great again.

The story in America was that the liberals were destroying the country. Then good President Trump cleaned all that up. He made America great again, strong again, Christian again. He reformed the nation and made it what God intended.

The story about England turned out to be wrong. Cambridge historian Eamon Duffy corrected all these misunderstandings with his monumental study called *The Stripping of the Altars: Traditional Religion in England 1400–1580*. Duffy was part of a group of English historians who looked again at the received account of the English Reformation, did some original research, and came up with the story of what really happened. Duffy shows that the state of the monasteries and of religious life in England was robust, dynamic, and strong. He explains how the ordinary people participated in church life and how it was central to the life of the family, the village, and the town. The monasteries might have been rich, but they funded the hospitals, schools, poorhouses, and social welfare programs. In addition, the friars, with their work in the towns and cities, were bringing renewal to the church. Duffy also outlines the almost universal attendance at Mass, the people's love and participation in pilgrimage and devotion to the saints, as well as their appreciation for the possible pains of hell and purgatory. The Catholic religion in England before Henry VIII's reign was, for the most part, vital and strong. It was broken and bereft not out of a will to cleanse and reform, but out

---

62. Krawczyk, "Giuliani calls for 'trial by combat' at D.C. rally."

of royal greed, vanity, and lust. Henry and his commissioners had also spotted that the monasteries and churches provided rich pickings. The king himself grabbed vast amounts of land for the crown and he awarded his faithful subjects with rich prizes of religious houses and their lands and goods.[63]

Meanwhile, Donald Trump became president in 2016 and it was more about wanting to be president for life than the good of democracy. The English Reformation destroyed a thousand-year-old culture in a few short decades. If Trump returns to the presidency in 2024, democracy may be destroyed in four years. Neither history nor the present are ever what they seem.

On January 6, a Trump sidekick, Representative Mo Brooks, Alabama, roused the crowd with fiery, combative words that it was time "to start taking down names and kicking ass."[64] When the "Jesus flag" people smashed through the doors and windows to enter the Capitol, they entered the cathedral of their own idolatrous faith. They trampled on holy ground and destroyed scared objects. Iconoclasts were loose in the offices of members of the House and the Senate. The very notion of being iconoclastic suggests ways of defining this mob: critical, skeptical, questioning, heretical, irreverent, nonconformist, dissident, dissenting, dissentient, malcontent, rebellious, subversive, renegade, mutinous. This was not a Jesus crowd; it was an anti-Christ crowd.

Trump himself had offered an "unwitting prophecy"[65] about his presidency on the campaign trail. He would read a poem about a snake, which he associated with immigrants, a venomous snake that, after biting the kind woman who had given it shelter, declared: "You knew damned well I was a snake before you took me in."[66] The evangelicals, blinded by resentment and anger, didn't recognize the snake they welcomed into their house, and he bit them and left them poisoned and bereft. In this case, there was no healing because for evangelicals to look, to really look, at the snake was impossible. You cannot help but be sympathetic with the evangelicals. They are being asked to look at a man they ordained as God's anointed and see him as the agent of death.

63. Duffy, *Stripping of the Altars*.
64. Bort, "Rep. Mo Brooks on Incendiary Jan. 6th Speech."
65. Ivie, "Trump's Unwitting Prophecy," 711.
66. Ivie, "Trump's Unwitting Prophecy," 711.

INTRODUCTION

There are two images that will never leave my mind: President Trump holding a copy of the Revised Standard Version of the Bible in front of St. John's Episcopal Church in response to peaceful protests, and those Jesus flags waving in the breeze alongside the snake flag and the Confederate flag as the invasion of the capital started. And somewhere in the basement of my mind I am haunted by scenes of ragged, barefoot, Confederate soldiers—four years of violence, pain, near starvation, death painted deep in their scarred, scared faces—marching one last time into the center of Yankee cannons at Gettysburg, marching to certain destruction. The mob at the Capitol appeared before my eyes as Confederate ghosts rising from the fog-shrouded bayous of Louisiana. But this was not the Battle of Bull Run. This was Petersburg, Atlanta, Richmond, Savannah—all bitter defeats, and at the bitter end, Appomattox. The tragedy of the "Lost Cause" is that the South lost then, and it will lose again.

My lasting hope is that when the last Trump storm trooper puts down his weapons, there will still be democracy in this house. When the last demagogue is swept from office, I pray some true patriot will shout, "There is still democracy in this house." I saw a glimpse of that hope in the voices of our elected representatives while under siege. They were voices of determination and dissent from the invaders. As fragile, divided, and confused as democracy was on January 6, the house of democracy did not fall before the attack of Donald Trump and his troopers. As Cornel West puts it so well, "Democracy matters."[67] To lasting gratitude for all of us, this was not *White House Down*.[68]

Donald Trump, the whispering, accusing, faultfinding, quibbling, caviling, mocking, insulting, carping, hypercritical spreader of doubt and suspicion has exacerbated the confusion between good and evil. There has arisen a contentious disagreement about what constitutes good and evil. Until recently, we have mostly thought that we can name what has gone wrong in the world. Hauerwas says, "Christian and non-Christian now believe that even if we do not share a common belief in God, we can at least agree about actions that are evil."[69]

The temptation to see Trump's supporters as fatuous can be overwhelming. Line up the synonyms to produce a verbal collage of how Trump supporters are perceived: silly, foolish, stupid, nonsensical,

---

67. West, *Democracy Matters*.

68. *White House Down* was a 2013 film depicting a terrorist attack on the White House.

69. Hauerwas, *Working with Words*, 10.

childish, puerile, infantile, idiotic, brainless, vacuous, imbecilic, asinine, witless, and empty-headed. All this accomplishes is to reinforce the evangelical commitment to Trump. MAGA people swallow liberal criticisms as if they were vitamins fueling their energy. Such a conclusion also ignores what rhetorical theorist Kenneth Burke calls the "total identification" of Trump and his followers. I think I failed to grasp the sheer ability of Trump's dark rhetorical skill that built a relationship with his followers that silenced dissent, precluded criticism, and was grounded in the subversion of critical thinking to pure identification. Only after immersing myself in the Facebook postings of MAGA people did I begin to grasp how much they perceive Trump as "superhuman" but deeply persecuted, how blindly they follow him, how they unconditionally comply to his wishes and how they give him unqualified emotional commitment even when they know he is lying. Somehow Trump manages to project as superman or "strong man" and as victim. It's no easy task but such trickery places Trump squarely in the wheelhouse of evil. On the one hand, Trump insists that only he can save the nation from chaos. Then he portrays himself as under vicious attack by larger forces. He has gone so far as to insist "no politician in history—and I say this with great surety—has been treated worse or more unfairly."[70]

Trump's followers abdicate judgment to him and allow him to define what is truth. Followers accept and believe that the past was as Trump portrayed it (America was losing; didn't have victories anymore), that the present is as he depicts it (wonderful and beautiful), and that the future will be as he predicts it (America will be great again). This is the marriage of good and evil, and when evil masquerades as goodness, we should know that we have a problem. There is no evil like religious evil. Donald Trump, the personification of evil, receives his most loyal support from people with a history of goodness—the evangelicals. This is not a moratorium of Donald Trump, because neither he nor his influence will diminish soon. I have not come to bury Trump, but to accuse him of evil.

Rhetorical scholars have not been kind in evaluating the rhetoric of Donald Trump. Like prophets of the Old Testament, these diligent scholars have repeatedly warned of the dangers of Trump's rhetorical strategies. Bonnie Dow says that the election of Trump threatened her teaching of the principles of rhetoric "that words matter, that reasons matter, and that rational deliberation should be central to how American culture makes

---

70. Steudeman, "Demagoguery and the Donald's Duplicitous Victimhood," 201.

decisions."[71] Paul Johnson argues that Trump's incoherent vacillations between strength and victimhood enable his white audiences to disavow hegemonic whiteness and align themselves with a marginalized, politically exiled subjectivity. Robert Ivie focuses on demolition as the "guiding trope" of Trump's apocalyptic rhetoric. Jennifer Wingard portrays Trump as the "product of a spoiled bunch" rather than just a "spoiled apple in the barrel." Ryan Skinnell says "Donald J. Trump is a notorious liar."[72] "Trump's rhetoric is centered on the preservation," says Michael J. Steudeman, "of a conception of American identity rooted in whiteness, masculinity, and heteronormativity."[73] Anna Young labels Trump "a populist,"[74] and Jennifer Mercieca declares him "a demagogue."[75] Joshua Gunn adds that Trump's political style is perverse.[76] Michael J. Steudeman: "Trump's rhetoric operates demagogically."[77] It is "centered on the preservation of a conception of American identity rooted in whiteness, masculinity, and heteronormativity. He makes sweeping condemnations of media, politicians, and public figures based on their perceived alignment with"[78] liberals. "

There's not a single good reason for disputing any of these rhetorical markers of Donald Trump. Rather I gather all these critiques into one tropological rotten barrel of apples and extend these assertions to a basic claim: Donald Trump is a secular revivalist, an evangelical preacher who traffics in evil, flaunts evil, and makes evil appear good. As Isaiah lamented, "Ah, you who call evil good and good evil, who put darkness for light and light for darkness, who put bitter for sweet and sweet for bitter!"[79] I argue that an embodied evil lies at the heart of Trump's personhood. I pay attention to all matters Trump, especially Trump as evil preacher. I go beyond these critiques to claim that there has never been a president that acted and spoke in terms that can be described as so completely saturated

71. Dow, "Taking Trump Seriously," 136.
72. Skinnell, "What Passes for Truth in the Trump Era," 83.
73. Steudeman, "Demagoguery and the Donald's Duplicitous Victimhood," 8.
74. Young, "Rhetorics of Fear and Loathing," 25.
75. Mercieca, *Demagogue for President*. Mercieca, in the Introduction, says, "The day after the election I sent Jay a note asking him if I could really write a book calling the president of the United States a demagogue, Jay stood by me."
76. Gunn, "Donald Trump's Perverse Political Rhetoric," 171.
77. Steudeman, "Demagoguery and the Donald's Duplicitous Victimhood," 71.
78. Steudeman, "Demagoguery and the Donald's Duplicitous Victimhood," 71.
79. Isa 5:20.

by evil. This is, of course, a serious charge, but with apologies for risking rhetorical infidelity, I attempt to make the case for the evil secular preacher that inhabits the persona of Donald Trump. Trump's persona and person are the same—"Trump on the stump is all there is—that there is nothing more to Trump than his spectacle. As co-creators of popular perception, this spectacle includes us, too."[80] In short, I think that judgments of Trump's character (ethos) are unavoidable. This makes my case a study in the Aristotelian mode of proof known as ethos.

No matter how evangelicals shrug off Trump's famous refusal to repent, it remains a real theological problem for evangelical faith. Trump makes no mention of the tears of confession or of the sacrifice that God will never reject, a broken spirit, a heart that is humbled and contrite. "You give your mouth free rein for evil, and your tongue frames deceit."[81] He has never addressed his besetting problem, which is his pride. The lesson untaught or unlearned "simply being that we are cured of our pride only through following the Word, the Truth, which surpasses even the highest parts of creation by becoming one with us."[82] Evangelicals had the tools to teach Trump, but instead they adored him and followed him.

I do not doubt that evangelicals believe they are acting morally. Nor do I doubt their sincerity. In *The Nazi Conscience*, Claudia Koonz argues that the mass murderers of the Jews understood themselves to be acting morally. Koonz argues, "The popularizers of Anti-Semitism and the planners of genocide followed a coherent set of severe ethical maxims derived from broad philosophical concepts."[83] The fierce denials of racism and antisemitism today are as passionate with Trump as they are with the evangelicals. Trump declared, "I'm the least racist person in this room."[84] At a South Carolina rally in March 2022, Trump told parents they had to be willing to fight to the death against Critical Race Theory.

Theologian Stanley Hauerwas says that our only defense against the "Nazi conscience" "will depend on whether communities exist capable of discerning their own propensities for the evil so often done in the name of good."[85] When evil is done in the name of evangelical "values," we have

---

80. Gunn, "Donald Trump's Perverse Political Rhetoric," 179.
81. Ps 50:19.
82. Hauerwas, *Working with Words*, 51.
83. Quoted in Badiou, *Saint Paul*, 18.
84. Amatulli, "Trump Says He's the Least Racist Person."
85. Hauerwas, *Working with Words*, 31.

moved beyond restraint. Evangelicals proudly assume they know what is wrong with the world. They are so frightened of the dangerous world in which we live that they are willing to put the world in handcuffs and attempt to enforce their moralism on all.

In this respect *Good and Evil in the Garden of Democracy* attempts to advance a biblical and rhetorical construct for ripping the cloak of invisibility from the racist and sexist ideology, constructs, and conventions of our culture. In the chapters that follow, I will argue that the differences between evil and good are visible and understandable. We can locate evil in Trump's character, words, and actions not only in ordinary ways of violating decorum, but in a deep structural sense pulling an entire people along the track that leads to death. Trump has managed to turn the seven cardinal vices into lively capitalist virtues. The evil stares back at us and we have eyes that do not see and ears that do not hear.

Like the evil he incarnates, Trump is a phantom, an image, a specter, a shadow. There's nothing real there. According to St. Augustine, there can be no evil "where there is no good. Nothing evil exists in itself, but only as an evil aspect of some actual entity."[86] Augustine's account of evil as "nothing," as "the privation" of good, can be applied to Donald Trump. Paul J. Achter says, "Trump is a shadow figure, a representative of our cultural unconscious, the unspoken 'true spirit' of life, a character whose actions offer constant contrasts to the thoughtful and democratic people we profess to be."[87] As a television character, Trump can move back and forth "between the pariah and the icon, the hated and the worshiped," because, loved or hated, the dramatic potential of a figure is the common currency of television drama.[88] Trump is addicted to television news and television news is addicted to Trump. "Trump's shadow archetype—his characterization as a bigoted, TV-obsessed lightweight—is proving irresistible for cable news. Like the anti-hero of fictional dramas, the typically male character who is celebrated for rule-breaking, the shadow character is immoral and impulsive but attractive to audiences."[89] There's little difference between the cancer-stricken chemistry teacher who mastered the production of crystal methamphetamine on *Breaking Bad* and Donald

---

86. Augustine, *Confessions and Enchiridion*, 344, 4.4. (References to Augustine will first include the page number, followed by chapter and paragraph numbers.)

87. Achter, "Great Television," 117.

88. Achter, "Great Television," 117.

89. Achter, "Great Television," 117.

Trump, the main character in a story that is personal, dark, novel, dramatic, and full of conflict.

Steven Marche writes, "Trump is not imposing distortion on American voters. He's just catching up with the marketplace. A people of screens will inevitably choose screened people to lead them."[90] Trump won in 2016, and so did the morality of the screen. Like Trump the screen has no morality. Television's famous "neutrality" doesn't exist. There's only ratings and clicks. Television and television news doesn't act as the guardian of civic norms and institutions—it acts as a profit-making business. "Show me the money." Television feasts on bad news. Television loves villains and evil. Television will miss Donald Trump but will help keep him on-screen for the next four years, paving the way for another run at the presidency. "The news networks and shows may deny that they are aligned with any political party, but they share with Trump the ideology of the marketplace, where making money is the goal."[91] Trump and his evangelicals perpetrate evil; the media reports the evil and deposits the profits. They may all be losing their souls, but they are certainly making a killing. As Cornel West puts it, "How ironic that in America we have moved so quickly from Martin Luther King Jr.'s 'Let Freedom Ring,' to 'Bling, Bling!'—as if freedom were reducible to having material toys, as dictated by free-market fundamentalism."[92] Trump and the media are economic partners in the dogmas of free-market fundamentalism as the idol and fetish of America.

In the spirit of Quintilian, I can only say, "Vileness and virtue cannot jointly inhabit in the selfsame heart and that it is impossible for one and the same mind to harbour good and evil thoughts as it is for one man to be at once good and evil."[93] As an embodied notion of the inability of vileness and virtue to coinhabit, consider what the Epistle of James says of the tongue: "So also the tongue is a small member, yet it boasts of great exploits. How great a forest is set ablaze by a small fire! And the tongue is a fire. The tongue is placed among our members as a world of iniquity; it stains the whole body, sets on fire the cycle of nature, and is itself set on fire by hell . . . From the same mouth come blessing and cursing."[94] A man

90. Marche, "Celebrity Warfare."
91. Achter, "Great Television," 126.
92. West, *Democracy Matters*, 5.
93. Quintilian, *Complete Works*, Kindle ed., loc. 12991.
94. Jas 3:5–11.

is either good or evil, but in television the only requirements are fame, fortune, and ratings.

Trump provides an excellent template for understanding what is evil and what is good. He represents a form of evil that finds withering condemnation in Scripture, philosophy, and rhetoric. Trump is the most conspicuous advocate of the evil that often lurks in the religious realm, posing as goodness, greatness, strength, and wisdom. The real focus of this book, however, is the danger Trump has created for democracy.

Chapter 1 focuses on good and evil in Proverbs and Plato. Proverbs offers two major tropes: the wise woman and the loose woman. Plato, in *Phaedrus*, has a philosophical pair of like-minded tropes: the evil lover and the good lover.

I turn to a more specific understanding of evil in the biblical context in chapter 2. This is an overview of the picture of evil provided in the Psalms. The evil one has more than 112 identifications in Psalms. The descriptions offered in this book of praise and song often stick to the machinations of Donald Trump. The primary artifact of this view from the psalter is Andre Chouraqui's "Introduction to the Psalms."

Chapters 3 and 4 turn to rhetorical understandings of evil and good. In chapter 3 there is what may seem like a daring consideration of history's most evil creature—Adolf Hitler. Hitler's rhetoric and the emerging desire of some Americans for a form of fascism lead to comparisons with Trump. I am not saying Trump is Hitler; I am arguing that Trump follows in Hitler's wake in disturbing ways. Chapter 4 offers a vision of the good in a democratic leader—Vaclav Havel. As the opposite of Trump, Havel demonstrates the power of "folly," humility, empathy, and irony in leading a democracy.

Chapter 5 sings the songs of democracy with Walt Whitman, songs from the African American prophetic tradition, and the Song of Solomon. In what I consider the most important part of the book, I conclude with suggestions of what we can do to preserve democracy, to produce good in the garden of democracy.

The vision amplified by the verbal—singing, screaming, and fighting (nonviolently)—combine to offer a way for democracy to recover vitality and hope. The stark pictures of destruction, the strident rhetoric of dissent, gives way to the songs of democracy. This is the way that leads to life. Walk in it!

CHAPTER 1

Good and Evil Rhetoric in Proverbs and Plato

American democracy now resides in precarity. I propose that this precarity is a matter of the difference between the good and the evil. Sarah Repucci and Amy Slipowitz, in *Freedom in the World 2021: Democracy Under Siege,* argue that democracy has been rendered vulnerable. "The expansion of authoritarian rule, combined with fading and inconsistent presence of major democracies on the international stage, has had tangible effects on human life and society."[1] This sounds a persistent alarm not only about democracy's precarity, but also about the precaritization of human life. If we only consider the possibility of nuclear war (Putin has made this clear) or climate change, we are on the edge of rendering all publics precarious. Humans are on the endangered species list because so many humans refuse to take seriously decades of climate and geological research that demonstrates that humanity itself may be on the endangered species list. This overwhelming precarity has surfaced with the rise of hardwired, right-wing nationalist populism. In *Precarious Rhetorics,* Wendy Hesford, Adela Licona, and Christa Teston suggest that the rise of "hard-right populism is cultivated through the sowing of fear and suspicion."[2] I will argue that the deliberate placing of all humanity into the state of precarity is a virulent form of evil on a parallel with war crimes and even genocide. Our anti-science, right-wing American populists have brazenly resisted the science of vaccination and masks and given assistance to the death of over one million Americans. This stubborn resistance hasn't receded. Tucker Carlson, attacking the

1. Repucci and Slipowitz, *Freedom in the World 2021,* 9.
2. Hesford, Licona, and Teston, *Precarious Rhetorics,* 1.

US support of Ukraine, compared it to mask wearing. Speaking of public health measures during the pandemic, Carlson said, "Masks were a training exercise. Mandatory masking was a shock collar designed to teach Americans unquestioning obedience and, of course, it worked because shock collars do work." Carlson went on: "In a single day last month we watched, for example, our entire professional class dutifully changing their Twitter avatars from 'mask up' to the now mandatory Ukrainian flag."[3] On the other hand, nothing underscores the precarity of human life like climate denial. Donald Trump has almost total control over the Republican Party and he is a climate denier. "Dangerous climate change is a white swan; it will destroy us, unless we intervene to stop it. It is utterly reckless to play politics with it in the way Trump is doing."[4] Somehow conservatives have linked climate denial to freedom. They seem to think that liberals are trying to control their lives with doomsday predictions about the dangers of climate change. "Climate-denial pretends to give the denier a power greater than that of nature . . . freedom from truth itself . . . an ultimate freedom."[5] Questions of truth and freedom land us in the territory of good-and-evil ethics, in other words. The alleged right to complete individual liberty is expressed by strongly in the rhetoric and behavior of Donald Trump.

The real danger of Donald Trump is that he isn't really a Republican; he's a renegade libertarian. He believes that he has the absolute freedom to do as he pleases about anything he pleases. In the last six years, he has infected his evangelical devotees with the spirit of libertarianism. Now, libertarians and evangelicals seem to be birds of a feather. When this dubious alliance was sealed is hard to discern. Did evangelicals first start talking like libertarians or did libertarians first start talking like evangelicals? I believe that libertarianism is the "heresy" that invaded evangelical churches in the last three decades and turned the churches into political arms of the libertarian ideology.

Michael Gerson, in a *Washington Post* op-ed, argues evangelicals have become libertarians, which has nothing whatsoever to do with Christianity. Gerson says, "They have replaced Jesus' moral and ethical teachings (which, you might recall, emphasized taking care of our neighbors, and everybody is a neighbor) with a libertarian position that

---

3. Kilander, "Tucker Carlson Doubles Down on Ukraine."
4. Read, "What Is New in Our Time," 90.
5. Read, "What Is New in Our Time," 81.

individual rights supersede everything else, including the well-being of others. And that the greatest evil in the world is government coercion, no matter what purpose is being served. This is heresy compounded by lunacy." E. J. Dionne makes a similar argument when he suggests that evangelicals see hostility to government (including science) as a way of fighting back against a secular culture. The reasoning is that scientists are liberals, and climate change is a liberal doctrine, promoted by the government. It must be false because it is just a secular conspiracy.

My previous research for my book *The Immaculate Mistake* discovered a simmering resentment of evangelicals against all things liberal that went back at least to the founding of fundamentalism in the late nineteenth and early twentieth centuries. William V. Trollinger, in reviewing William Bell Riley's work *The Menace of Modernism,* says that the book is "saturated with Riley's sense of alarm about an American culture in grave danger." Trollinger also argues that the fundamentalists "deeply resented the modernists, not simply because they held heretical ideas or even because they threatened America," but that they "arrogantly designated themselves the 'solitary progressives of the hour,' the men 'who really think.'"[6] This intellectual chip on the shoulder cut deep. William Bell Riley observed that conservative ministers had "about as good a chance to be heard in a Turkish harem as to be invited to speak within the precincts of a modern State university."[7]

I argue that evangelicals and libertarians, directed by Donald Trump, have now morphed into one entity by examining the case of climate denial. Philosopher Rupert Read says, "Climate-denial is certainly the most 'epic' form of fake-news our culture has ever known." One reason for looking at climate denial is that Donald Trump is the most powerful man in the Republican party; and he is a climate denier. Another reason for using climate denial as a primary example is that it involves issues that are of utmost importance to libertarians and evangelicals: freedom and truth. In fact, there is a clash between freedom and truth. American historian William Trollinger, in an email correspondence, told me, "Over the past century white evangelicals have become increasingly unmoored from the constraints of truth, and the constraints of their faith, and the constraints of the biblical text."

---

6. Trollinger, *God's Empire*, 35.
7. Trollinger, *God's Empire*, 35.

The seeds for climate denial were planted much earlier by politicians and preachers opposing environmental laws. Senator James Inhofe (R-OK), will always be remembered for his stunt of throwing a snowball in Congress as he tried to discredit climate science. Then there was the Acton Institute for the Study of Religion and Liberty, a Christian-right and free-market economics think tank. In an editorial on that site called "Global Warming or Globaloney? The Forgotten Case for Global Cooling," we hear echoes of todays' vigorous climate denials. The article calls climate change "a shrewdly planned campaign to inflict a lot of socialistic restriction on our cherished freedoms. Environmentalism, in short, is the last refuge of socialism."[8] And in a real blast from the past there's Jerry Falwell, who said on CNN, "It was global cooling 30 years ago . . . and it's global warming now . . . The fact is there is no global warming."[9]

Southern Baptist preacher, presidential candidate, former governor of Arkansas, and Fox News host Mike Huckabee has insisted that global warming was not a reality but a distraction from the real dangers the country faced. As Huckabee quipped in January 2015, "A beheading is a far greater threat to an American than a sunburn."[10] When quips and tweets replace truth and facts we should know we have a problem.

The Illusion of Freedom

Climate denial gives deniers freedom from truth itself. "The most crucial of all the attractions of climate-denial is . . . that it provides would-be libertarians an ultimate freedom" (Rupert Read).[11] This raises a serious epistemological issue in that they are unwilling to be bound by anything, even truth itself. Freedom has replaced truth as the driving force for libertarians and many evangelicals. The irony here is that this epistemic sea change rises from an attitude of individualism and consumerism regarding truth. This marketing of truth as something that can't be nailed down, ironically, is a foundational principle in the political philosophy of liberalism.

Libertarians and evangelicals trafficking in liberal notions of subjectivity takes some adjustment. The demand for individual freedom

8. Desai, "Detractors Say."
9. Falwell, Sermon.
10. Kumar, "Huckabee Says ISIS Beheadings Greater Threat Than Climate Change."
11. Read, "What Is New in Our Time," 90.

energizes libertarians and evangelicals. The chorus of evangelical voices raised in protest of COVID restrictions mirrors that same disregard for truth. When COVID-19 first hit our shores, a significant number of evangelical pastors refused to close their doors on Sunday and defied orders by local governments to do so. A Louisiana pastor defied coronavirus order and drew over one thousand people to services. The pastor, Tony Spell of Life Tabernacle Church in Baton Rouge, said he does not believe his congregation is at risk of getting COVID-19, the disease associated with the coronavirus. "The virus, we believe, is politically motivated," Tony Spell said. "We hold our religious rights dear, and we are going to assemble no matter what someone says."[12]

Climate deniers are cut from the same cloth: "How dare you interfere with my rights, my freedom?" This misuse of a classic liberal political idea now passes for common sense: "even though it threatens to cut off at the knees action to prevent" the existential threats caused by climate change.[13]

The claims of absolute freedom and rights make up a large portion of the current political noise. It is hard to tell if the voices are more from libertarians or from evangelicals. It sounds like a combined choir. It is mostly a male choir. Many evangelicals are committed to a male-dominated view of life, and most of the preachers are males. Libertarians are overwhelmingly white and male.[14] Libertarianism and evangelicalism share a commitment to individualism and consumerism. Both of these components are dependent upon a notion of absolute freedom and "growthism." The danger lies in the social and ecological limits that we are encountering and will increasingly encounter with climate change. The reality is that continuing with unlimited economic growth over the coming two decades is incompatible with meeting our international obligations on climate change. As Kevin Anderson and Alice Bows-Larkin have said, "Avoiding dangerous climate change demands de-growth strategies from wealthier nations."[15] "The evidence is crystal clear: Nature is in trouble. Therefore, we are in trouble," says Sandra Díaz, one of the co-chairs of the UN Global Assessment Report on Biodiversity and

---

12. Rddad, "Pastor Tony Spell."
13. Read, "What Is New in Our Time," 83.
14. See Heer, "Why Are Libertarians Mostly Dudes?"
15. Anderson, "Avoiding Dangerous Climate Change."

Ecosystem Services.[16] Evidence, facts, scientific data sound like whistling in the dark to libertarians and many evangelicals.

The right to complete individual liberty is expressed most clearly in a bastardized version of the Baptist concept of the priesthood of the believer. Too often, the priesthood of the believer ignores the priestly aspect, which suggests a church hierarchy and a community of faith, to put all the focus on the individual believer. In politics, the priesthood of the believer has become the right to have opinions. "I have my opinion and you have yours" is a constant refrain. People professing to believe in the priesthood of the believer would probably be shocked by J. Whyte's article, "Sorry, But You Are Not Entitled to Your Opinion."[17] In the hierarchy of persuasion, beliefs occupy a higher rung than mere opinions, but now opinions have been elevated to a primary argument as in, "Well, you have your opinion and I have mine."

Libertarianism sets people free from truth. It gives them a licentious freedom of thought. The truth has now been packaged by a marketing firm and comes in more sizes, shapes, and colors than can be imagined. Truth is on sale at Walmart—a sort of consumerism of the mind. This is the ultimate freedom. Unwilling to be bound by anything, libertarians feel free to deny and reject anything they dislike. They are willing to concoct stories with no factual basis to trigger liberals. Florida governor Ron DeSantis has made up a "humdinger" of a lie about "woke" math textbooks. He claims that math textbooks are teaching Critical Race Theory.[18] He offers no evidence for his outrageous claim. Perhaps equilateral triangles made DeSantis suspicious. An equilateral triangle is a triangle that has all its sides equal in length. Is a triangle where all sides are equal a threat to the worldview of Governor DeSantis?

Two forces of irrational thought drive the libertarian/evangelical emotion machine: 1) The ability to churn out personalized propaganda and pass it off as the truth has gone into overdrive. The driver of this engine that turns truth into lies is Donald Trump. As a result, we may be in danger of losing the public sphere altogether. 2) The rise of individualist ideology. Aided by an evangelical theology of individual freedom, libertarians and many evangelicals are destroying the public sphere by

16. United Nations, "Global Assessment Report on Biodiversity."
17. Whyte, "Sorry."
18. Burnside, Sottile, and Chavez, "Florida rejects 41% of new math textbooks."

undermining our shared sense of the value of truth and our trust in the anchor institutions of democracy.

Disdain for truth and the mass marketing of lies has produced a nation of Pilates: "What is truth?" Faced with the absolute truth as revealed by Jesus, Pilate responded with one question, "What is truth?" It is absurd that we are walking into the mass genocide of climate catastrophe, asking, "What is truth?" Our sneering "How dare you?" couples with our insistent cries, "Who are you to tell me I must wear a mask?" Credibility, in the eyes of libertarians and evangelicals, has not only been undermined; it has been replaced with the absolute freedom to do anything based on their beliefs.

The Illusion of Rationality

Libertarians and evangelicals insist on a philosophy that is rigorously objective. Both claim they are welded to the truth and rationality. Evangelicals have long insisted that rationality and morality were the major ideas of American ethos. They applied the "scientific method" of Francis Bacon to the Bible, even though the Bible—a book of symbolic, metaphorical language—resists such a method. The nineteenth-century evangelicals were such thorough rationalists that they believed the higher critics of the Bible represented a conspiracy of intellectuals. Today, many evangelicals go on and on till doomsday that there is something elitist, deceptive, and dishonest about climate change, science, and history. This hard-wired claim to rationality and objective truth defines libertarianism and evangelicalism.

Herein lies the conundrum. Libertarian and evangelical commitment to rational truth clashes with the equally intense commitment to absolute freedom. Truth imposes restraints and constraints on one's ability to do and believe and think whatever one wants. Evangelicals sound suspiciously like they have been drinking from the liberal political fountain of John Stuart Mill and his principle of liberty. Mill argued that freedom from social interference was the best way to produce strong individuals. To interpret this to mean that freedom of thought provides us with complete license suggests a contradiction, especially for evangelicals. No card-carrying evangelical would ever suggest that moral freedom requires complete individual license, but that is exactly what they are implying with this insistence on complete freedom.

Read puts it exactly right, in my view: "Libertarians [and many evangelicals] can't stand to be told that they don't have as much epistemic right as anyone else on any topic that they like to think they understand or have some 'rights' in relation to. Thus, the cry rings out: 'Who are you to tell me that I have to defer to some scientist?'"[19] The demand for individual freedom rebounds across the evangelical churches. This sense of feeling free has never been as dominant or more potentially dangerous.

The Prophets of Doubt and Cynicism

This is the heart of the matter and helps explain the tragic spectacle of evangelical preachers—claiming to have the truth, the whole and literal truth, and nothing but the truth—becoming climate deniers, history deniers, science deniers, COVID restriction deniers. The preachers of truth have become the prophets of doubt, cynicism, and skepticism. The libertarian and evangelical love of truth and reason has crashed into a limit: their love of the unfettered pursuit of Mammon and the freedom to their own opinion, come hell or high water. And according to the scientific data it's the high water that's coming first, i.e., rising tides, melting ice caps.

The scientific consensus is clear: more than 95 percent of climate researchers agree that human activity is causing global warming, and that without action to combat it we are on a path to dangerous temperature rises from pre-industrial levels.[20]

The evidence that climate change is real gets discounted by a bit of trickery. Climate deniers claim that all these elitist scientists and radical left-wingers are agreeing with one another because they are scratching each other's backs. The argument turns scientific knowledge into a form of elitism. The scientist is not now seen as an expert, but as a suspect. The argument reduces to over-educated snobs attempting to tell common people what to think. The tricksters have convinced many people that climate change is another political con. This makes sense to an already mistrustful public.

The fight over climate reveals how easily politics can get in the way of the facts, and how hard it can be to escape once cynicism exerts its grip. In many ways, climate science is particularly vulnerable to political

---

19. Read, "What Is New in Our Time," 88.
20. Bawden, "Scientists."

distortion. But the issue of climate change also shows that it is a false comfort for liberal elites to think that the facts will win in the end. If they do, it won't be because we woke up to the science. It will be because we woke up to the politics.

Given the choice between the truth that we are going to have to rein in our appetites for "more" and our absolute freedom to do as we please for as long as we please, then the truth is that truth itself is crucified on the scaffold labeled freedom. The obsession with individual freedom increases mistrust among the public. Libertarians and many evangelicals become voluntaristic and contrarian because they can. It feels good and in the new culture of "feeling good," nothing matters more than emotions, affects—pathos. They end up believing what feels good, what feels right, what they want to believe. Not wanting to accept the scientific reality of ecology and climate science, they deny it. They end up looking like people standing in a church on the Atlantic ocean singing "Kum by yah my Lord" while the waters of the sea fill the building.

Absolute freedom aligned with a pretentious rationality and a strong insistence on doubt, cynicism, and mistrust put libertarians and many evangelicals on a downward spiral that also endangers the entire planet. To sum up, I think that the libertarian-evangelical alliance has been raging for decades and only recently has become so obvious. The politics of libertarianism, the politics of Donald Trump, have overwhelmed the theology of evangelicalism.

The total disregard for truth, facts, and rational deliberation puts us squarely in the realm of the rhetorical principle of ethos—a consideration of good and evil. When a people are no longer willing to be constrained by anything, even the truth, we are on the precipice of a new dark age in civilization. Aristotle's ancient concept of ethos claims center stage at a time when a sizeable portion of the American population insists that character doesn't matter. What matters is a strong leader, a strongman who will rule with an iron fist.

The intellectual class has weighed in from every available form of communication to sound the alarm about the dangers we face. A veritable Paul Revere army of political scientists, rhetorical critics, sociologists, historians, philosophers, and even the psychiatrists that first warned that Trump was mentally ill, have outlined the symptoms of a democracy at best in decline, at worst on the precipice of falling apart. Cornel West has spoken with clarity on the issue: "The great dramatic battle of the twenty-first century is the dismantling of empire and the deepening of democracy."[21]

West identifies three dominating, antidemocratic dogmas that threaten democracy: free-market fundamentalism, aggressive militarism, and escalating authoritarianism. Intertwined with these three dogmas is the militant crusader mentality of evangelical Christians—the bulwark of Trump support. Free-market fundamentalism has come back into style like an old tie hidden in the closet for so many years. "Taking as an article of faith that unfettered markets are self-correcting,"[22] the free-market fundamentalists have lambasted all government regulation as interference and resisted spending and tax legislation. They have engaged in the attempt at rehabilitating the reputation of an unregulated, small-spending, low-tax economy existing back in the day. These Market God worshipers acquitted the policies of the Coolidge years and decided that government intervention caused the Great Depression.

West's vision of reclaiming and saving democracy relies on three key components: the Socratic tradition, the Hebrew prophets, and the African American struggle against white supremacy. I have tweaked those to suggest that our response should also include Proverbs and Psalms, especially the pictures of good and evil that appear in these Hebrew texts. The Socratic tradition includes the rhetorical theory that finds expression throughout this study. The African American struggle emphasizes the importance of pathos—affects—in the battle to restore democracy. The archetypal pathos rises from the cry of the Israelites when they were slaves in Egypt: "The Israelites groaned under their slavery, and cried out. Out of the slavery their cry for help rose up to God. God heard their groaning, and God remembered his covenant with Abraham, Isaac, and Jacob. God looked upon the Israelites, and God took notice of them."[23] The cry of the slaves has been drowned out by the cries of American evangelicals pretending to be victims, pretending to be in a state of precarity. They have attempted to co-opt the powerful cries of the oppressed and now insist they are persecuted, misunderstood, and deprived of natural rights.

From the right there are jeremiads about a fracture that would be like a civil war, and from the heart of Texas spasmodic cries for secession. From the left there are illuminating studies of what's wrong with

---

21. West, *Democracy Matters*, 22.
22. McElvaine, *Great Depression*, xviii.
23. Exod 2:23b–25.

democracy. So many scholars have congregated at the "last-one-turn-out-the-lights" party, I thought I would attend in clerical robe and stole to offer ancient wisdom from Proverbs, Psalms, prophets, and ancient philosophers. As a generalist I dabble in theology, ethics, philosophy, history, and rhetoric. This study encapsulates these disciplines in an attempt to focus on the issues of good and evil in the garden of democracy. From Proverbs and the prophets we hear the primal scream of the evil that stalks the land. From the Psalms rises the songs that we must sing for life, for democracy. "O Democracy, for you, for you I am trilling these songs," wrote our most exuberant democrat, Walt Whitman.[24] From Plato and a long line of philosophers we are endowed with our fighting spirit for what matters in human life. This is a battle for ethos—for the reality that character counts, character matters.

The lies have to be fought with the truth. "A lying tongue lasts only for a moment,"[25] but in that moment the danger multiplies. No matter how contestable the truth may be, there must be ongoing attempts to keep saying, "This is the truth. Walk in it." Proverbs has a clear vision of what is good and what is true. Proverbs can serve as a political manual for democracy. While the context of Proverbs is the monarchy of Solomon, the universal principles of good government are written large on its pages. There's sheer goodness at our disposal in the embodiment of the "wise woman" of Proverbs. She presents herself as a wise teacher of rhetoric who will teach "the ropes" to young people destined for leadership roles in national politics.[26] How many Americans will come to a training in goodness with the wise woman of Proverbs and help create a blueprint for American renewal?

The subjects of good and evil dominate Proverbs and Plato's *Phaedrus*. Each presents a pair of dominant tropes. In Proverbs, there's the wise woman and the loose woman; in *Phaedrus* there's the good lover and the evil lover. In both cases, the tropes deal with good speakers and evil speakers. This is rhetorical battle royal.

A word about method: My use of Proverbs as a trope banquet rises from my belief that texts do not have a single meaning limited to the intent of the original author. A major reason for this interpretative principle is the symbolic language of the Bible. "The most difficult aspect of

---

24. Whitman, "For You, O Democracy," 99.

25. Prov 12:19b.

26. Prov 1:5 (in McKane translation, *Proverbs*). Hereafter simply indicated with "(McKane)."

the Bible's complexity is its use of symbols."²⁷ At the literal level, Proverbs seems to be a series of repeated warnings about sexual conduct and avoiding loose women, but the book of Proverbs is not about sex. In the rich world of symbols and tropes, Proverbs has richer meanings and inspired teachings about good and evil speech. In a 1983 review essay on Harold Bloom, James Arnt Aune explains that tropes are strategies of cultural invention used by lexical innovators who propel culture forward by formulating meanings different from those already in circulation. "Meaning, any meaning," notes Aune, "occurs as part of an agon or struggle with previous meaning."²⁸ According to this account, historical progress or cultural development depends in part on the struggle one has with and against the possibility that everything worth saying about important subjects has already been said and one risks only regurgitating the thoughts of previous thinkers. Thus, one turns to tropes "as a defense against literal meaning and the powerful presence of a precursor's meaning," both of which "are equivalent to death in that they prevent the impulse to communicate further."²⁹ To trope is to fight the anxiety of influence of one's precursors. Cultural progress depends, in this view, on memes: new words and new meanings for old words, phrases, and metaphors. Tropes are strategies for producing new meanings different from those already in circulation. "Meaning, any meaning," notes Aune, "occurs as part of a struggle with previous meaning."³⁰

Our pair of archetypal tropes dominate: Lady Wisdom and Loose Woman. One is the true Wisdom, the pure bride adorned for her husband; the other is the Loose Woman who is the incarnation of evil and disaster. This chapter describes the nature of good and evil in politics and rhetoric by investigating the biblical book of Proverbs and Plato's *Phaedrus*. Both works concern what constitutes the good life and the evil life, perhaps suggesting Proverbs as a biblical Plato. I read Proverbs as a rhetoric/ethics training manual for young adults who will become political officials.

Building on the work of Old Testament scholar William McKane, I suggest that the biblical book of Proverbs may be read as a work of rhetoric and may be compared with classic studies of rhetoric. McKane notes

---

27. Davis and Hays, eds., *Art of Reading Scripture*, 12.
28. Aune, "Burke's Late Blooming," argument throughout paraphrased.
29. Aune, "Burke's Late Blooming," 328.
30. Aune, "Burke's Late Blooming," 329.

that Proverbs has two distinct literary origins, and one is older than the other. The older of the two forms is represented by the "old wisdom" and the second by the language of piety and morality. In no sense am I making light of the moral implications of Proverbs, but my interest here is the vocabulary of the old wisdom, "with its robust intellectual content and its preoccupation with skill and aptitude."[31] The instruction offered is not a religious authority but a rhetorical one. "The wisdom teacher distills the sagacity of generations for the benefits of her pupils, basing her authority on what has proved best in the past and on her own judgement."[32] The old wisdom, in a proper sense, is "amoral" and concerns how to be not only a good person but also how to be a good citizen. It thus deals with politics and rhetoric. Chapters 1–9 of Proverbs present a "strenuous educational discipline which is productive of rigorous intellectual attitudes."[33]

Proverbs 1–9, 22:17–24:22, and 31:1–9 contain rhetorical instruction. The instruction is as early as Solomon, when a class of officials came into existence to serve the new structure of the state. In Egypt this instruction "was located in schools where an elite was trained for the service of the state; likewise, when Solomon created a civil service there would have been a demand for a similar type of school and for such an instrument of vocational education."[34] My only adjustment to this development is the suggestion that the more general school founded in Israel was a school of rhetoric. The students were taught not only how to speak "right" but to speak the language of right policies and politics. The school included instruction in knowledge and wisdom, but also was an embodied rhetoric.

Paramount in the ethos of the practical political instruction of wisdom was the telling of truth and the refusal to indulge in lies. Any consideration of good and evil in democracy investigates whether a politician is telling lies. "A faithful witness does not lie, but a false witness breathes out lies."[35] "A truthful witness saves lives, but one who utters lies is a betrayer."[36] Lies indicate the presence of evil as a parasite on goodness. Everywhere in the ethos of the Loose Woman there is a strong element of deception.

    31. McKane, *Proverbs*, 264.
    32. McKane, *Proverbs*, 264.
    33. McKane, *Proverbs*, 264.
    34. McKane, *Proverbs*, 9.
    35. Prov 14:5.
    36. Prov 14:25.

In the deep of winter, when the leaves are long missing in action from our trees, there are splotches of greenery scattered here and there. It's mistletoe, a leathery-leaved parasitic plant. No parasite has ever received as much acclaim as mistletoe. Mistletoe is believed to possess a magical affinity for seizure disorders. To prevent seizures, carry a piece of mistletoe in your pocket or within a conjure bag. Jewelry and charms carved from mistletoe wood can also be worn or carried. During the Christmas season, a piece of mistletoe hanging over the door invites a kiss to those standing beneath its sexual magic. But it's a parasite—an organism that lives in or on an organism of another species and derives nutrients at the expense of the host.

Setting aside magical beliefs and the joy of kissing under the mistletoe, I suggest that the parasite of human cruelty attaches itself to Christian beliefs. The tree of Christian belief is a life-giving tree with unparalleled generosity and receptivity. As Jesus says of the tree, "When it grows up and becomes the greatest of all shrubs, and puts forth large branches, so that the birds of the air can make nests in its shade."[37] The words of Ezekiel 31:6 are suggestive: "All the birds of the air made their nests in its boughs." All the birds of the air nesting in the tree posits an inclusiveness that is belied by the parasites that also embed themselves in the tree of life. Christian belief is always susceptible to parasites.

Evil impacts bodies in destructive and hurtful ways. "He goes like an ox to the slaughter, as a hart skips into a noose."[38] Evil has a way of existing as if it was part of some gnostic scheme to denigrate, abuse, misuse, and deny the material, the bodily, the fleshly. Evil does its dirty work in bodies, but in its rhetoric, it speaks from the high and lofty mountains of freedom, patriotism, and goodness. Connecting thought with materiality and positing sensuousness as communication unmasks the evil within the body. When we consider the ways in which bodies are treated because of hard-core beliefs we bump into racism, sexism, nativism, heteronormative toxic maleness—all having to do with bodies. Beliefs can manufacture cruelty. "At its most broadly productive, a move to the body also engages the multiple scientific, musical, or religious perspectives that most carefully contemplate bodies, rhythms, and movements, none of which can or need to be easily disentangled from sociocultural or economic forces, but all of which bear importantly on meaning making,

---

37. Matt 13:32.
38. Prov 7:23 (McKane).

language use, and, yes, thought itself."[39] Those engaged in evil are free to do their worst under the protection of a theological belief system.

The attachment of cruelty to belief has precedents much older than Christian beliefs. The proponents of beliefs often interpret the Bible "in ways that authorize appalling abuse, even murder, of Jews, slaves, colonized peoples, homosexuals."[40] The Bible, stitched together over the centuries, has a stark historical honesty in showing where all the bodies are buried. Nothing is covered up even when there are official scribes of the king involved in telling the stories. Alongside the official version of the truth, there are the songs and speeches of prophets, psalmists, poets—telling the subversive, counter truth. Walter Brueggemann says that other truth "is carried by song, oracle, and narrative that continually subvert official truth."[41] There's no hiding from the reality that the Bible "emanates from a culture that was . . . xenophobic, patriarchal, classist, and bloodthirsty."[42]

The "true believers" make no connection between what they believe and how the bodies of others are treated. This leads to strange stances like evangelical pastors defending the separation of migrant children from their parents at the border and putting children in cages. When beliefs are more important than bodies, bodies suffer. David Livingston Smith has lucidly demonstrated our capacity to be "less than human" as we trample across the terrain demeaning, enslaving, and exterminating others.[43] Always attached to the Christians "marching as to war" is the parasite of cruelty—slavery, colonialism, racism, sexism, toxic masculinity, and a host of other harmful cruelties against the bodies of others. A crusade may sound righteous, but its impact on bodies is evil.

There needs to be a reckoning about the nature of cruelty and its intimate ties to religious belief—especially white Christian beliefs. "As intensity, or an emotional force which acts upon the body, cruelty emerges out of an encounter between the self and the Other. It is in that encounter, or infliction, that cruelty is dependent on affective identification of a body as deserving cruelty."[44] For example, when Christians believe that homo-

---

39. Hawhee, *Moving Bodies*, 2.
40. Davis and Hays, eds., *Art of Reading Scripture*, 165.
41. Brueggemann, *Truth Speaks to Power*, 2.
42. Davis and Hays, eds., *Art of Reading Scripture*, 165.
43. Smith, *Less than Human*.
44. Levina, "Whiteness and the Joys of Cruelty," 75.

sexuality is an abomination in the eyes of God, homosexual bodies are marked as the "other" not only as a sexual identifier, but more importantly, affectively, as a body to which cruelty can "stick." Beliefs do not exist in splendid isolation that simply give believers the euphoric feeling of being right. Beliefs are sticky things. Beliefs are characterized by their attachments. Cruelty sticks to beliefs in such deep ways that the cruelty seems justified by the beliefs. "Stickiness," after all, is a primary characteristic of the parasite. Objects become "sticky"—that is, "saturated with affects."[45] The believer receives a kind of perverse joy in the exercise of cruelty even when she says, "I have nothing against gays; some of my best friends are gays."

What can be easily forgotten is that harm has a history. In the short story, "This Is the Only Time I'll Tell It," an infant is saved from a drunken father's attempt to drown her in a bucket of icy water. The little girl was saved by a woman named Zelene. The church voted to give the child to Zelene and at the baby's baptism, "Zelene only ran one finger down the thin arm that crazy man had broken, saying in silence that the mark was made deep, that water meant for drowning had gone inside this child, that no grown body—at any size—would ever be fully dry of that knowledge."[46] As Sara Ahmed puts it, "Pain is the bodily life of that history."[47] Violence is not simply inflicted upon the body of the individual who was shunned or shut out from the family and faith community for being gay. The body of the family and the church are also part of the violence of the young man being torn apart. Here, the damage cares nothing for the rightness or wrongness of the belief responsible for the tearing apart. The righteous ones who expel the son, who rip him away from a lifetime of affection, community, and belonging, are also part of the violence. It is a blow to the basic tissues of social, family, and faith life that damages the bonds attaching people to one another. The "one another" is disrupted and becomes a "you" versus "them." This pain of separation, this hurt, this bereavement makes recovery so difficult, and it remains in the memory of the bodies forever.

The adhesive that gives the quality of stickiness is "disgust." Ahmed demonstrates how "disgust" produces those who are deemed

---

45. Ahmed, *Cultural Politics of Emotion*, Kindle ed., loc. 288.
46. Betts, "This Is the Only Time I'll Tell It," Kindle ed., loc. 3264.
47. Ahmed, *Cultural Politics of Emotion*, Kindle ed., loc. 829.

"disgusting—as the bodies that must be ejected from the community."[48] Disgust shapes the bodies into a community of the disgusted by sticking all these objects together. For example, when someone says of a young woman who reports a sexual assault, "You are disgusting," the blame transfers from the perpetrator to the victim and, often, with the consent of the establishment, sticks to the victim. The victim is "disgusting"; the young male perpetrator "is a good young man from a nice family." Cohesion demands adhesion. In other words, by creating a body of "others" who are disgusting, they all are stuck together as the rejected ones. This new category of the "disgusting" sticks to the entire group. This is a part of the "ickiness," the "tackiness," the enduring cruelty of stickiness.

"I believe that connectedness to joy is essential for theorizing cruelty."[49] Cruelty is the joy with which Christian beliefs about others assert themselves. For cruelty to exist, there must be bodies that are deemed unworthy of respect and deserving of cruelty. There are Christians promoting hard-core beliefs with cruelty attached and the horror of this is that it gives them the joy of power over others. Is not this part of the anti-abortion heartbeat?—power over women by making abortion a crime. Is not this part of the anti-gay movement?—power over gays by making gayness a crime. Cruelty attaches itself to power—a rush of good feeling. Levina suggests, "Cruelty is the joy with which whiteness asserts itself."[50] "It is not until we reckon with the intimate and joyful connection between whiteness and cruelty that we can make political, cultural, and economic choices that lead us toward empathy."[51]

The parasitical cruelty attached to Christian beliefs extends to hurtful condemnation of those who dare to dissent from certain beliefs. Some beliefs are themselves parasites and when they embed onto the tree of life, they bring along their natural cruelty. Examples include creationism and its insistence of creatio ex nihilo. Any person daring to suggest that creationism is a false doctrine will be subjected to verbal and emotional cruelty with an outburst of name-calling. There's no more basic form of cruelty than name-calling: heretic, blasphemer, liberal, unbeliever. A collection of negative labels are compiled by the name-calling community and they are repeated for each person that is to be culled out from the

---

48. Ahmed, *Cultural Politics of Emotion*, Kindle ed., loc. 399.
49. Levina, "Whiteness and the Joys of Cruelty," 76.
50. Levina, "Whiteness and the Joys of Cruelty," 76.
51. Levina, "Whiteness and the Joys of Cruelty," 77.

community of true believers. Name-calling is a subspecies of the cruelty parasite. It has the same "stickiness." Negative labels stick to persons demeaned, labeled, and called hurtful names.

When a group of Christians coalesce around a particular belief, make that one belief that crucial, primal, and the only acceptable mark of true Christianity, they have produced the kind of environment where cruelty thrives. Beliefs are weaponized and use to inflict pain on others. Belief and cruelty become a matched pair. Using belief as a force and a tool to gain compliance or to exercise cruelty over others is a perversion.

If our beliefs give life and breath to cruelty, we need to rethink and reject those beliefs. This is true if the cruelty resides in racism, sexism, or self-righteous judgmentalism of others. It is also true if the cruelty resides in attacking the alleged "Other" with name-calling and labeling that sticks to them and marks them as "disgusting." Beliefs, it turns out, are themselves sticky and what sticks to beliefs can be evil.

Proverbs as Rhetoric Text — Proverbs as Good Rhetor

Proverbs 1–9 is a sustained argument by a woman speech instructor named Wisdom. Her curriculum contrasts the good with the evil path. "Every good path," "walk in the of the good," "favor and good repute." Proverbs refers frequently to the path or the trail or the "tracks" of life and death. "There is a way that seems right to a person, but its end is the way to death."[52] I maintain that Proverbs 14:12 is the theme verse of Proverbs. This verse also offers insight into the power of the evil that now threatens democracy: "a way that seems right." There exists a template or rhetoric that "seems to be right." Such speech gives the impression of having the quality of rightness. This is the genius of Donald Trump's rhetoric. To millions of Americans, he gives the impression of being right, of being God's anointed, of standing up for America. His "seems to be" smacks, however, of illusion, as one of the primary viruses in the template of the Evil One. What makes this even more powerful is that any critique is automatically suspect. The wisdom of Proverbs suggests that "the one who first states a case seems right, until the other comes and cross-examines,"[53] but the opposite has been true with Trump.

52. Prov 14:12; 16:25.
53. Prov 18:17.

Wisdom extolls her virtue: "I have good advice and sound wisdom; I have insight, I have strength."[54] "The desire of the righteous ends only in good."[55] The analysis of these sections of Proverbs focuses attention on the rhetorical nature, vocabulary, and imagery of goodness. Since the "aim is to command and persuade," I believe the instructions include what is necessary for a person to not only be good and wise, but also to be a good speaker. Wisdom and speech are partners. The opening verses of Proverbs read like course objectives in a public speaking textbook. The objectives of public speaking from Proverbs are: "For learning about wisdom and instruction, for understanding words of insight, for gaining instruction in wise dealing, righteousness, justice, and equity; to teach shrewdness to the simple, knowledge and prudence to the young—let the wise also hear and gain in learning, and the discerning acquire skill, to understand a proverb and a figure, the words of the wise and their riddles."[56]

The Noble Lover and the Woman of Wisdom

In glaring contrast to the Loose Woman is the Woman of Wisdom. Here we are treated to the ethos of integrity, wisdom, goodwill, and goodness. Now ethos takes center stage because a politician's greatest strength is her moral/ethical character. The Lady of Wisdom resides in the home of the Noble Lover and the Good Rhetor. She is a good woman speaking well. She has given her life in service to the common good, which matters more than acquiring knowledge. She is a studious woman. Paul Griffiths, in his *Intellectual Appetite: A Theological Grammar*, argues that curiosity was, among the ancients, a form of greed. The desire for knowledge was an effort to give the knower control over that which they knew. Griffiths refers to this as "sequestered intimacy."[57] The curious, greedy for knowledge, are like the non-lover in the speech of Lysias, following the way of enlightened self-interest. The non-lover never has occasion for remorse, never says that he is sorry, and has no reason to repent. The non-lover never sacrifices himself and demonstrates his superiority by what he knows that others do not know. Knowledge, in this sense, is for the exclusive use

54. Prov 8:14.
55. Prov 11:23.
56. Prov 1:1–6.
57. Griffiths, *Intellectual Appetite*, 21.

of those who have come to know. The alternative to curiosity, according to Griffiths, is studiousness. This is a form of love because it is not the acquisition of knowledge to be owned or possessed. This is shared knowledge, participated in with the community lovingly as a gift. The knowledge paired with wisdom in Proverbs is studiousness. It is knowledge that makes possible a shared life. The willingness to share what we have learned has much to do with how much we are willing to give away. The Woman of Wisdom in Proverbs willingly offers all her knowledge to others for the good of all. This is a "participatory intimacy."[58] She guides her students into the land of wonder: the wonder of creation, the wonder that there is anything at all, the wonder that comes from knowing that we exist in a good world made by a good God who had made us to be good, and the wonder directed at particular creatures such as ants, "a darling hind," "a graceful doe,"[59] and birds.

The wise woman, the teacher of wisdom and truth is a gracious woman. "A gracious woman gets honor."[60] Or, as Plato might put it, "If wisdom could be seen with the eyes, it would arouse astonishing feelings of love for it." Proverbs presents Wisdom as a beautiful and righteous woman to be loved and cherished: "Do not forsake her, and she will keep you; love her, and she will guard you."[61]

The Wise Woman does everything within her persuasive power to lead her students to the likeness of and fear of the Lord. Instead of exploiting others, she releases them to lives of knowledge, wisdom, holiness, and goodness. In this reading all speech possesses a persuasive, seductive power and is a kind of love. Lady Wisdom is to be courted, wooed, and won. She is the good lover of Plato's *Phaedrus*. Look at her: more profitable than silver, a higher yield than gold, more precious than jewels. "Nothing you desire bears comparison to her."[62] Notice the sexual concept of desire. "Her ways are ways of pleasantness, and all her paths are peace."[63] "Wisdom comes first, get Wisdom and with all your getting get Insight. Hold her in high esteem and she will get preferment for

---

58. See Griffiths, *Intellectual Appetite*.
59. Prov 5:19 (McKane).
60. Prov 11:16.
61. Prov 4:6.
62. Prov 3:15.
63. Prov 3:17.

you."[64] "Take hold of Instruction (Wisdom), do not relax your grip (never let her go), mount a guard over her, for she is your life."[65]

In her most dramatic, rhetorical, and passionate presentation, the Wise Woman appeals to her students (Prov 8). Wisdom calls out, raises her voice. "On the high ground beside the road . . . she takes up her stance."[66] She makes her case to the men and insists "my words are for humankind." She offers those she is seducing, in the positive sense, shrewdness, wisdom, acumen, understanding, insight, and perception. Rather than engaging in a rhetoric that is all flowers and sweetness, she insists, "my speech is straightforward," "my utterances plain,"[67] "my mouth speaks the truth,"[68] "all my sayings are honest, nothing in them is tortuous or twisted,"[69] "they are all plain to the perceptive man and straightforward to the perceptive man."[70]

Her next words are the most rhetorical, in the highest philosophical sense: "I, Wisdom, am neighbor to shrewdness, I find out the right procedures. . . . I possess policy and competence, insight and power. By me kings reign, and rulers enact what is right. By me statesmen wield power, and nobles—all entitled to rule. I love those who love me and those who seek me will find me." "I walk in the path of righteousness, in the tracks of justice."[71] The wise woman knows that politics is about policies instead of performances. What is right can't be enacted by politicians whose every speech ends up being about nothing except anger, resentment, and attacks on the character of others.

Proverbs 8 is the career-defining speech of the Wisdom speech professor. She exclaims that she mixes with men in the most busy and public places of the town, where they gather for social intercourse, the transaction of business, and political discussion. She enters the public arena and assumes the role of a speaker in the public forum of the town. Her speech inspires men to goodness, not insurrection.

---

64. Prov 4:5–8a (McKane).
65. Prov 4:13.
66. Prov 8:2 (McKane).
67. Prov 8:6 (McKane).
68. Prov 8:7 (McKane).
69. Prov 8:8 (McKane).
70. Prov 8:9 (McKane).
71. Prov 8:12–17 (McKane).

That this is public and political is made clear in 8:14–16. "I possess policy and competence, insight and power. By me kings reign, and rulers enact what is right. By me statesmen wield power, and nobles—all entitled to rule." Wisdom presents herself and her speech as the example her students are to follow. One day they will be charged with the task of being statesmen and responsible for making both for righteousness and goodness in the world. Her speech is "firmly anchored in the ethos of the old wisdom."[72] She models tradition, decorum, manners, and dignity.

The vocabulary of verses 12 and 14 argues that wisdom "knows her way about the world and has expertise in earthy, hard-headed procedures and negotiations."[73] Here Wisdom speaks as a statesman using a vocabulary descriptive of the attitudes, skills, and executive abilities associated with good government. The Wisdom speaking to the men in the public sphere has a cosmic background. Wisdom declares, "Yahweh created me at the beginning, as the most primaeval of his acts in antiquity. In the distant past I was formed, at the beginning, before the world began to be." "I was beside him as his confidant." [74]

The sense of playfulness that dominates in verses 30–31 suggests the intimacy of Wisdom with God: "I gave him pleasure daily, jesting before him continually; jesting about his created world, and the pleasure I got from human beings."[75] Wisdom is the voice of God and her speech not only needs to be heard but put into action by good men who are also good speakers. Wisdom speaks with confidence. She is the voice of God.

Wisdom, in this speech of the lover, claims to be the lover of the divine, the Truth. There is an element of courtship involved with the Woman of Wisdom. The playful words sound strange to our ears, but it a pushing of the metaphor of the good lover to its maximum expression. "Love her and she will guard you."[76] "She will get you honor if you embrace her.[77]"

Socrates, also using personification for wisdom, makes the same sort of grand claims for the power of rhetoric: "I do not compel anyone to learn to speak without knowing the truth, but if my advice is of any

---

72. McKane, *Proverbs*, 343.
73. McKane, *Proverbs*, 347.
74. Prov 8:22, 30 (McKane).
75. Prov 8:30–31 (McKane).
76. Prov 4:6 (McKane).
77. Prov 4:8b (McKane).

value, he learns that first and then acquires me. So, what I claim is this, that without my help the knowledge of the truth does not give the art of persuasion."[78]

The Good Rhetor

Rhetoric is grounded in choice and carries with it a strong ethical consideration. This fits the theme of Proverbs 14:12 well. "The purpose of rhetoric," said Plato, "was to make the will of God known."[79] To Plato, truth was all that mattered in life. Truth existed in the minds of the gods. Truth originates in the divine. He illustrated this notion in *The Republic*. Rhetoric concerns goodness. The good speaker should know the truth of what she is going to speak. The good speaker defines her terms and knows that the terms are debatable. The nature of the soul must be shown; in other words, the speaker is a psychologist. The speaker will have such a high moral purpose in all her work that she will be constantly obsessed about saying that which is "acceptable to God." Rhetoric is an instrument for making the will of God prevail. "The perfect rhetorician, as a philosopher, knows the will of God."[80]

Proverbs insists "The fear of God is the beginning of knowledge."[81] Aristotle said that one of the functions of rhetoric was to make truth and justice prevail. Proverbs notes that the student's task is "to receive effective instruction, righteousness, justice, and uprightness."[82] Quintilian argued that a rhetor is a good man skilled in speaking. According to Proverbs, "To make an apt answer is a joy to anyone, and a word in season, how good it is!"[83] For example, Adlai Stevenson's goals were to "talk sense to the American people" and "to tell them the truth." In his 1952 acceptance speech as the Democratic nominee for president, Stevenson said, "Let's talk sense to the American people. Let's tell them the truth, that there are no gains without pains, that there that we are now on the eve of great decisions, not easy decisions, like resistance when you're attacked, but a long, patient, costly struggle which alone can assure triumph over the

---

78. Plato, *Phaedrus*, 260.
79. Golden, *Rhetoric of Western Thought*, 176.
80. Hunt, *Plato and Aristotle on Rhetoric and Rhetoricians*, 25.
81. Prov 1:7.
82. Prov 1:3.
83. Prov 15:23.

great enemies of man—war, poverty, and tyranny—and the assaults upon human dignity which are the most grievous consequences of each."[84] He approached the nomination for president with a deep sense of humility. He would not glibly seek the nomination for the presidency, because the burdens of that office stagger the imagination. Its potential for good or evil, now and in the years of our lives, smothers exultation and converts vanity to prayer.

"I have asked the Merciful Father—the Father of us all—to let this cup pass from me, but from such dreaded responsibility one does not shrink in fear, in self-interest, or in false humility. So, 'If this cup may not pass from me, except I drink it, Thy will be done.'"[85] Stevenson praised Winston Churchill and John F. Kennedy for their success in marshalling elements of rhetoric in educating and elevating their countrymen in moments of crisis—a far cry from the speeches of President Trump during the pandemic. Trump's speech fails to meet any of those standards. Robert L. Ivie says of Trump, "The language of excess—hyperbole, incivility, and an appeal to nostalgia that relies on significant erasures—threatens to become the enduring and defining feature of the nation's politics."[86] Bonnie Dow adds, "Trump . . . communicated most effectively through hyperbole, untruthful and often incoherent claims and threats against his opposition, using such strategies to whip huge crowds into a frenzy."[87]

Accepting Richard Weaver's contention that "language is sermonic" suggests that "speech" and "words" are obvious candidates for investigation.[88] Weaver insists that the communicator must function as a minister who urges people to make ethical choices about good and evil. In describing language as sermonic, he observes, "It is impossible to talk about rhetoric as effective expression without having a term giving intelligibility to the whole discourse, the Good."[89] Weaver reminds us that "there are but three ways for language to affect us. It can move us toward what is good; it can move us toward what is evil; or it can . . . fail to move us at all."[90] Karl Wallace adds that "the substance of rhetoric is 'good reasons,'

---

84. Baker, "Let's Talk Sense to the American People."
85. Baker, "Let's Talk Sense to the American People."
86. Ivie, "Trump's Unwitting Prophecy," 707.
87. Dow, "Taking Trump Seriously," 136.
88. Weaver, *Language Is Sermonic*.
89. Weaver, *Language Is Sermonic*, 80.
90. Weaver, *Language Is Sermonic*, 60.

and "the basic materials of discourse are ethical and moral values and information relevant to these."[91] Proverbs, structured in a poetic/rhetorical form, does not lend its wisdom to literal readings. "It is a limitation to suppose that the truth of the story lies in its historicity. There are no reasons to attempt to supplant poetic analogy with fact. It would be like an archaeologist saying that she was looking for the foundations of the Garden of Eden or for the ark of Noah." These empty searches play havoc with the truth. Weaver points out, "But while this sort of search goes on the truth flies off, on wings of imagination, and is not recoverable until the searcher attains a higher level of pursuit."[92]

One of the purposes of the Wisdom Teacher has to do with students learning the epistemic value of metaphors: "Acquire skill, to understand a proverb and a figure, the words of the wise and their riddles."[93] Proverbs 1:6 describes the forms of literary art in which the wise man has a competence.

The Wisdom Teacher wages war with language and with goodness. Richard Weaver wrote that rhetoric is "persuasive speech in the service of truth."[94] He also argued that rhetoric should "create an informed appetition for the good."[95] Aristotle insisted that the function of rhetoric was to make truth and justice prevail. Quintilian established the precedent with these words: "I am convinced that no one can be an orator who is not a good man, and even if anyone could, I would be unwilling that he should be."[96] Old Testament scholar Maurice A. Canny argues that the Hebrew word *melis,* used in Proverbs, means "fluent speaker," "advocate," "ambassador."[97] The Wisdom Teacher acts as a speech professor: "Wisdom cries aloud in the streets [like a public speaker], she raises her voice in the squares. At the busiest corner she cries out; at the entrance of the city gate she speaks."[98] The place of the speechmaking—the entrance of the city gate—suggests the political arena. Second Samuel 15:1 records that Absalom hatched his plot to overthrow King David "beside the road

---

91. Wallace, "Substance of Rhetoric," 240.
92. Weaver, *Language Is Sermonic,* 59.
93. Prov 1:6.
94. Weaver, *Life Without Prejudice,* 116–18.
95. Weaver, *Life Without Prejudice,* 116–18.
96. Quintilian, *Complete Works,* Kindle ed., loc. 285.
97. Canney, "Hebrew 'Melis,'" 135.
98. Prov 1:20–21.

into the gate." Discernment, knowledge, competence, wisdom, resourcefulness—all are necessary skills for the good rhetor. The student learns negotiating skills, soundness of judgement, and becomes a person who "knows the ropes."[99] The rhetorician of Proverbs educated men to make their way successfully in the world as it was.

Proverbs 1:5, by aligning wisdom with metaphor, suggests not only an epistemic power for metaphor, but also the rhetorical purpose of the book—"A wise man listens and appropriates more (wisdom) and a perceptive man learns the ropes." Learning the tropes is the rhetorical equivalent to learning the ropes. The Wisdom Teacher knows that truth is contestable and elusive. "The purposes in the human mind are like deep water, but the intelligent will draw them out."[100] Flannery O'Connor famously said, "The truth does not change according to our ability to stomach it."[101] Real investigation goes forward with the help of analogy, what David Tracy identified as the "analogical imagination,"[102] and Paul Ricoeur, "the mytho-poetic core of imagination."[103] No person can be wise who has not steeped himself in that wisdom which is the deposit of the best minds of many generations. The wise speech teacher instructs students how good people in the past have spoken. To learn the wisdom of the ages is to learn another language and becomes the foundation for learning how to speak as well as teach others how to talk, as we say in Louisiana, "right." Here we have a metaphor for the negotiating skills necessary for goodness in politics and personal life.

This aligns with Chaim Perelman's claim that the "goal of all argumentation is to create or increase the adherence of minds to the theses presented for this assent."[104] "Epideictic oratory", Perelman argues, "has significance and importance for argumentation because it strengthens the disposition toward action by increasing adherence to the values it lauds."[105] There is no doubt the tradents of Proverbs expect students to act in righteousness and justice. A speaker's message is a moment akin to courtship—an attempt to create a relationship. The speaker, in effect,

---

99. Prov 1:5b (McKane).
100. Prov 20:5.
101. O'Connor, *Habit of Being*, 100.
102. Tracy, *Analogical Imagination*.
103. Ricoeur, *Freud and Philosophy*, 35–36.
104. Perelman and Olbrechts-Tyteca, *New Rhetoric*, 45.
105. Perelman and Olbrechts-Tyteca, *New Rhetoric*, 50.

woos his listeners. This wooing can result in total identification and good or evil results. The speaker's responsibility is to eliminate this division through identification based on courtship. The speaker woos the audience with a common language and shared values.

Ethos always lurks here because the "wooing" may be for good or for evil. The Loose Woman practices the art of rhetoric, but she is deceptive and harmful. Her words are smooth, her purpose is deceit, and her end is death. In this act of at-onement or reconciliation, understanding becomes the key element. I. A. Richards makes the remarkable claim that rhetoric deals with meaning. "Rhetoric, I shall urge, should be a study of misunderstanding and its remedies. It should concern itself with 'How much and in how many ways may good communication differ from bad?'"[106] Rhetoric, when noble, results in action. Proverbs announces from the beginning her intention to train her rhetorical students in the art of understanding. "For learning about wisdom and instruction, for understanding words of insight, for gaining instruction in wise dealing, righteousness, justice, and equity."[107] These are worthy rhetorical goals. Burke shows the relationship between understanding and persuasion: "Wherever there is persuasion, there is rhetoric . . . And wherever there is 'meaning' there is 'persuasion.'"[108] Understanding and meaning are thus synonymous and a rhetoric ground in understanding, insight, and wisdom is essential to goodness.

Speech and Words

The obvious connection between Proverbs and rhetoric is speech. Proverbs often refers to the act of speaking: "At the busiest corner she cries out; at the entrance of the city gates she speaks."[109] "Hear, for I will speak noble things, and from my lips will come what is right."[110] "Speak out for those who cannot speak, for the rights of all the destitute."[111] Proverbs is more speech acts than epigrams, more reality-making metaphors of wisdom and folly than an ancient collection of tweets. Proverbs centers

---

106. Richards and Constable, *Philosophy of Rhetoric*, 3.
107. Prov 1:2–3.
108. Burke, *Rhetoric of Motives*, 72.
109. Prov 1:21.
110. Prov 8:6.
111. Prov 31:8.

on a pair of personified metaphors: A Wise Woman and a Loose Woman. "It is necessary, therefore, to be alert for what takes place through the analogical mode."[112]

These two women engage in the art of seduction in Proverbs. Proverbs provides echoes of the "subtle" creature of the garden of Eden, the talking snake. Both offer a course in rhetoric, values, ethics, choices, speech, conduct, obligation, and duty. Proverbs is an epistle of ethos wrapped in the tropes of eros. This puts the Wise Woman in direct competition with the strange woman who is in the streets, in the squares, and "beside every corner she skulks."[113] The wise woman "takes up her stance."[114] Her voice rings out with declarations that are all rhetorical in nature in chapter 8. There are these scenes where the tradents seem to be a bunch of sexists, sounding like the headmasters of private schools for boys, counseling the young men to behave themselves with the girls. The advice seems to veer into the ditch of an authoritarian, patriarchal, petty bourgeois, puritanical, old-fashioned, narrow-minded, negative morality. In a literal reading, Proverbs is thus rendered as a sex manual to warn against adultery and fornication.

In analogical imagination, however, the Wise Woman and the Loose Woman become personifications of good rhetoric and evil rhetoric. Why, we may ask, is so much of Proverbs about the sexual relationships of men and women? The same question, in a different form, has been raised about *Phaedrus*. Why is so much said about the relationship of the lover and the non-lover? Far from seeing a sex manual stated in ethical terms, the two women represent evil love/evil rhetor and good love/good rhetor. In both Proverbs and the *Phaedrus*, we encounter two understandings of rhetoric: Rhetoric that can move us in the direction of what is good or rhetoric that can move us in the direction of evil. Weaver calls "the evil lover" a "base rhetoric" because its end is shame and death. "Base rhetoric is always trying to keep its objects from the support which personal courage, noble associations, and divine philosophy provide a person."[115]

Socrates delivers a speech that centers on the point that the lover is an exploiter. Love is defined as the kind of desire that overcomes rational

---

112. Weaver, *Language Is Sermonic*, 58.
113. Prov 7:12 (McKane).
114. Prov 8:2 (McKane).
115. Weaver, *Language Is Sermonic*, 66.

opinion and moves toward the enjoyment of personal or bodily beauty. This is the picture of the evil lover. Weaver says,

> The lover wishes to make the object of his passion as pleasing to himself as possible; but to those possessed by this frenzy, only that which is subject to their will is pleasant. Accordingly, everything which is opposed, or is equal or better, the lover views with hostility. He naturally therefore tries to make the beloved inferior to himself in every respect. He is pleased if the beloved has intellectual limitations because they have the effect of making him manageable.[116]

For a similar reason he tries to keep him away from all influences which might "make a man of him," and of course the greatest of these is divine philosophy. While he is working to keep him intellectually immature, he works also to keep him weak and effeminate, with such harmful result that the lover is unable to play a man's part in crises.[117] (Say hello to McCarthy, Gaetz, Graham, and Jordan, to name only four of Trump's "lovers.")

The lover is, moreover, jealous of the possession of property that he does not wish him to have. Thus, the lover in exercising an unremitting compulsion over the beloved deprives him of all praiseworthy qualities, and this is the price the beloved pays for accepting a lover who is "necessarily without reason."[118] In brief, the lover is not motivated by benevolence toward the beloved, but by selfish appetite; and Socrates can aptly close with the quotation: "As wolves love lambs, so lovers love their loves."[119] (Similarly, Trump only cares about himself.) The speech is on the single theme of exploitation.

As we look now for the parallel in language, we find ourselves confronting the second of the three alternatives: speech that influences us in the direction of what is evil. (Trump's January 6 speech influenced his followers in the direction of what was evil and criminal.) As noted already, Weaver calls this "base rhetoric."[120] The purpose of base rhetoric is exploitation, and it hates all that is opposed. The base rhetor knows only his own will. He will bend every rule to overcome the objective, stubborn

---

116. Weaver, *Language Is Sermonic*, 65.
117. Weaver, *Language Is Sermonic*, 65.
118. Weaver, *Language Is Sermonic*, 66.
119. Weaver, *Language Is Sermonic*, 66.
120. Weaver, *Language Is Sermonic*, 66.

restraint of the truth, to the point of denying the truth and producing an alternate truth.

We find that base rhetoric hates that which is opposed or is equal or better because all such things are impediments to its will, and in the last analysis it knows only its will. Truth is the stubborn, objective restraint that this will endeavors to overcome. Base rhetoric is therefore always trying to keep its objects from the support that personal courage, noble associations, and divine philosophy provide a man.

The base rhetorician, we may say, is a man who has yielded to the wrong aspects of existence. He has allowed himself to succumb to the sights and shows, to the physical pleasures that conspire against a noble life. He knows that the only way he can get a following in his pursuits (and a following seems necessary to maximum enjoyment of the pursuits) is to work against true understanding of his followers. Consequently, the things that would elevate he keeps out of sight, and the things with which he surrounds his "beloved" are those that minister immediately to desire. The beloved is thus emasculated in understanding in order that the lover may have his way. Or as Socrates expresses it, the selfish lover contrives things so that the beloved will be "most agreeable to him and most harmful to himself."[121]

Examples of this kind of contrivance occur on every hand in the impassioned language of journalism and political pleading. In the world of affairs that these seek to influence, the many are kept in a state of pupillage so that they will be most docile to their "lovers." The techniques of the base lover, especially as exemplified in modern journalism, would make a long catalogue, but in general it is accurate to say that he seeks to keep the understanding in a passive state by never permitting an honest examination of alternatives. Nothing is more feared by him than a true dialectic, for this not only endangers his favored alternative, but also gives the "beloved"—how clearly here are these the "lambs"[122] of Socrates's figure—some training in intellectual independence. What he does therefore is dress up one alternative in all the cheap finery of immediate hopes and fears, knowing that if he can thus prevent a masculine exercise of imagination and will, he can have his way. By discussing only one side of an issue, by mentioning cause without consequence or consequence without cause, acts without agents or agents without agency,

---

121. Weaver, *Language Is Sermonic*, 67.
122. Weaver, *Language Is Sermonic*, 67.

he often successfully blocks definition and cause-and-effect reasoning. In this way his choices are arrayed in such meretricious images that one can quickly infer the juvenile mind that they would attract. Of course, the base rhetorician today, with his vastly augmented power of propagation, has means of deluding that no ancient rhetor in forum or marketplace could have imagined.

Loose Woman/Evil Lover/Evil Rhetor

Proverbs warns often of evil. Do not keep company with evil people. Do not give your consent to evil persons. Proverbs 1 outlines the speech of an evil person: "Come with us, let us lay an ambush for blood, let us waylay the innocent at our whim; let us swallow them as Sheol swallows life . . . We shall find the rarest wealth, we shall fill our houses with spoil. Throw in your lot with us, there is one purse for all."[123] Here is the speech of evil. At times, evil can be more subtle and can sound as if she is being honest. Sweet talk that drips honey; smooth words pretending to be about freedom and rights and dignity.

The Loose Woman appears in Proverbs 2:16–19; 5:3–23, 7:7–27, 9:13–18; and 22:14. She makes her first appearance in chapter 2 and returns again and again. There's an extended visual metaphor of a "loose"/"strange" woman. "You will be saved from the loose woman, from the adulteress with her smooth words."[124] "For the lips of a loose woman drip honey, and her speech is smoother than oil."[125] "That they may keep you from the loose woman, from the adulteress with her smooth words."[126] "Then a woman comes toward him, decked out like a prostitute, wily of heart."[127] "The foolish woman is loud; she is ignorant and knows nothing."[128] The strange/loose/evil woman will teach you smooth speech that is deceitful. She offers speech that is twisted from the truth. "The lips of the evil lover drip honey, her speech is smoother than oil; but in the end she is as bitter as wormwood, as sharp as a two-edged sword. Her feet do down to death. She has no regard for the path of life,

---

123. Prov 1:14.
124. Prov 2:16.
125. Prov 5:3.
126. Prov 7:5.
127. Prov 7:10.
128. Prov 9:13.

her tracks waver, she is never at rest."[129] "A foolish woman is wanton and seductive and is restless. She sits at the door of her house, on her seat at the heights of the town, to call to those who pass by who walk with purposeful step, 'Whoever is untutored, let him turn in here.'" To him who lacks sense she says, "Stolen waters are sweet, and bread of stealth is delicious." And he does not know that dead men are there, "her guests are in the depths of Sheol."[130] Thus, the battle of persuasion is joined.

The object of the persuasive efforts of the Wise Woman and the Loose Woman is "the simple."[131] Here we discover the primary description of the young men that are exposed to the path of life and the path of death. Both the Wise Woman and the Loose Woman are acutely aware of how many young men are "simple." Both implore, "You are simple, turn in here!"[132] The goal of the Wise Woman is to teach shrewdness to the simple. "How long, O simple ones, will you love being simple? How long will scoffers delight in their scoffing and fools hate knowledge?"[133] The wisdom teacher considers those who have no training in the ethos of rhetoric as the simple ones.

One of the marks of the Trump rhetoric is simplicity. Waywardness kills the simple as they wander off into myths, conspiracy theories, quips, memes, tweets, and the maze of social media. The simple is a young man without sense, one who is imprudent, lacks intelligence, and flies by the seat of his pants. The Wise Woman offers to teach those without sense. "You that are simple, turn in here."[134] "The simple believe everything."[135] What a perceptive description of how easily the Loose Woman, the evil lover, seduces her audience. In an age of mistrust, people will believe anything. No wonder conspiracy theories are so powerful. The simple never see the danger. They plunge headlong into the deception, fall for the rhetorical tricks, imbibe the hyperbole, and accept the emotional appeals even when evidence is lacking.

I have tried for years to give some reasonable explanation for Donald Trump. Proverbs has helped me land on the word *simple*. Trump sees

---

129. Prov 5:3–6.
130. Prov 8:13–18 (McKane).
131. See Prov 1:32; 7:7; 8:5; 9:4; 9:16; 14:15; 14:18; 22:3; and 27:12.
132. Prov 9:4, 16.
133. Prov 1:22.
134. Prov 9:4.
135. Prov 14:18.

himself as an honest, straightforward, intelligent person. Yet he is simple in the Proverbs sense. He is the uncle who comes to Thanksgiving dinner and explains the meaning of everything with certainty. He is that group of men sitting on feed sacks in a farmer's supply store and exclaiming, "If we were president, we would clean this mess up in a week and still have time for a wild weekend. This is simple, easy, and those idiots make such a mess out of it all." Trump is simple, impulsive, and emotional. He is the embodied metaphor of social media: simple, impulsive, emotional.

The dominant impression of this rhetorical trope is that the Loose Woman is seductive, smooth, and persuasive. This serves to mask the evil that she intends. Here the seductive and deceptive ethos of Trump flashes before our eyes. His larger-than-life media persona—"reality television star"—suggests a pleasurable eroticism and fits with the description of the Loose Woman. The tragic part of Donald Trump's rhetoric is that it is also seductive and deceptive in negative and destructive ways. His rhetoric is profane and pornographic. It is raw, chaotic, loose, excessive, dangerous, undemocratic, deceptive, angry, and violent. He seduces with power—heteronormative, masculine power. "Its caustic bent reinforces a militant mindset."[136] Proverbs suggests that he is a man of "twisted speech." He produces a hyperpolarizing discontent and antagonism.

Trump's message oozes a sexual message of precarity (in a sexist, macho male sense). He presents the nation as helpless and feminine and himself as the powerful male prepared to save the weak female. He has seduced his followers and they have responded with, "We love you. We love you. We love you." At least four times during Trump's January 6 rally speech, the crowd broke into "We love you" chants that suggest more adoration and worship than mere political support.[137] With the pathos of an apocalyptic evangelist Trump preaches a repeated theme that can be paraphrased: "Be afraid, be very afraid. Enemies are everywhere. They are 'Legion.' They are out to get you and destroy our way of life. They are raping the nation on trade and at the border. We are losing. We are in deep trouble." The tragedy here is that Trump has no offer of actual national salvation. Ivie claims that Trump's rhetoric is deceptive because it "hinges on a facile promise of national salvation"[138] and "re-

---

136. Ivie, "Trump's Unwitting Prophecy," 709.
137. Trump, "Donald Trump Speech 'Save America' Rally."
138. Ivie, "Trump's Unwitting Prophecy," 708.

demption by demolition and deal making."[139] It vows to restore lost glory, but never delivers. It promises a swift, simple, and emotionally satisfying renovation of a "system" rigged against white men. It plays to the fantasy of bootstrapping individualism and the braggadocio of "good old boys" from down home. Ivie reminds us, "It dominates the public agenda in a mercurial display of political clownery and racist innuendo that demonizes opponents without regard for constituency or truth."[140]

In an passage important for my argument, Ivie says: "The belligerent tone of Trump's Harrisburg rally was palpably vicious. Michael Gerson insisted that Trump's speech was the most hate-filled speech in modern history.[141] Ivie says, "The belligerent tone of Trump's Harrisburg rally was palpably vicious."[142] He then cites Trump's violent language directed at watching a protester being removed: "That's right, get him out of here, get him out."[143] Ivie writes,

> Throughout the talk, Trump stitched a thematic thread of militancy, linking military, police, and border patrol into a single motif of personal safety and homeland security achieved by building a border wall and deporting "illegals." . . . He spoke in the language of war. It was a war to stop crime that Democrats refused to fight. Democrats "don't mind drugs pouring in. They don't mind, excuse me, MS-13 coming in." They must either "vote to help American citizens and American families be safe" or "to help drug cartels and criminal aliens trying to enter the United States."[144]

Trump has managed to make affluent, influential, powerful white males feel precarious. The nation, in the Trump version, has become a loser. "We are number one" has been replaced by "losers." America has become a weak woman, and is in need of a strong man. George Lakoff, in *The Political Mind*, argues that the dominant metaphor of conservatives is the "strict father model."[145] Trump has become the father of a feminized, weak, and endangered nation. Mapped onto politics, this is the

139. Ivie, "Trump's Unwitting Prophecy," 708. See also Ivie, "Rhetorical Aftershocks of Trump's Ascendency."
140. Ivie, "Trump's Unwitting Prophecy," 709.
141. Gerson, "Trump's Harrisburg speech."
142. Ivie, "Trump's Unwitting Prophecy," 711.
143. Ivie, "Trump's Unwitting Prophecy," 711.
144. Ivie, "Trump's Unwitting Prophecy," 709.
145. Lakoff, *Political Mind*, 76.

appeal of "Make America Great Again," because only the strong, strict, authoritarian father can be the savior.

While it is unlikely that Trump will ever actually make America great again, his followers are not put off by that possibility. The truth-value of the slogan offers multiple interpretations. Perhaps Trump supporters feel great as a result of Trump's rhetoric and that is enough for them. It's all about feeling good and feeling free. Or maybe Trump supporters interpret him as saying that he will put America first. In short, a lot of trust is being placed in a vague slogan that makes people feel great and feel as if America is finally being put first. "Or maybe it's less even than that. Maybe what Trump supporters care about is merely that they will get to feel good about someone as prominent as it is possible to be saying they'll put America first."[146]

The power of Trump's "Make America Great Again" trope doesn't lie in its truthfulness or even its fulfillment. Trump voters are not indifferent to the truth-value that Trump will make America great again. I seriously doubt Trump's ability to make America great again. The trope is so unstraightforward and Trump's action, especially on January 6, suggests that he is only interested in what is good for him. Therefore, the trope of greatness suggests evil intent. There is here the phenomenon of the seeming indifference to the truth by many of Trump's supporters. Here we are as close to the garden of Eden experience as possible, where Eve repeats the truth and then believes the Big Lie that she will not die. Trump makes a promise, and no one cares whether he can cash that check. Therefore, they don't care about him lying and being caught lying. If a Trump follower admitted that Trump tells lies, he would then have to be concerned that the promise of making America great again was a lie. "But there is another interpretation available of their not caring about his lying . . . They are not put off by him lying . . . [because] they like it."[147] Trump demonstrates that he is their divinely appointed strongman because he can lie and not be finished by it. He gets away with it, and this is perceived as a sign of strength. Trump, like the main character in the movie *Catch Me If You Can*, gathers fans and supporters who are excited about just how much he can get away with and still be standing. When the millions of Trump supporters share an active mistrust of the truth, a cult-worshiping adoration for a serial liar, a naïve relationship to truth-seeking and

---

146. Read, "What Is New in Our Time," 83.
147. Read, "What Is New in Our Time," 83.

truth-taking, "We are quite close to a neo-fascist situation here."[148] Even Trump's tropes are deceptive and dangerous.

The strategy reeks of an abuse of love that is vividly portrayed in the *Phaedrus*: Love as exploitation. The evil lover attempts to make his beloved "inferior to himself in every respect."[149] "While he is working to keep [the beloved] intellectually immature, he works also to keep him weak and effeminate."[150] The relationship suggests the dynamics of an abusive husband, who after beating his wife, wins her back by saying, "You know I love you. I have always loved you."

In the "strict father" metaphor of Lakoff,[151] Trump as the strong "father of Trump nation" is the moral leader of the family and is to be obeyed at all times.[152] There is evil in the world (liberals, socialists, mentally sick Nancy, demons, secret powers, a swamp full of odious creatures) and the strong father has to protect the family because Mommy can't do it. The primordial father is precultural: a prehistorical, all-enjoying, incestuous, devouring father who had to be done away with to enable the formation of culture proper (complete with its constitutive taboos). What we have in the case of the rise of Trump (and other similar figures) is the regression of this process.[153] The sense that America is slipping, in trouble, and in a precarious position pervades Trump's rhetoric. The irony is that all humanity now lives in precarity even as Trump derides the climate change that puts humanity in this situation. Trump manages to reverse the precarity and blame it on people who are teaching climate change, Critical Race Theory, and engaging in political correctness. This is a particular kind of rhetorical evil.

The result of this fake precarity, as Casey Ryan Kelly illustrates, is an articulation of white masculinity taken up by wealthy and poor white men alike, that can only be explained as the illusion of fixing the male image in the present by restoring a time when men were not wounded by feminist and civil rights movements. The final chapter of *Apocalypse Man* addresses the apex of white masculine victimhood's melancholia and repetition of trauma through the death drive: the sadomasochistic

---

148. Read, "What Is New in Our Time," 84.
149. Weaver, *Language Is Sermonic*, 65.
150. Weaver, *Language Is Sermonic*, 65.
151. Lakoff, *Political Mind*, 77.
152. Lakoff, *Political Mind*, 77.
153. Andrejevic, "Jouissance of Trump."

rhetoric of President Donald J. Trump. In chapter five, "Midnight in America: Donald J. Trump and Political Sadomasochism," Kelly suggests that Trump's "dark portraiture of American life, under siege by treacherous enemies, provides an exigence for cruelty and national regeneration through violence."[154] In a review of Casey's book, Evin Groundwater notes, "Trump's oft-repeated narrative wherein he and his followers are simultaneously unjustly persecuted, oppressed, and cheated but ready to lash out and overcome their oppression through violence creates a fantasy of being wounded in ways that warrant the destruction of their supposed dominators. This sadomasochistic relationship to identity, however, requires its subject to *always* suffer."[155] Kelly argues that Trump's "rhetorical challenge is to find new ways for his adherents to coalesce around suffering and stay on the margins while also taking back their country."[156] Otherwise, strong and powerful males are wounded and dominated by feminists in Trump's world.

Trump produces precarity by convincing white males they are powerless against the elites, the politically correct, the establishment. Democracy is endangered by all this diversity. He presents an overt bigotry toward persons of other races, and he sells himself as a charismatic leader who is the only one who can get the job done. In other words, he is a con artist selling a mixed bag of evil lies, misconceptions, and misdirected feelings. The promises mask the consequences of following the "Loose Woman." "Come, let us take our fill of love till morning, let us delight in each other's embraces" (7:18) entices but in the end not so much: "Her victims are a great company. Her house is the road to Sheol, going down to the hall of death" (7:26–27).

The deception of Trump lies in his masterful use of tropes that have deep meaning for his evangelical followers in particular, the flag and the Bible being two of such examples. Trump uses the language and images of democracy, but his deception lurks beneath the words. For example, in his January 6 rally speech, the "exclamation" politician shouted, "The 75,000,000 great American Patriots who voted for me, AMERICA FIRST, and MAKE AMERICA GREAT AGAIN, will have a GIANT VOICE long into the future. They will not be disrespected or treated unfairly in any way, shape or form!!! . . . Hundreds of thousands of American patriots are

---

154. Kelly, *Apocalypse Man*, 133.

155. Groundwater, "Review of: *Apocalypse Man*."

156. Kelly, *Apocalypse Man*, 141–42.

committed to the honesty of our elections and the integrity of our glorious Republic. All of us here today do not want to see our election victory stolen by emboldened radical left Democrats, which is what they're doing and stolen by the fake news media.... If you don't vote, the socialists and the communists win. They win. Georgia patriots must show up and vote for these two incredible people."[157] McCarthy and his paranoid populism that saw a communist in every room has been disinterred from the grave. One of Trump's minions has even built her congressional record on calling all Democrats "communists"—Marjorie Taylor Greene.

Greene provides material evidence that even if Trump never again runs for president, the evil he unleashed is alive and well. Greene came to Washington, saw "red" everywhere, and painted Democrats as communists. "They have been running this plan for decades now, because the same people running this country—Bernie Sanders, Joe Biden, Nancy Pelosi—oh, let's not forget Hillary and Bill Clinton, because they're not out of the picture. Barack Obama," Greene said. "All of these people swore themselves to the communist agenda back when they were in college." She added, "Democrats are actually communist. Every single elected Republican should say no to every single thing they want and never give them a damn thing because they're ruining our country."[158] Greene tore into Rep. Alexandria Ocasio-Cortez in a speech: "She's not an American. She really doesn't embrace our American ways." Greene claimed the "Green New Deal" is being pushed by "the little communist from New York City."[159]

Marjorie took the sizzle, the razzle dazzle, and the humbug along with the glaring lights of the performance motif. All she had to do was be herself and say whatever was on her mind—a perverse reality show where the actor has no lines to memorize. All that is required is wallowing in the gutters, the murky underworld of disgust and delirium, and thinking of the worst accusations that can be made. Such a role was "tailor"-made for Marjorie Taylor Greene, because the highest rated currency in politics now is "saying whatever is on your mind," and Greene has no restraints in this venue. No one seems to notice that "saying what's on her mind" is a like dumping a batch of $100 counterfeit bills in town as if they were real. Behold the "Loose Woman" of Proverbs in all her demonic rhetoric.

---

157. "Donald Trump Speech 'Save America' Rally Transcript."
158. Slisco, "Marjorie Taylor Greene Says."
159. Slisco, "Marjorie Taylor Greene Says."

Dismantling Greene's lapses of logic, her shameless unoriginality, her torturing of evidence, her half-truths, her ugly barbarisms, her crazy conspiracy theories, and her unforgivable uncouthness is not difficult, and that should be the end of it, but Greene has the support of the new breed of Christians who are out for blood. Greene is a performer in an age that lusts for the spectacular, the illusion, the fantastic, the trickery, the sleaziness of the modern media. There's a sense in which much media has all become *The National Enquirer*. But instead of "inquiring minds want to know," the slogan has become, "sleazy minds want to know." The deliciousness, the jouissance of Greene's performance, plays well in the media.

Greene uses rhetoric for no purpose—with no regard for ethos to get what she wants—publicity and notoriety for her cause. Her entertainment consists of mocking—and her audience finds mockery hilarious. Her entertainment intimidates and threatens because her audience likes intimidation and threats. Her rhetoric means to demean and degrade because her audience revels in demeaning and degrading, especially evangelical preachers who made this rhetoric an art form long before Greene started her first year in the school of insult.

Does this leave us with anything to say about the Greene ethos? She is guided by no self-evident truths, no sacred canon. She never suffers the burden of her lies and insults but reaps the personal rewards for her message—notoriety, money, and political power. Greene has lost all her committee assignments in Congress, but she doesn't need to be a public servant because she is a performing siren. Now, she's facing a challenge to running for reelection in Georgia because of her alleged involvement in planning the January 6 insurrection.

Marjorie Greene proves that a woman may go a long way in politics—without much in the way of convictions. Green proves a woman can talk her way to power with nothing worth saying. She only needs the strength to maintain her own sense of righteousness. When there's a moment of silence, Greene fills it with something trashy. She's a tragic figure, a cipher in the gutter that has become national politics, a bit player in the fantastic, the spectacular, the sizzling. She participates in the epistemic crisis of our time—the denial of truth—to the point of psychosis. Her shallow responses possess no content, no reason, no humanity. Her hyperbole produces nothing, grows nothing, helps no one, heals no wounds. She is sound and fury, a performance, in the end, about nothing. Marjorie Taylor Green, as one of many aspiring Trump-imitators, suggests that Trump is more than one rotten apple in the barrel. He has managed to rot the entire barrel.[160]

More specifically, the rhetoric of the loose woman is deceptive. She uses every trick in the rhetorical handbook to trap her victim. Her speech is "smooth." With much seductive speech she persuades him; with her smooth talk she compels him. Persuasiveness means more than charm. That is the vulgar understanding of rhetoric. The Loose Woman has considerable verbal skills, and she seduces the man with her ample words and he is putty in her hands. He is convinced by her lies and promises. Her smoothness completely covers up the danger. He follows her impulsively. Two figures of speech make clear the danger into which he has fallen. He goes "like an ox to the slaughter" and "like a stag towards the trap."[161] "The youth is likened to an animal which is caught and tied by a cord to a stake ready for killing."[162] It's ambush from which there is no escape.

The loose woman is "uninhibited because she defies religious and social sanctions and conventions and is a law to herself. She will say and do anything to get what she wants. As such she is particularly deadly to young men who become embroiled with her."[163] She can indulge her appetites with impunity. To the men she is fascinating, alluring, and mysterious. "She speaks in accents which ooze seductive charm and her voice, which is smoother than oil, draws her victim irresistibly towards mystery, excitement, and delight."[164] In the end, the victim will be cut to pieces by the sharp edge of her cruelty.

The evil lover in the *Phaedrus* parallels the Loose Woman of Proverbs. Socrates offers speeches from the non-lover and the evil lover. In Proverbs the two are combined in the Loose Woman. This is "speech which influences us in the direction of what is evil."[165] The results of an alliance with the Loose Woman are presented in stark, devastating descriptions. "Her house inclines toward death . . . None who visit her return, they do not regain the paths of life."[166] "Her feet go down to

---

160. Wingard, "Trump's Not Just One Bad Apple," 42.
161. Prov 7:22.
162. McKane, *Proverbs*, 340.
163. McKane, *Proverbs*, 285.
164. McKane, *Proverbs*, 314.
165. Weaver, *Language Is Sermonic*, 66.
166. Prov 2:18–19.

death, her steps set course for Sheol. She has no regard for the path of life, her tracks waver, she is never at rest."[167] To follow her will give your honor to others, your dignity to the cruel. Strangers will feed on your strength and consume your hard-earned wealth. "Can a man put fire in his breast pocket without his clothes being burned? Or can he walk on coals without his feet being scorched?"[168]

In *Phaedrus* and Proverbs, "The base rhetorician is a man who has yielded to the wrong aspects of existence. He has allowed himself to succumb to the sights and shows, to the physical pleasures which conspire against noble life."[169] "The sights and the shows" of the base rhetorician suggests the persona of Barnum and the rhetoric of artful deception. "We are supposed to believe . . . that campaigning is a put-on, a crafted, artful deception, which is the tactic that made P. T. Barnum rich with the Fiji mermaid."[170] As Jennifer Mercieca characterizes Barnum's style, it is hyperbole and humbug. This has Trump written all over it: "Donald Trump, creature of television."[171] The persona, the presentation, and the props are the affects of the "Trump emotional machine." Mercieca explains why we are easily misled by artful deception: "We love to be amused and we love excess, and so we reward showmen with our attention. Some have said that we're 'amusing ourselves to death' and that we live in the 'society of the spectacle.'"[172] Or as Socrates phrases it, the selfish lover contrives things so that the beloved will be "most agreeable to him and most harmful to himself."[173] Likewise, the evil rhetor's interest is making the alleged "beloved" (his followers) inferior to himself in every respect. Trump works to keep his followers intellectually immature, weak, and effeminate so they will believe that Trump and Trump alone can save them. Weaver suggests that such tactics deprives the beloved of all praiseworthy qualities, "and this is the price the beloved pays for accepting a lover who is necessarily without reason."[174] For example, Trump often attacks his own followers (the beloved). His speeches are sprinkled with "America doesn't

---

167. Prov 5:5–6 (McKane).
168. Prov 6:27–28 (McKane).
169. Weaver, *Language Is Sermonic*, 66.
170. Gunn, "Donald Trump's Perverse Political Rhetoric," 170.
171. Achter, "Great Television," 115.
172. Mercieca, "Greatest Story Ever Told."
173. Weaver, *Language Is Sermonic*, 67.
174. Weaver, *Language Is Sermonic*, 66.

win anymore," "Our country is going to hell," and "America is weak and ineffective." Trump attacks allies like Senator Mitch McConnell. Prior to the Senate vote on impeachment, McConnell sent a message to his fellow Republicans that he would vote against impeachment. In effect, McConnell saved Trump's presidency. Yet when McConnell, on the floor of the Senate, said that Trump was the cause of the riot, it was only a matter of time before Trump unleashed his "temper tantrum" on McConnell. "Mitch is a dour, sullen, and unsmiling political hack," said Mr. Trump, "and if Republican Senators are going to stay with him, they will not win again."[175]

The lover is not motivated by benevolence toward the beloved, but by selfish appetite. No wonder Socrates can quote: "As wolves love lambs, so lovers love their loves."[176] As Trump presents himself as a messiah-savior, a suffering servant (of all the discordant images), his followers go forth like lambs led to the slaughter.[177] Trump's rhetoric seduces in negative and destructive ways. The pleasure he provides, according to Ivie, is a kind of violent entertainment, a terrifying performance, a mixture of skepticism with fantasy, and violence with authoritarian impulses. It is raw, chaotic, loose, excessive, dangerous, undemocratic, deceptive, angry, and violent. He seduces with power, heteronormative, masculine power. "Its caustic bent reinforces a militant mindset."[178] "Its undemocratic leaning threatens a political regression away from an already thin democratic culture."[179] The Wise Woman of Proverbs offers the perfect tag for Trump: a man of "twisted speech." He produces a hyperpolarizing discontent and antagonism. As much as his followers applaud this excessive rhetoric of resentment, "its end is bitter as wormwood, sharp as a two-edged sword" (Proverbs 5:4). Here we see the rhetorical exhibitionist, the politician who engages in rhetorical indecent exposure in city park rather than in dark, smoky rooms. The Wise Woman of Proverbs makes abundantly clear that becoming a person of perverse and twisted speech is the road to destruction. Her students are constantly warned to avoid perverse speech. Discernment will save you "from those who speak perversely."[180] "The

---

175. Gregorian, "Trump blasts McConnell as a 'hack.'"
176. Gregorian, "Trump blasts McConnell as a 'hack.'"
177. Isa 53:7b.
178. Ivie, "Trump's Unwitting Prophecy," 709.
179. Ivie, "Trump's Unwitting Prophecy," 708.
180. Prov 2:12.

perverse are an abomination to the Lord."[181] "Whoever allows perverse ways will be found out."[182] "The perverse tongue will be cut off."[183] "A perverse mind is despised."[184] "A perverse person spreads strife."[185] "The crooked of mind do not prosper, and the perverse of tongue fall into calamity."[186] "Better the poor walking in integrity than one perverse of speech who is a fool."[187]

What the Loose Woman does is dress up her offer in all the cheap finery of immediate hopes and fears. Her rhetoric majors in pathos over logos and ethos. In two specific ways, Trump has dressed up his rhetorical offer: He has promised change that seems to promise an undoing of the status quo, but this is a lie. Ivie says, "Trump's rhetoric is deceptive about change in particular. He is a harbinger of change in the sense that he channels and redirects much of the public discontent that seems to call for a turnabout."[188] Then he promises to take away the shame that evangelicals endure from the political correctness of liberals, but this too is a failure because the shame is rooted in the reality of a racist, homophobic, sexist crowd. Trump is a rhetorical one-way street. There's his way and only his way. He promises redemption only through demolition. He gives his followers permission to express fear, anger, bigotry, and hatred. Rhetorically, "by discussing only one side of an issue, by mentioning cause without consequence or consequence without cause, he . . . . blocks definition and cause-and-effect reasoning. In this way his choices are arrayed in such meretricious images that one can quickly infer the juvenile mind which they would attract."[189] Weaver observes that the base rhetorician today has "means of deluding which no ancient rhetor [or Loose Woman] could have imagined."[190] The Loose Woman and the evil lover "strives to possess and victimize the object of their affections."[191] The goal, after all, is for Trump to have his way.

181. Prov 3:32.
182. Prov 10:9.
183. Prov 10:31.
184. Prov 12:8.
185. Prov 16:28.
186. Prov 17:20.
187. Prov 19:1.
188. Ivie, "Trump's Unwitting Prophecy," 707–8.
189. Weaver, *Language Is Sermonic*, 67.
190. Weaver, *Language Is Sermonic*, 68.
191. Weaver, *Language Is Sermonic*.

Trump's rhetoric has major themes identified with evil by our civic virtue and ethical consciousness: racism, nationalism, xenophobia, and militarism combine with a polarizing rhetoric that is "coarse, non-deliberative, illiberal, deceitful, and destabilizing."[192] Trump massages the mistrust of government that was decades in the making. He stole the legitimate grievances of generations of populists and used only fear, mistrust, and resentment to his personal advantage. It would be a mistake to say that Trump was just another populist. If he qualifies as a populist, he is a paranoid, dangerous one. As John Feffer has noted: "The electorate collaborated in its own disenfranchisement. In the public's view, all politicians were corrupt, all civil servants inept, and every government little more than a Mafia plus an army."[193] Trump added to this rhetorical Molotov cocktail an unexpurgated attack on the press—"fake news" and a doubling down on the insistence that whatever he did, the Democrats were worse. The argument that "Dems do it too" became a Trump follower's favorite. No one seems to notice that this is but a flowery version of "two wrongs make a right." Once the public has accepted mistrust and suspicious as the status quo, "the real Mafias took over."[194]

This brings to the level of consciousness the consequences of following the Loose Woman, evil lover, or evil rhetor. It imperils democracy, which is now battered by those following Trump in the way that "leads down to death."[195]

Two Rhetorical Theorists and the Perverse Rhetor of Proverbs

In an effort to complicate the rhetorical understanding of evil, I move to rhetorical scholars Joshua Gunn and Roderick Hart, both of whom have made major contributions to an understanding of Trump and his perverse ways. While both these rhetorical scholars see Trump in a gentler light than I do, the picture is still a dim one. Since "perversity" is a major concern of the rhetoric of Proverbs, perhaps the major trope, an overview of Gunn's *Political Perversion* serves to draw out the concerns of the rhetoric professor of Proverbs.

192. Ivie, "Rhetorical Aftershocks," 61.
193. Feffer, *Splinterlands*, 92.
194. Feffer, *Splinterlands*, 92.
195. Prov 2:18.

Joshua Gunn and Perversion

Twisted speech is biblical language for perverse speech. Twisted speech may be defined as speech that sounds good, seems right, and offers a return to some sort of paradise bathed in innocence. Donald Trump and his followers have given dark meaning to the scriptural admonition of "What seems to be good."[196] The phrase, "what seems to be good," bespeaks of a kind of evil perversion. To mention the word *perversion* in our cultural milieu conjures sexual images, profanity, and an excess of both. Perversion means showing a deliberate and obstinate desire to behave in a way that is unacceptable, often in spite of consequences. It means to act contrary to the accepted or expected norms of culture. Synonyms include *contrary, difficult, unreasonable, uncooperative, obstructive, tiresome,* and *annoying*. This common understanding of perversion is set aside here. I have little interest in revisiting the sexual braggadocio and exploits of Donald Trump. His dalliance with a porn star and the resultant "hush" money payments are garden variety perversions that serve only to divert attention from the much more damaging perversion at play in the persona of Donald Trump. Joshua Gunn says that Trump is a "political pervert"[197] utilizing a rhetoric of perversion. That doesn't go far enough in my estimation. Donald Trump is a pervert in the biblical sense; in particular, I have in mind the book of Proverbs. The "Loose Woman" of Proverbs functions as a rhetorical trope for an evil, deceitful, and perverse leader/speaker.

In the same way that Americans consume piles of junk food, which we know is bad for us, we have and are consuming the rhetoric and persona of Donald Trump, the junk food of politics. Donald Trump is a double quarter pounder from McDonald's. Trump is exhibit A of a person whose appetites have been unchecked for decades. He doesn't merely trend toward excess; it is his middle name, his reason for being. And in his excesses, Trump defines perversion.

Trump often, perhaps unconsciously, provides unexpected tropes that underscore his excesses and perversion. When he provided the University of Clemson national championship football team a banquet of "junk food"—McDonald's, Wendy's, and Burger King cheeseburgers, and some pizza—the picture provided an unintentional trope of Trump's "junk food" rhetoric. Trump has sold himself as a product, a "junk food"

---

196. Prov 14:12; 16:25.
197. Gunn, *Political Perversion*, 6.

supreme to a consumer-based culture. Trump invites his audiences to treat themselves to a feast of their worst perversion, including but not limited to sexism, nativism, and racism. "Let yourself go!" "Trump fits the criteria of perversion as being unfit and immoral. Trump's perversion denotes acts and behaviors that violate and transgress political norms and expectations."[198] This became the expectation for Trump. He was praised for "Trump being Trump." The media couldn't get enough of Trump and his tweets and his outrageous behavior. All his lies were counted, catalogued, and printed in the *New York Times* and the *Washington Post*. Trump's perverse ways became the new norm. Such behavior is now expected, and in some locales celebrated and embraced. Governor Abbott of Texas, Matt Gaetz of Florida, Lauren Boebert, and Governor Santos of Florida are four of the many examples of this trend. Perversity is now trending in front of the 2022 midterm elections.

Evangelicals, having embraced Trump, can't be at ease with the perversity that covers Trump World like a fog on a Louisiana bayou, yet they seem like a people at ease in Zion. Evangelicals have historically ranted against all forms of perversity. Now, there is a "pervasive and palpable permissibility for all sorts of perversions,"[199] particularly in politics and entertainment (the two have merged into a perverse performative genre). It's difficult to find a rational explanation for how Trump is allowed to "get away with" any obnoxious behavior, but others are still held to the older standards. Jennifer Mercieca explains how Trump gets away "things other candidates can't."[200] She notes that "what sets Trump's campaign apart is his reliance upon paralipsis, a device that enables him to publicly say things that he can later disavow—without ever having to take responsibility for his words. Paralipsis (*para*, "side," and *leipein*, "to leave") is a Greek term that translates to "leave to the side." It's thought to be an ironic way for a speaker to say two things at once."[201]

As a case in point, consider the righteous indignation pouring forth from ESPN about the video of Urban Meyer, the coach of the Jacksonville Jaguars in the NFL, dancing with a young woman at a restaurant in Columbus, Ohio. Cries for his dismissal frequented the diatribes of sports

---

198. Gunn, *Political Perversion*, 16.

199. Gunn, *Political Perversion*, 16.

200. Mercieca, "How Donald Trump Gets Away with Saying Things Other Candidates Can't."

201. Mercieca, "How Donald Trump Gets Away with Saying Things Other Candidates Can't."

reporters on ESPN. This sort of behavior by Donald Trump would not even make the news. It's just not explosive enough for Trump. There's another level of perversity involved in the way Trump can get away with any kind of behavior or speech. Trump may be the only president in the history of the USA to actively despise the truth, be able to do as he pleases, not be finished by it, and then have it seen as a sign of strength. Philosopher Rupert Read argues that this perverse behavior puts us close to a neo-fascist situation.[202]

Trump now obsesses about the loss of the 2020 election. His obsession that the election was somehow stolen reaches the level of a "fixation" and that of a pathological pervert obsessed with overturning the 2020 election. This dominates his thinking in such a way that it has caused harm (the January 6 insurrection). Gunn says, "At this juncture, we can distinguish among three categories of perversion plotted along Freud's post-natural continuum: a common perversion, which is universal and orbits permitted forms of enjoyment, culturally cultivated and moderated; a juridical perversion, which is identified through fixation and the lack of mutual informed consent; and an ideological perversion, which concerns aberrations in the unspoken beliefs, attitudes, and values of a given community."[203] Trump' perversion, enabled by the growing common perversion of culture, smacks of an ideological perversion with a sense that it is also a juridical perversion and worthy of criminal investigation and imprisonment of the former president. The confusion surrounding the description of January 6 indicates that one person's insurrection is another person's tour of the capital. Trump's perversion lies in the fact that his violations of norms and even laws may remain unpunishable if he is backed by evangelicals and Congress, especially Republican senators. Trump is the most visible picture of the rupture of expectation and political norms. A major charge repeated over and over, on the internet, in op-ed pieces, and television news reports is that Trump is unfit for office. Hilary Clinton claimed Trump was unfit for the presidency during the 2016 election, but she failed to win. Members of Trump's cabinet concluded he was unfit.[204]

In the same vein, Suzanne Lachmann concluded,

---

202. Read, "What Is New in Our Time," 84.
203. Gunn, *Political Perversion*, 18.
204. Kirk et al., "230 Things Donald Trump Has Said and Done."

GOOD AND EVIL RHETORIC IN PROVERBS AND PLATO 73

> In my view, Mr. Trump cannot uphold the duties of this office because even in his first 100 days, his insight and judgment have disintegrated to the point at which his public statements, accusations and tweets seem delusional. Not surprisingly, Trump feels otherwise, declaring, "I think my strongest asset maybe by far is my temperament. I have a winning temperament." His distorted thinking, disorganized conduct, and erratic, impulsive behavior—combined with his fixation on his own importance—directly impacts our safety as citizens of the United States and has led me to conclude that he should be removed from the line of duty.[205]

In addition to previously claiming to be the smartest person in the world and the least racist person in the world, Trump recently asserted, "I think I'm the most honest human being, perhaps, that God has ever created."[206] His defenders, as usual, claimed that Trump was joking or speaking ironically.

Indeed, in excerpts published by the *New York Times* and *Washington Post*, Bob Woodward captures Trump's dislike for military officials and his impulsive, personality-driven approach to foreign policy—and officials' concerns about his leadership. In one episode, Trump rails against military leaders for putting allies over his hard-line negotiation strategy. "My fucking generals are a bunch of pussies," Trump told trade adviser Peter Navarro in 2017, per Woodward. "They care more about their alliances than they do about trade deals."[207] "The president has no moral compass," Dan Coats told Jim Mattis, who believed Russia had "something" on Trump.

"True," Mattis, then-director of National Intelligence replied. "To him, a lie is not a lie. It's just what he thinks. He doesn't know the difference between the truth and a lie." "There may be a time when we have to take collective action," Mattis told Coats last year, in a separate conversation. "He's unfit."[208]

In the eyes of the writer of Proverbs, perversity is a synonym for evil. "Trump is perverse in a structural and uncommon sense, and as such his person betrays a compulsive need to violate perceived norms as

---

205. Lachmann, "Why I Think Donald Trump Is Unfit to Be President."
206. McDonald, "Trump Says He's 'The Most Honest Human.'"
207. Lutz, "Trump Saw His Generals As 'Pussies.'"
208. Lutz, "Trump Saw His Generals As 'Pussies.'"

a core component of his character."[209] While this political perversion is not unique to Trump, it is much more pronounced in his rhetoric. Trump is the politician who turns left on a red light, the oncoming traffic be damned. Gunn recasts these behaviors as rhetorical genres and suggests that Trump's *perversion*—his contagious obsession with flouting conventions and transgressing taboos—is the motor that drives his rhetorical success. The focus here is on the statement and the style.

Proverbs, as an embodied rhetoric, indicates a symbiotic relationship between discourse and bodies: "how a rhetorical repertoire accrues and coheres through repeated statements that are both verbal (speech, tweets, tone), and visual (looks, body comportment, gestures, and so on)."[210] "Even the most dismissive gesture betokens a body. As a craft or producerly art, Friedrich Nietzsche taught us that the stuff of rhetoric is gestural and rhythmic, a bodily act, a kind of singing and dancing. Rhetoric is not only bodily, it also sends forth bodies, 'like so many lovely lips setting off a thousand scripts.'"[211] Trump speaks and his body speaks a stern message: "What I say goes." He doesn't make suggestions but speaks every thought as a completed act. There's no nuance in Trump's rhetoric, there's the statement of fact wrapped in a thousand lies, delusions, feints, and destructive rhetorical tropes.

Trump's rhetoric, as inartful as it often appears, taps into deep cultural and political phenomena. There appears to be an endless communication loop between Trump and his followers. He appears to repeat what this audience already believes and says, and they repeat it back to him in slogans at Trump rallies. This suggests the relationship between a ventriloquist and his dummy. Trump's "people" are the ventriloquists; Trump is the fake person on their lap mouthing their perverse rhetoric. Ventriloquism, or ventriloquy, is an act of stagecraft in which a person (a ventriloquist) creates the illusion that their voice is coming from elsewhere, usually a puppeteered prop known as a "dummy." The act of ventriloquism is ventriloquizing, and the ability to do so is commonly called in English the ability to "throw" one's voice. Originally, ventriloquism was a religious practice.[212] The ventriloquist act of Trump's followers and Trump combines religion and entertainment.

209. Gunn, *Political Perversion*, 4.
210. Gunn, *Political Perversion*, 23.
211. Gunn, *Political Perversion*, 25.
212. Connor, *Dumbstruck*, 3–43.

Gunn says, "If Trump is perverse in the popular sense of violating civic expectations, such violations only begin to make sense as such when the racist and sexist norms of US culture are foreclosed, disavowed, or repressed: 'I'm not racist, but . . .'"[213] Even in this statement the racism shines through in black and white. Despite white defiance, the racism still sticks to them as they deny it. Trump's entire campaign can be summed up with his promise to build a great wall and have Mexico pay for it. Evangelicals flocked to the great wall builder, construction genius, and made him president. The wall, the wall, the wall. Nothing makes an evangelical more comfortable than walls. This is despite the lesson of Ephesians: "For [Jesus] is our peace; in his flesh he has made both groups into one and has broken down the dividing wall, that is, the hostility between us."[214] Jesus destroys walls; Trump promises to build a great wall. Trump is the vindicator, a scion of defiance. Gunn says, "Trump is less a discrete person than he is a kind of cultural gallbladder on autosecretion . . . His campaign an uncanny channeling and redirecting of social bile, but not in any studied way . . . Trump is epiphenomenal, a fungible figure."[215]

The most focused study of Trump, affect, and communication to date comes in Brian Ott and Greg Dickinson's *The Twitter Presidency*, which expressly argues that the aesthetic dimensions of Trump's style are designed to resonate with what they refer to as "white rage."[216] They locate white rage in "the fear and anxiety surrounding the social decentering of white privilege and hegemonic masculinity."[217] Trump, they propose, is effective as a communicator precisely by virtue of his ability to ignite this latent fund of frustration. They further suggest that Twitter was a uniquely effective tool for Trump by virtue of its medium-specific affordances in favor of simplicity, impulsivity, and incivility.[218] Richard Harvey Brown observed that our culture has turned the seven cardinal sins into the lively virtues of capitalism.[219] Trump as a crony capitalist becomes the embodied trope of excessive capitalism. His perversions embody more vice than virtue.

213. Gunn, *Political Perversion*, 23.
214. Eph 2:14.
215. Gunn, *Political Perversion*, x.
216. Ott and Dickinson, *Twitter Presidency*, 3.
217. Ott and Dickinson, *Twitter Presidency*, 29.
218. Ott and Dickinson, *Twitter Presidency*, 61.
219. Brown, *Society as Text*.

Gunn suggests that our society is becoming increasingly psychotic. He argues that we have lost the "Third Thing"—a governing set of logics and meanings that render discourse intelligible to members of any given society.[220] The Third Thing is what allows some people to call the events of January 6 an "insurrection" rather than a "tour"; it is what allows us to distinguish "facts" from "alternative facts" (or, simply put, "lies"). Yet, as demonstrated by those who call the insurrection a "protest" and any sort of anti-Trump news "fake news," the Third Thing is not quite as authoritative as it once was. This absence of a shared Third Thing—a recognized authoritative ethos or psychoanalytical parental figure—corresponds with a "decline in symbolic efficiency"[221] wherein language and meaning become even more slippery than they already were. Now, there's a sense that we are all working in the narthex of the asylum. As Barry Hannah puts it, "We have all worked in the foyer of the lunatic asylum. But we pray and beg for something else across the river and into the shade of the trees."[222] This state of psychosis then drives people to seek out other forms of authority, a new Third Thing, to replace the one they have lost. Donald Trump has become the "Third Thing" for millions of his followers. He replaces previous authorities in the minds of evangelicals, including the teachings of Jesus about forgiveness. How odd that a people who have banked on the authority of Scripture as the touchstone of faith have now embraced a different kind of authority—secular political authority in the persona of Donald Trump. As Ivie says,

> An excessive rhetoric of exclusion is rampant in contemporary U.S. politics (and politics elsewhere in the world). It is a dangerous and undemocratic trend. I also agree that Trump is as much a symptom of rhetorical disorder as an agent of it, although political power is ceded to individuals rather than institutions in unstable times. Trump's political agency cannot be overlooked, nor should its rhetorical import be underestimated. The significance of Trump's rhetorical excess for democratic polity and politics extends, beyond incivility, to deception and unwitting prophecy.[223]

Perhaps nothing seems more out of kilter for evangelicals than replacing their old "Third Thing"—the authority of Scripture—with the

220. Gunn, *Political Perversion*, 54.
221. Gunn, *Political Perversion*, 54.
222. Hannah, "Christ in the Room," 74–75.
223. Ivie, "Trump's Unwitting Prophecy," 707.

rhetoric of Trump. This undoing of the evangelical "Third Thing" also rears its ugly head as many evangelicals replace a commitment to truth with an obsession with absolute freedom. How's that for a strange version of the priesthood of the believer? Now, it's as if Christians in Congress are shouting: "Forget the teachings of Jesus. They aren't working. Collude with white supremacists. Ignore loving your enemies and lump them all together as 'communists.'" In the 1990s Christian members of Congress were obsessed with apocalyptic visions of a Rapture and the end of the world. Now, the new kind of Christian unleashes apocalyptic terrors on democracy. Instead of a Rapture, these new Christians pray for and work for a rupture in deliberative democracy. As earlier noted, American historian David Blight laments, "American democracy is in peril and nearly everyone paying attention is trying to find the best way to say so. Should we in the intellectual classes position our warnings in satire, in jeremiads, in social scientific data, in historical analogy, in philosophical wisdom we glean from so many who have instructed us about the violence and authoritarianism of the 20th century? Or should we just scream after our holiday naps?"[224]

These are not Christians cut from the cloth of suffering servants or the bearing of daily crosses. These are violent zealots, intent on the destruction of democracy and an authoritarian replacement government. Some are rabidly anti-gay, anti-transgender, and anti-immigrant.

It is hard to tell which came first, evangelicals acting like Donald Trump, or Donald Trump acting like evangelicals. In my earlier volume *The Immaculate Mistake*, I argued that evangelicals came first, and nothing has happened to change my conclusion. In psychoanalytical language, the patient on the couch may be the people or it may be Trump. Gunn favors the people as patient. He sees the people embedded in a tradition of racism, sexism, and nativism. Trump, the creature of reality television, contemporary media technologies, and the obsession with speed in a twenty-four-hour news cycle, and the anger and disgust in internet posts, gives voice to this body politic. Trump has addressed the message of the people back to the people in a repetitive cycle: "I am your voice." The man and the people are connected in a pipeline of vitriol and bile that has the pumping mechanism turned to wide open. Addressing this loss of a dependable authority to tell us what (to think) is true, Trump emerges as an embodied distillation of a new Third Thing. The distinction is significant

---

224. Blight, "Trump Has Birthed a Dangerous New 'Lost Cause' Myth."

for Gunn, as he is keen to point his psychoanalytical lens at the society, our society, that has *produced* Trump, rather than at Trump himself. Trump may only reflect this "people," but I don't think anyone saw Trump coming. He is more than a reflection, but his ability to seem like a reflection is part of his evil genius. He has helped produce an unsustainable state of psychosis that, in its foreclosure of communicative reflection for the sake of speed, produces perverse rhetoric. In other words, psychosis, and its inevitable path to perversion, has produced a "'Fuck it' electorate"[225] that simply cannot be bothered to care about what they say, do, or tweet, because there is always and constantly something new being said, done, or tweeted that demands our attention. Trump, in his campaign and presidency, threw so much humbuggery at the media that they spent every waking moment repeating it, rehashing it, and reproducing it for the people's consumption. Trump used the media to make sure he was the subject, and it didn't matter what he said. Gunn argues that today there is "a pervasive and palpable permissibility for all sorts of perversions."[226] What was a slow drip of grudging cultural acceptance has now become a flood of perversion. People feel they are free to say anything, do anything. Trump comes as the culmination of this cultural perversion. The "shock meter" has broken and can't be repaired. As it was in the day of Judges, "all the people did what was right in their own eyes."[227]

Trump, seemingly an honor graduate in the most destructive rhetorical tropes of the Greeks, produces a verbal, physical, political, and "pleasing" style (for his followers). Trump's major trope is occultatio. He acknowledges and disavows in the same sentence. He gives and he takes away. For example, "I would never call Kim Jong-un short and fat."[228] Trump never allows his left hand to know what his right hand is doing. He speaks out of both sides of his mouth. Gunn labels this rhetorical trick as "disavowal and demand."[229] Trump verbalizes a larger longing for a newer order, a new Third Thing, a new authority, and at least 70 million people agree with him.[230]

---

225. Gunn, *Political Perversion*, 135.
226. Gunn, *Political Perversion*, 16.
227. Judg 17:6; 21:25.
228. Papenfuss, "Trump Attacks Kim Jong Un."
229. Gunn, *Political Perversion*, 24.
230. Gunn, *Political Perversion*, 117.

Trump's rhetorical performance brings Proverbs 5:12–15 into clear focus as a definition of his perverseness: "A scoundrel and a villain goes around with crooked speech, winking the eyes, shuffling the feet, pointing the fingers, with perverted mind devising evil, continually sowing discord; on such a one calamity will descend suddenly; in a moment, damage beyond repair." Trump's use of destructive rhetorical tropes has been brilliantly catalogued by Jennifer Mercieca in *Demagogue for President*. Trump's dividing strategies are argument ad hominem, argument ad baculum, and reification, according to Mercieca. His strategies for unifying his followers are argumentum ad populum, American exceptionalism, and paralipsis. This demagogic style, this populism on steroids, has morphed into a perverse style, or "a mode of political presentation characterized by innuendo and irony, misdirection and contradiction, and deliberate instabilities in look, speech, and deed."[231]

Trump, in Gunn's view, is symptomatic of a society-wide state of perversion supported by reality television and constant media spectacle. I am convinced that Trump is more creator than imitator, and the perversion, the bad seed having come from evangelicals, has been brought to full manhood by Trump himself. He is the rhetorical pervert of our time. The "Loose Woman" of Proverbs may be perceived as the primary trope of evil and the evil incarnated by Donald Trump. How odd that such a sexist would be represented by a "Loose Woman," given that Trump seems to see all women as loose and promiscuous and for his personal satisfaction.

After all, Trump got away with words and actions that prior to 2015 would have ended political careers in a single news cycle. Philosopher Rupert Read argues that an "emotive subjectivism combined with populism" have put us on the slippery slope towards fascism. He notes, "Perhaps the reason why Trump supporters are not put off by him lying or bullshitting is that they like it. Because being able to do this and not being finished by it (i.e.: getting away with it) are a sign of strength."[232] Ten years ago, even the most cynical of us likely could not have predicted that a president who openly invited a white supremacist insurrection on the US Capitol and called for the deaths of his colleagues would be acquitted. Trump has been a full participant in and creator of a miasma of political apathy, a political landscape of polarization, and a mentality that

---

231. Gunn, *Political Perversion*, 83.
232. Read, "What Is New in Our Time," 84.

in Gunn's words "disavows both the presumed, dominant social order as well as any need to fundamentally and systematically change it."[233]

Evangelicals are his willing co-conspirators because they want their "culture" back. They want to rid the nation of the "liberal" diseases that they feel forced to endure. Evangelicals embrace Trump, in part, because they can't abide the secular virtue that embraces gay marriage, has "loose" morals, and is so open to diversity. Imagine a moralistic, sex-obsessed, judgmental bunch of Christians endorsing, embracing, and idolizing a president who is the walking, talking, acting version of the Loose Woman of Proverbs. A people that has been too interested in what is between people's legs undergoes a metamorphosis in following the perverted rhetoric of Donald Trump. The perverseness is double-edged because a Christian people now embrace a politician who embodies everything they have always considered an abomination.

On January 6, white supremacists attempted a coup in the (supposed) heart of global democracy to avenge an allegedly "defrauded" president. The insurrection illustrates Gunn's thesis that US society is becoming increasingly perverse, evinced by our ever-increasing tolerance and sustenance of psychically and structurally perverse events. While I waited for the publication of *The Immaculate Mistake*, I knew there would almost certainly be more perverse horrors dominating headlines. Trump was not at all finished by his defeat even as he was diminished. The alarm I sounded in *The Immaculate Mistake* seemed like an overreach by my detractors, but I now feel, more than ever, that my arguments then were not strong enough. My warnings may be too early for some, but this is not an indication that they are wrong.

Gunn puts it in the right framework:

> Political perversion is the name for public demands that simultaneously disavow—fights over gun rights, same-sex marriage, abortion, immigration, and on and on—and thus are representative of a collective longing for a new order, newer fundamentalisms, newer belief systems, renewed racisms, outbursts of violent individuals or groups laying down their own rules (e.g., mass shootings), forms of radical conformity, and, in the end, the demand for a powerful master who will cut through all the crap. Trump says what he means, except that he doesn't. Trump's the real deal, except that he isn't.[234]

---

233. Gunn, *Political Perversion*, 115.
234. Gunn, *Political Perversion*, 116.

Roderick Hart: Trump as Us

Roderick Hart, in his perceptive study *Trump and Us: What He Says and Why We Listen*, makes the case for how dangerous Trump really is. Hart argues that "Donald Trump is one of us and ought not be dismissed as a cultural alien. Trump emanated from the land of reality television, for example, and that would be sinful if it were not for the fact that 52% of the American people watch such shows. Trump has no sense of history, no aesthetic taste, and no moral complexity, sins committed from time to time by everyone we know."[235]

Trump has been so outrageous that there is a sense in which he is protected by all the outrage. People simply can't believe what they are hearing and seeing from Trump. Critics have had a field day labeling Trump with nearly every possible human transgression. He has been called the example of how one man can ruin the country; a traumatized child who refuses help; an example of the stupid psychopath problem; an extreme narcissist; and a big baby. These charges have often been deflected. The Trump as an infant trope has been a go-to for liberal critics. Liberals invite scorn when we substitute actual criticism of Trump with contempt and scorn. Like Christians who have reduced the devil to a cartoon character complete with pitchfork, horns, and a tail, Trump has been reduced to a mostly harmless character who merely says what he says. Christopher Gilbert argues that infantilization constitutes comic diminution by dampening the magnitude of Trump's presidency with mockery and contempt. Gilbert makes use of the rhetorical trope of reduction ad bairn—the comic reduction to the infantile—that does little to demystify the tyrannies and evil of Trump.[236] There's nothing of the comic in Trump's rhetoric. A presidential cartoon figure has no value to democracy. "Baby Trump stands out as an exemplar of comic infantilization."[237] Liberals come across as resentful, as resentful as Trump. "[Comic]caricature ... doesn't put the president in his place."[238] It's just a liberal version of conservative efforts to trigger liberals. The game is outrage and all the outragers are attempting to out-rage one another. Trump and the anti-democracy force he has unleashed are no laughing matter.

235. Hart, *Trump and Us*, 12.
236. Gilbert, "Diapered Donald."
237. Gilbert, "Diapered Donald," 328.
238. Gilbert, "Diapered Donald," 347.

"If Donald Trump was summoned from the gates of hell, then, he was summoned by us."[239] This disquieting indictment sounds like a biblical text: "The Lord looks down from heaven on humankind to see if there are any who are wise, who seek after God. They have all gone astray, they are all alike perverse; there is no one who does good, no, not one."[240] Yet if Trump really does represent us, if he is the culmination of what America has become, then we are in bigger trouble than I thought. But it is not as if we were not warned. The rhetorical scholars, like ancient prophets, investigated Trump in every way and found him grandiose and shameless, "firmly rooted in the pugilistic, impatient culture that raised him."[241]

Hart understands Trump as the product of "structural racism, institutional sexism, and a carnivorous right-wing media,"[242] and as the result of Americans' declining trust in national institutions, leaders, and each other. He positions Trump as a product as well as a cause of the nation's political maladies. Trump, in Hart's analysis, is something of an "emotional revolutionary" who is proud of his feelings, unafraid to express them, and who understands and reaches out toward his supporters' emotions as well.[243] Hart attributes Trump's electoral success and his ability to sustain support to that connection.

The symbiotic partnership between Trump and his followers surges with all sorts of negative energy: feeling ignored, trapped, besieged, and weary. Trump doesn't talk or act like a normal politician. Somehow this makes him more authentic for his followers. This is one of the ways that Trump capitalizes on the ruptures in American politics as he raves about lack of trust in institutions, leaders, and the liberal culture of political correctness. Trump's perverse rhetoric labels all negative reports about him as "fake news," perceives all critics as "losers," and insists that he is the only person in the world who can solve all the apocalyptic problems facing the United States. In his perversity, Trump comes across as both the victim and the savior. He is the sacrificial lamb on the altar and the savior who will restore his followers to a sense of pride and dignity. This perverse use of the dominant Christian trope concerning Jesus, instead of disgusting evangelicals, turned them into whimpering exaggerated

239. Hart, *Trump and Us*, 12.
240. Ps 14:2–3.
241. Hart, *Trump and Us*, 13.
242. Hart, *Trump and Us*, 18.
243. Hart, *Trump and Us*.

biblical comparisons of Trump as "God's anointed." This stretches the idea of what "seems to be good" to the virtual breaking point. Trump has mastered the ancient art of the jeremiad: No one can produce such long, mournful complaints and lamentations, such a list of woes as Trump. He sounds like a Puritan preacher warning of moral decay. The problem is that the Trump jeremiads are inapposite. Trump's rally speeches, since he lost the 2020 election, are increasingly noxious, a fog-filled room of grievances, an kind of "Agent Orange" rhetoric that poisons the mind and hardens the heart and murders the better angels of our spirits. President Trump's rhetoric is a noxious pathology, an inability to find common ground for the sake of democracy.

Trump, in Hart's view, uses four kinds of populism to win the loyalty of his followers. Those four kinds of populism are monetary populism, needy populism, banal populism, and divisive populism.[244] Trump converts evangelicals to a worship of his wealth, however exaggerated it might be. Evangelicals fawn over the billionaire in an odious display of adoration and allegiance to the one god that opposes the true God of the gospels: Mammon. The perversity thickens in this exchange. Trump evokes a specific kind of political neediness, in which Trump exposes his vulnerabilities and relies on claims to victimhood; banality, in that Trump avoids the language of values in favor of the prosaic; and divisiveness, through which he has "exploited the nation's fault lines."[245]

The primary affects and ethos of Trump's rhetoric are anger and hurt. Hart says, "Trump consistently talked about the Anger (sic) Americans were feeling and, by so doing, he added to it."[246] Not only were the people angry, but they were also deeply hurt. Evangelicals felt damaged and displaced by gay rights, women's rights, immigrant's rights. They were hurt by the vast liberal abominations. This gave Trump supporters a righteous indignation to help vent their anger, while also promising that their hurt would be healed. Trump promised to take all their hurts, and in a perverse incorporation of the suffering servant of Isaiah, Trump would bear their infirmities and be stricken, and struck down by God, afflicted, and treated worse than any president in history, including the assassinated Lincoln. Here the sickening alliance between perversity and religious suffering feels unbearable. "But he was wounded for our transgressions,

---

244. Hart, *Trump and Us*, 50–61.
245. Hart, *Trump and Us.*, 59.
246. Hart, *Trump and Us*, 75.

crushed for our iniquities; upon him was the punishment that made us whole, and by his bruises we are healed."[247] Trump as suffering servant presents a far worse case of heresy than Trump as God's anointed. The irony is that Trump promised to heal through anger and revenge, a complete reversal of any actual suffering servant themes. Trump relied on the rant as his signature rhetorical form. He gathered the "bloody heirloom"[248] of evangelical racism and made it "white as snow."[249] Trump conveyed both the anger and hurt through stories, the subject of Hart's chapter 5, that relied on narratives of national disintegration that also conveyed a real sense of optimism that what ails the nation can be healed. This of course explains how liberals are targeted by Trump and his supporters, for their mistreatment is the precondition for the national purification required to restore the nation to its mythological former greatness.

"Paranoia"—the requisite malady of the populist—exhibits the trait of a viral surge. Trump stoked anger and fear with a paranoia that evangelicals have been nursing since at least the 1920s. Having lived in fear that evolution would destroy civilization (massive overkill), evangelicals are attuned to paranoia. Trump shouts "paranoia" to the evangelical ear. Hart maintains that Trump rose "from the tacky underside of American culture."[250] What happens feels like watching an apocalyptic movie of the undoing of democracy as Trump and his minions encourage, support, and engage in undemocratic acts and speech. If any of the fervor and loyalty that Trump manages to inspire in his followers translated into good government, he would be unbeatable, but sadly, Trump's passion, simplicity, and outside-the-norm wackiness is not good for the nation. Hart, like Gunn, sees Trump as more symptom than cause of the disease in democracy and its possible destruction, but like an Old Testament prophet, warning Judah of a coming invasion, I warn that Trump may be symptomatic of a culture reeling in disarray, but he is an arsonist pouring more fuel onto the fire. His ability to produce mini-Trumps shows that even when he is no longer on the scene (the sooner the better), the danger to democracy will still be there. Perversity, after all, has a long shelf life.

Trump barks more than he speaks. Authoritarian commonplaces, conventionalisms, aggression toward norms, mystical stereotyping,

---

247. Isa 53:5.
248. Coates, "First White President."
249. Isa 1:18.
250. Hart, *Trump and Us*, 133.

tropes of the strong and the weak; hostility toward an array of enemies, projection toward nonwhite Others and Islam, and sexual obsessiveness. One looks in vain for any valid policies in Trump's rhetoric. It is so monotonous that one meets with endless repetitions. Here is a man with a limited number of tropes and stock devices. His rambling speeches serve to either intoxicate or numb the senses of his followers while creating an inseparable bond between him and them. Trump is hooked on his followers; his followers are hooked on Trump. They are enabling drug addicts in a weird political dance of endless repetitions. To listen to Trump is to sense that he has a list of common words designed to incite his memory and keep the speech going, as if he were some sort of inebriated rhapsode presenting an evil version of the *Iliad*.

For example, the wall was never meant to become a national policy. Trump's aides were trying to keep him on the subject of immigration in his campaign speeches. "How do we get him to continue to talk about immigration?" Sam Nunberg, one of Mr. Trump's early political advisers, recalled asking Roger J. Stone Jr., another adviser. "We're going to get him to talk about how he's going to build a wall."[251] According to Nunberg, the entire idea of a wall along the US-Mexico border was only meant as a way to remind Trump, "who hated reading from a script but loved boasting about himself and his talents as a builder," to "remember to talk about getting tough on immigration."[252]

Evangelicals wanted a win and they wanted it any way possible. They were galvanized by the idea of building a wall to keep out immigrants (an odd stance for Jesus people) and Trump took a symbol of racism and made it the center of his presidency—because he liked the attention it got him at rallies. Evangelicals didn't notice. Trump offered victory and a demoralized evangelical community leaped at the promises of Trump. As a result of this deal with the "devil," evangelicals are becoming more generally perverse or culturally pyretic, rejecting the worn-out idea that "you can't always get what you want." Evangelicals, tired of losing to the rights of every Other that rolled down the political turnpike, embraced the disruptive Trump who promised to change everything back to the evangelical normal. Evangelicals grieve the loss of their special Third Thing—the authority of Scripture. This loss, felt and experienced by

251. Martin, "Wall Was Never Meant to Be a Literal Thing."
252. Martin, "Wall Was Never Meant to Be a Literal Thing."

evangelicals since at least the 1920s, has been one of their major illusions along with creationism, and America founded as a Christian nation.

Trump massaged all the evangelical tropes to win their allegiance. For example, evangelicals loved Trump raising the Bible at St. John's Episcopal Church in DC because what the Bible says doesn't matter as much as the Bible as a symbol of power. Evangelicals have put all their eggs in the scriptural authority basket for so long that it becomes the dominant argument in any of their presentations. For example, Own Strachan, in his attack on wokeness, runs short of actual evidence and falls back to the scriptural authority trope: "Our dependence on Scripture is intentional and unmissable . . . The Bible is sufficient for all things that pertain to life and godliness . . . The answer to the problems that ail us—and they do really ail us—is not wokeness. It is biblical truth."[253]

When this argument fails to convince, evangelicals repeat the argument. In these turbulent times, evangelicals have faced the reality that scriptural authority has no standing in the political and secular culture. They long for a return of this authority. The longing has been so intense and overwhelming, evangelicals have fallen for a con man promising to give them back their authority, and his promises are not rooted in Scripture, but in the words of a talking snake saying, "You will not die." Gunn argues that conspiracy theories, emotional rhetoric, and perversions of logic are part of a longing for an authoritative, agreed-upon speech that will make sense of the unraveling of democracy.

The anti-democratic impulse depends upon a perverted understanding of the good, where good becomes "what seems good" to the purveyors of demolition. After every lie, "do what seems good to you."[254] After every racist attack, "do what seems good to you." After every attack on the free press, "do what seems good to you." Even after January 6, "do what seems good to you." After the big lie that the election was stolen, "do what seems good to you." Trump, assuming that what is good for him is good for the Republican Party, and what is good for the Republican Party is good for America, has no scruples about doing what "seems good" to him. Trump has taken his license to do what seems good to him and carried out his demolition of democracy at will. Maybe the wood undergirding the façade of the House of Democracy is rotted to its core and there's nothing left to be done.

253. Strachan, *Christianity and Wokeness*, 7.
254. Judg 10:15.

To describe Trump as a demagogue, a psycho, or a fascist retreats to a rhetorical safe zone. To assert as I do that Donald Trump is evil, the incarnation of evil, is to say something about the ethos of an actual human being. Trump's habits are the habits of an evil person. His perverseness, accentuated by his serial lies, promise to be the beginning of a new order, except that he is only reinforcing the old order. Trump's "agenda looks more like crony capitalism than a consistent turn from neoliberal norms," notes Joelle Gamble. [255] There is a way that seems right, but it is not only wrong, it is evil.

Trump mirrors the rest of us but goes far beyond most of us in his will to do evil. What is more concerning is the way Trump's evil works to destroy the foundations of democracy. Rhetorical analyses of Trump hedge against claiming that Trump is evil, but they have, like the ancient Israelites approaching the promised land, at least dipped a toe into the River Jordan before retreating.

The evil lies in the saying and doing of what seems to be good. The end of this evil is death—of good government, of truth, of democracy. A collage of texts from Proverbs offers a summary of the challenge of the evil loose in the garden of democracy. In the Age of Trump, "our eyes have seen strange things and our minds have uttered perverse things."[256] There has always been a biblical confidence that "the crooked of mind do not prosper, and the perverse of tongue fall into calamity,"[257] but Donald Trump has challenged this truth in destructive ways. Now, with a toxic social media, an addicted-to-pleasure-and-violence national media, and a perverted Trump, we have a people "who rejoice in doing evil and delight in the perverseness of evil."[258] "A perverse person spreads strife, and a whisperer separates close friends," and democracy twists in the violent winds.[259]

With what I consider prophetic realism, I hear the Lord saying, "See, I am setting a plumb line in the midst of my people; I will never again pass them by; the high places of corporate America shall be made desolate, and the sanctuaries of the evangelicals shall be laid to waste,

---

255. Gamble, "Populism Ascendant."
256. Prov 23:33 (McKane).
257. Prov 17:20.
258. Prov 2:14.
259. Prov 16:28.

and I will rise against the house of Trump with the sword."[260] I accept that I may be perceived as a preacher who has conspired against the nation and evangelicals, and that there are those who will not be able to bear my words. Perhaps I will be told, "O preacher, go, flee away to the land of Ireland, but never again prophesy in the USA, in Washington, DC, because it is Trump's sanctuary, and it is a temple of the kingdom." I'm good with that judgment.

Bodily, Physical, Material, Fleshly Rhetoric

The personification of the "Loose Woman" strengthens the argument that Proverbs offers an embodied rhetoric. The Loose Woman lurks at street corners after dark and speaks in secretive, seductive, dangerous rhetoric of whispers, gossip, and innuendo. There is a physicality to rhetoric that goes beyond attention given in public speaking courses about gestures. As a direct competition to the bodily "love" of Wisdom, there is much in Proverbs of the nature of the evil lover. This is a sinister indication of how a rhetor "speaks" with eyes, tongue, hand, mind, and feet. "A scoundrel and a villain goes around with crooked speech, winking the eyes, shuffling the feet, pointing the fingers, with perverted mind devising evil, continually sowing discord; on such a one calamity will descend suddenly; in a moment, damage beyond repair."[261] "There are six things that the Lord hates, seven that are an abomination to him: haughty eyes, a lying tongue, and hands that shed innocent blood, a heart that devises wicked plans, feet that hurry to run to evil, a lying witness who testifies falsely, and one who sows discord in a family."[262]

Trump embodies the trope of the Loose Woman. Instead of embracing the Wisdom of Proverbs and Plato, Trump seized on fear and anger. He deployed a paranoid, perverted rhetoric with distinct bodily rhetorical markers that include "winking the eye," "pointing the finger," "running the mouth," "lying of the tongue," "scoffing and mocking." The Loose Woman, the mischief-maker of Proverbs, shows up in Donald Trump.

As Michael Wyschogrod argues, the being of Israel is embodied being.[263] The wisdom of Proverbs cannot be pious, pure self-consciousness.

260. Amos 7:7–9.
261. Prov 6:12.
262. Prov 6:12–19; see also 6:10; 16:30.
263. Wyschogrod, *Body of Faith*, 26.

Proverbs refuses to allow the category of the "spiritual"—that stuff that is too deep to understand but thought to be important—to dominate the scene. This is flesh and flood, material perversity. Proverbs deals with the stuff that really matters to us—that is the body, sex, money. An irony is that while Trump embodies an evil rhetoric, he is followed slavishly by millions of evangelicals whose default theological setting is Gnosticism. The lethal combination of the bodily evil and the spiritualized evangelicalism intensifies the danger we face.

The truth we seek is the rhetoric of the body. The biological being of rhetoric comes first. The embodiment of rhetorical evil plays large visual roles in the persona of Donald Trump.

Winking the Eye

"He who winks his eye makes mischief." The mischief-maker in this pericope is a "model of malevolence, and all his energies are bent to destructive and divisive ends."[264] The person described sows the seeds of confusion promiscuously. His conduct is polluted and his speech is perverted. "He is a model of malevolence, and all his energies are bent to destructive and divisive ends. All he says and does is informed by a spirit of evil, and a deep-seated moral perversion."[265] He employs a sinister sign language—he winks with his eye and points with his fingers. Old Testament scholar William McKane suggests the reference here is to the antisocial practice of magic and may mean "to devise magic."[266] "An aspect of his expertise as trouble-maker and agitator is his capacity to initiate the alienation and misunderstanding between man and man which comes to a head in litigation"[267]—Trump's post-election loss strategy in more than fifty court cases.

In Proverbs 6:16–19, the described behavior is disruptive in tendency, "characterized by self-assertiveness or malice or violence, and they break the bond of confidence and loyalty between man and man." Trump uses the abuse of inventiveness for evil ends and in the contempt for law and the rights of others in a serial pattern of lying. Proverbs describes a man who employs his talents to destroy the basis of common life. "What

264. McKane, *Proverbs*, 325.
265. McKane, *Proverbs*, 325.
266. McKane, *Proverbs*, 325.
267. McKane, *Proverbs*, 326.

is described is a malicious malevolence that has no capacity for hospitality or neighborliness. This chronic ill will is aligned with deceit and assumes it most dangerous shape by wreaking havoc in a community." From a Christian perspective, it is Trump's inability to be a good neighbor that creates the most trouble. This extends from his militant announcement that he would build a wall to keep out the undesirables to his refusal to condemn white supremacy in Virginia. Trump's actions diametrically oppose what the Bible says about the treatment of immigrants, about the meaning of neighbor, and tramples on Jesus' command to love our neighbors as ourselves. In the end, Trump is a bad neighbor.

The Proverbs author may be specifically targeting litigation as the typical outcome of the malign activities of the mischief-maker: "He who says to a guilty man, 'You are innocent,' peoples curse him, nations fume at him; but it is well with those who exact the right penalty."[268] The suggestion is that that mischief-maker observes with satisfaction the widening of the gulf between himself and others, the hardening of attitudes, and the refusal to be reconciled, and the bitterness of legal strife which makes the alienation irrevocable. Donald J. Trump, the forty-fifth president of the United States, has been involved in over four thousand legal battles in some capacity. From his beginnings in the real estate and gambling industries during the 1970s and 1980s, to his entrepreneurial and entertainment ventures in the 1990s and early 2000s, all the way to his baffling transition into politics in the 2010s, Trump has been fighting courthouse battles every step of the way.[269]

Our culture's ambivalence to the idea of innocence or guilt has devolved into the belief that a presidential pardon bequeaths innocence. Two convicted felons pardoned by President Trump are Roger Stone and Michael Flynn. Both spoke at a rally in Washington, DC on December 13 to subvert the legal results of the 2020 election. In Flynn's case he has gone so far as to encourage the president to declare martial law and send US troops into the streets of American cities. The former national director of security petitioned that "limited Martial Law is clearly a better option than Civil War!"[270]

Trump's winking of the eye at the anchor institutions of democracy, has done untold damage to our nation. There is a deep struggle (agon)

---

268. Prov 24:24–25 (McKane).
269. Democracy Now!, "Donald Trump Has Sued."
270. Kerr, "Michael Flynn Promotes Petition."

in democracy concerning what is good and whether the good is that of the people or the politicians, and the expressing of this struggle often exacerbates the tensions. The language of excess and emotion denigrates democracy. "It short circuits the rationality that is crucial to self-rule and republican governance."[271] Only a democracy based on deliberation can handle these difficulties. Trump's evil rhetoric has failed to ensure truthful speech, and instead, has contributed to the decline of democracy. Ivie argues that Trump "subverts democratic values and process," "alienates the policy from democracy," and fails to advance the cause of the people.[272] His blustering, bragging, bootstrapping individualism, unfettered capitalism, and contempt for the rule of law stretches the ability of democracy to survive. "It dominates the public agenda in a mercurial display of political clownery and racist innuendo that demonizes opponents without any regard for consistency or truth."[273] Evil speech divorced from truth is not an act of courage; it is a pathetic display of cowardice. Trump has managed to create a howling mob of adherents. Some critics have reached for descriptions of Trump followers as being like members of a cult. Trump supporters are accused of the stereotypical mantra of "drinking the Kool Aid." This may or may not be overreach, but on December 12, 2020, at a Trump protest rally in Washington, DC, the crowd cheered, pointed, and shouted as Trump buzzed overhead on Marine One. Trump buzzed the Saturday rallies in Marine One, circling twice over the roaring crowds as he departed on a trip to attend the annual Army-Navy football game. "That's pretty cool," Flynn said admiringly as the president flew overhead. "Imagine being able to just jump in your helicopter and go for a joy ride around Washington, DC. I love it."[274] The adoration, the worship, the willingness to do what Trump requests, suggests that the psychology of the cult deserves consideration.

In any event, the resulting confusion is one between good and evil. The confusion about the good and the evil permeates all our politics. Anti-abortionists insist that if you don't agree with them, you can't be a Christian and you are a "baby-killer." Stark lines are drawn on some issues and there's murky fog on other issues. President Trump at times seems to endorse white supremacy and then issues statements insisting

271. Ivie, "Trump's Unwitting Prophecy," 707.
272. Ivie, "Trump's Unwitting Prophecy," 708.
273. Ivie, "Trump's Unwitting Prophecy," 709.
274. Linge, "Violence Erupts at Trump."

he's not a racist. There's good and there's evil, but in our politics the two have merged. The psalmist would feel like a stranger with his insistence that there are only two ways: "Happy are those who do not follow the advice of the wicked, or take the path that sinners tread, or sit in the seat of scoffers; but their delight is in the law of the Lord, and on his law, they meditate day and night." Today the path tread by the wicked seems more clogged than an LA freeway. Led by the scoffing and mocking of the "Humiliator-In-Chief" Trump, evangelical Christians have filled the seat of the scoffers. Evil is good; good is evil. The atmosphere fits the strategy of President Trump perfectly.

Is Trump merely a mischief maker, a man devising drama, scenes, situations for the sport? Proverbs 10:23 reads "It is like sport to a fool to make mischief."[275] In Alison Hearn's terms, Trump's hustle is a symptom of, and alibi for, a "failing political economic system marked by perpetual crisis, where traditional jobs are disappearing, and employment is ever more precarious."[276] Ivie adds, "He advances the agenda of a corporate capitalist. His act is political theater that stymies rather than presages positive change."[277] Is Trump pulling our leg or is he really attempting a coup? Trump seemed to observe with satisfaction the activities of January 6. He smugly looks on at "the widening of the gulf [between Republicans and Democrats], the hardening of attitudes, the refusal to be reconciled, and the bitterness of legal strife . . . which may make alienation irrevocable."[278]

Graphic, Erotic Pictures of Good and Evil in Proverbs

The embodied rhetoric of Proverbs reaches its zenith with the erotic pictures of good and evil. What is the point of all this sexual rhetoric about love? The words of the lover in the Song of Solomon suggest the Wise Woman of Proverbs:

> Upon my bed at night I sought him whom my soul loves; I sought him, but found him not; I called him, but he gave no answer. "I will rise now and go about the city, in the streets and

275. Prov 10:23 (McKane).
276. Hearn, "Trump's 'Reality' Hustle," 658.
277. Ivie, "Trump's Unwitting Prophecy," 708.
278. McKane, *Proverbs*, 326.

in the squares; I will seek him whom my soul loves." I sought him, but found him not. The sentinels found me, as they went about in the city. "Have you seen him whom my soul loves?" Scarcely had I passed them, when I found him whom my soul loves. I held him, and would not let him go until I brought him into my mother's house, and into the chamber of her that conceived me.[279]

While conservative Christian commentators interpret the Song of Solomon as a love story about Jesus and his church, this is overreach, since neither Jesus nor the church exist in the Old Testament. It is a love poem; it is an erotic love poem. And it shares much with the Wise Woman and good lover of Proverbs.

The Wise Woman encounters her students in the public arena and encourages them to follow her, to love her, to marry her. The Loose Woman attracts young men from the dark shadows of corners and back streets and seduces them into her bedroom. This is a dramatistic presentation of a major theme—the siren call of true love and false love. Beneath the surface of the back and forth between the Wise Woman and the Loose Woman, Proverbs asks whether we ought to prefer the speech of the wise to the rhetoric that is ever getting us aroused over emotional nothingness and provoking an excess of mistakes and consequences.

Proverbs goes to every possible method to expose the Loose Woman's rhetoric as the politics of nothing—the politics that come to nothing, the politics that end in death. There is no hope, no light, no life in the politics of nothing. There are appearances, pretension, emotion, but nothing of substance.

There's a politics loose in our democracy that is all about nothing. It suggests a biblical text: "The grass withers, the flower fades; but the word of our God will stand forever."[280] Isaiah speaks here of humanity, but his dreary truthful tropes can apply to what I call "the politics of nothing." While the politics of nothing has its chimera of glory, it will wither and fade like flowers and grass.

The politics of nothing sells the public a bill of goods, empty bags, inflated promises, and so much rage. The politics of nothing is riding humanity hard now, and its purveyors think it will last forever, but the grass withers, the flower fades. The politics of nothing is not the future of our democracy, but unless we see it for its uselessness it may be the end.

279. Song 3:1–4.
280. Isa 40:8.

The politics of nothing is like a frontier medicine man peddling bottles of liquor pretending to be miraculous healing medicine but actually worthless except for a temporary moment of feeling high.

What is the politics of nothing? It is emotionally laden speech that has no policies attached. It is a rage against how bodies act and interact in culture, with no goods offered to bodies in return. The politics of nothing has allergic reactions to policies—substantive policies designed to empower, enable, protect, and assist humans. Our current outbreak of the politics of nothing has no place for policy. The Wise Woman of Proverbs reminds, "I possess policy and competence."[281]

The politics of nothing uses pathos to induce feelings of freedom and goodness in the audience. Ironically, the "feel good, feel free" theme of the politics of nothing relies on the rhetoric of demonization, evidence-flouting, and repudiation of institutions. Somehow the politics of nothing manages to be entertaining and terrifying at the same time. The pathos is that of a stand-up comedian getting people to laugh nervously at the destruction of others who can safely be made fun of and put down in nefarious and hurtful ways. The politics of nothing churns out shame on the bodies of those who are different. It channels anxiety, narcissism, and alienation to attract supporters who are now given the signal that it is OK to rage against the dreaded others.

The politics of nothing turns out to be a labeling company that spends all its time and energy on ginning up protests—an entire list of emotional issues that amount to nothing. These efforts are more than quips, slogans, or tweets. They are determined propaganda efforts to sway the nation's voters to support Republicans. The labeling factory at the politics of nothing has churned out political correctness, CRT, wokeness, don't say gay, anti-LGBTQIA legislation, and "All Democrats are communists." The purpose is to engender rage at, well, nothing.

The politics of nothing offends all human compassion. When the politicians of nothing entice us, we should resist. They say, "Come with us, let us lay an ambush for the transgender, the poor, the immigrants, the women, the children, let us waylay the oppressed, let us swallow them as Sheol swallows life. Let us undermine the teaching of biology and the life-saving research of science, let us revise American history to make light of our nation's flaws, ignore them." When they say, "We shall

---

281. Proverbs 8:14a (McKane).

enrich ourselves and fill our houses with spoil. Throw in your lot with us," resist.[282]

The Wise Woman of Proverbs eviscerates the politics of nothing as twisted speech, as politicians who forsake straight paths, who take pleasure in evildoing, who journey on ways of darkness. Their tracks are labyrinthine and tortuous. Smooth speech, empty rhetoric, promises without policies—this is the way of the politics of nothing. The Wise Woman uses straightforward speech, plain utterances, and her mouth speaks truth, her sayings are honest: "I, Wisdom, am neighbor to shrewdness, I find out right procedures . . . I possess policy and competence, insight and power. By me kings reign, and rulers enact what is right . . . I walk in the path of righteousness, in the tracks of justice."[283]

Bottom-line fact: The politics of nothing does nothing to improve people's lives. The politics of nothing doesn't advocate for the poor or pass legislation that would feed the poor. Being anti-science, anti-history, anti-mask, anti-vaccine, or anti-CRT doesn't put food on anyone's table. The politics of nothing has nothing to say about the comfort of persons of color, persons of precarious economic standing, and persons who are living in fear and want.

The tradents of Proverbs, aware of the seductive possibilities in rhetoric, chose the analogy of love to make the case in a similar vein to Plato's Phaedrus. Perhaps Proverbs should be read in conjunction with The Song of Solomon, another of the books of Wisdom literature. I can imagine the "wise woman" of Proverbs saying, "I am a rose of Sharon, a lily of the valleys" (Song 2:1).

The Wise Woman accumulates wisdom, gives instruction that is effective. She keeps company with righteousness, justice, and uprightness. She teaches the young the ropes. Like Plato, the Wise Woman could have easily said, "I shall never stop practicing philosophy and exhorting you and elucidating the truth for everyone that I meet, I shall go on saying . . . Are you not ashamed that you give your attention to acquiring as much money as possible, and similarly with reputation and honor and give no attention to the truth and understanding and the perfection of the soul? . . . I shall do this to everyone I meet, young or old, foreigner or fellow citizen, but especially to you, my fellow citizens."[284]

---

282. Prov 1:11–14. Paraphrase from McKane translation.
283. Prov 8:12–16, 20 (McKane).
284. Plato, *Apology*, 29d–30a.

The Wise Woman constantly exhorts her students to attentiveness. "Be attentive and receive my words."[285] "Keep your eyes fixed ahead."[286] "Go to the ant, O sluggard, observe her ways and be wise."[287] Paying attention becomes the mantra of the wise. Only in this way can students avoid falling into heedlessness.

There's another voice I offer, not a democratic one, but the moral imperative of a Hebrew prophet, Isaiah: "On this mountain the Lord of hosts will make for all peoples a feast of rich food, a feast of well-matured wines, of rich food fill with marrow, of well-matured wines strained clear. And he will destroy on this mountain the shroud that is cast over all nations; he will swallow up death for ever. Then the Lord God will wipe away the tears from all faces, and the disgrace of his people he will take away from all the earth."[288] With a wondrous sense of attentiveness and thoughtfulness, perhaps we can ponder and discern that heedless living leads only to destruction. Rather than denying ontological interconnectedness, perhaps we can embrace the vision of Jesus: a feast of enemies. Rather than keeping America for America, with secret codes like "civilizational self-confidence" and "What's wrong with Western civilization?," we can offer the banquet of democracy to everyone. This might be a truly inclusive feast that links former enemies around a single table as an emblem of mature and flourishing democracy.

I sing the glory of attentiveness, thoughtfulness, discernment, and the danger of heedlessness. In our battle between tyranny and democracy, heedlessness is not a viable option. Tyranny is the enticing way of sinners (Prov 1). We can't afford to go with them. The end is destruction. Public commitment to democracy must claim our full attention. The evil of heedlessness is that it casts itself as the defender of democracy when it works to destroy it. For the Wise Woman of Proverbs, every citizen must aspire to the love of wisdom, to a vigilant questioning that transforms the unruly mob into mature seekers of the tougher, deeper truths that sustain individuals, communities, and nations.

Perhaps I am compelled to face the question of whether I have exaggerated the nature of evil in Donald Trump. Fair enough. I feel more than

---

285. Prov 4:11.
286. Prov 4:25a.
287. Prov 6:6.
288. Isa 28:24–26.

adequately prepared to face that criticism with a comparative study of Putin and Trump.

There is a way that leads to death; that way is the slippery slope of evil. There are road signs, billboards, visual images available as warnings. For example, the charge of "evil man" sticks to Vladimir Putin in his war against Ukraine. His human rights violations and war crimes mark him as evil. His nefarious example should be a warning to America because Donald Trump has taken the same road as Putin. There is evidence that Trump has copied Putin's political performance. The danger here is that once the slippery slope of evil becomes the road taken, there's no turning back from the inevitable disaster.

Putin is a right-wing populist whose political performance hides his agenda in an ostentatious masculine posturing that has the virtue of being relatively malleable. This advantage dissolved when Putin invaded Ukraine. While Putin established himself as a transgressive outsider he later developed the image of being a good father of Russia. He fostered a conservative gender order while attacking the masculinity of his opponents and casting them as outsiders. "The result is a Janus-faced masculinity of outsiders-yet-insiders, bad-boys-yet-good-fathers, which establishes that the leader is both the same as other men and also different from them standing above the citizenry, mediating and fostering a conservative political order."[289]

Putin, as a right-wing populist, authoritarian "strongman" in charge of a nuclear armament endangers all humanity. The more ominous problem for us is that Donald Trump has followed Putin's political performance in his own campaigns, and is still a viable candidate for president in 2024. Trump projects the same ultimate bad boy strongman image, who in has case wields his anger and macho rhetoric in defense of America. Like Russians, evangelicals share feelings of resentment over their losses. The rise of "hard-right populism," they note, "is cultivated through the sowing of fear and suspicion." Politicians in the West have exploited feelings of disaffection among those who believe globalization has left them behind—white, American blue-collar workers, for example. These leaders have amplified appeals that blame the global and cultural other for the vulnerability those who were previously privileged may now face. Whether it be immigrants that allegedly "take (y)our jobs"; corporations who are perceived to enjoy unfair competitive advantages because the

---

289. Eksil and Wood, "Right-Wing Populism as Gendered Performance," 733.

countries in which they operate extend financial, legal, or other subsidies; or those whose cultural practices seem otherworldly when compared to received wisdom relative to, say, gender, this scapegoating of the cultural and foreign other evokes inchoate feelings some have associated with "tribalism" both positively and negatively. That affective register of precarity—feeling at once exposed to, vulnerable to, dependent upon, and impinged upon by others—is itself a function of a sociability Judith Butler recognizes as a condition of living. This cultural or socialized precarity, in other words, is an inescapable fact of being human and of the publics humans constitute.

The sense of being left behind and left out of everyone else's "rights" movements and wealth has produced a community of "white rage" that Trump successfully has tapped and managed. Putin, with his transgressive language, his masculinity, his promises to make Russia great again offered Trump the road map to election. Putin projects a nativist discourse that castigates outsiders as deficient in terms of their masculinity. With the war in Ukraine not going as well as Putin expected, his rhetoric has become filled with angry attacks on fellow Russians. Putin likened opponents to "gnats" who try to weaken the country at the behest of the West—crude remarks that set the stage for sweeping repressions against those who dare to speak out against the war in Ukraine. "The Russian people will always be able to distinguish true patriots from scum and traitors and will simply spit them out like a gnat that accidentally flew into their mouths—spit them out on the pavement," Putin said during a call with top officials. "I am convinced that such a natural and necessary self-purification of society will only strengthen our country, our solidarity, cohesion and readiness to respond to any challenges."[290] The coarse language carried ominous parallels for those familiar with Soviet history. During show trials of Stalin's Great Terror, authorities disparaged the declared "enemies of the people" as "reptiles" or "mad dogs." Putin's language also has parallels with Trump's own coarse, weaponized rhetoric.

The Nazis were explicit about the status of their victims. They were Untermenschen—subhumans—and as such were excluded from the system of moral rights and obligations that bind humankind together. It's wrong to kill a person, but permissible to exterminate a rat.

---

290. Reuters, "Putin Warns."

To the Nazis, all the Jews, Gypsies, and the others were rats: dangerous, disease-carrying rats.[291]

Trump's rhetoric slowly descends to the depths of Putin, Stalin, and the Nazis as he demeans all who oppose him as "stupid," "crazy," "weak," "mentally ill," and "cowards." He gives the appearance of strong, male-dominated, and conservative set of ideas that appear to restore an imagined and idealized gender order based on male dominance that will make America great again. At the same time, he has deliberately undermined public institutions on the grounds that he is the one person best qualified to meet the needs of the people.

Putin convinced the Russian people that he was the only person who could make things right, that he was the strongman and the masculinity of everyone else was rejected, and he was prepared to be the father that the nation needed for protection. "The good father" plays a key role in Putin's legitimacy. Trump, following the same blueprint, poses as the savior of the nation.

Putin used angry, aggressive, even profane language to show his authenticity. Trump has been labeled the "Profanity President." Trump's language signals the tough stance of an aggrieved, underdog nation tired of losing to China and Mexico. His rhetoric helped him earn his image as a decisive and masculine leader. In his speeches he dwelt on the terrible sense of humiliation plaguing the nation, and he emphasized the supposed failure of President Obama and his own determined approach to face the humiliation and put an end to it. In an interview with Greta Van Susterin, Trump said, "When was the last time on trade, on war. We can't beat ISIS. We can't beat anybody. Iraq is a disaster. Afghanistan with the hospital and you see what's going on with that, with such a tragedy. And everything we do is wrong. We are like the gang that couldn't shoot straight. We just—everything we do is wrong. And, you know, I say it, we don't have victories anymore."[292] Putin said, "Russia can rise from its knees and fight back as it should."[293] Putin told the world he was going to make Russia great again. Military analysts now suggest that Putin's dream of greatness includes reconstituting all the new nations that were once part of the USSR back into a single nation ruled by him. Putin insisted that he alone (not courts, press, or other institutions, economics, or larger

---

291. Smith, *Less than Human*, 14.
292. Susteren, "Trump Under Obama."
293. Eksil and Wood, "Right-Wing Populism as Gendered Performance," 9.

social forces) could be the champion of the people. Putin said he would "rub out the bandits in the outhouse," and his popularity skyrocketed. "No politician has ever been so fantastically vulgar. Ordinary people love it because it's the way they speak themselves. They think he's less hypocritical than other politicians."[294]

Putin was giving Russians a lost sense of pride. It was like Nikita Khrushchev banging his shoe at the United Nations. Putin was standing in for the nation as a whole. Putin's speeches insisted that the Motherland was a "man's affair" and remarks to women rejecting public debates on the grounds that he did not need to engage in public debates on which was better, "Tampax or Snickers." Putin quoted Stalin: "We showed weakness and the weak get beaten."[295] He projected an air of grandeur as he talked often of the "might" of Russia. He claimed himself as the strongman who would not show weakness and would not let others show it.

A populist leader must define the nation by casting out some people and groups as "others." The elites are often feminized, identified with derogatory female qualities. Other groups such as ethnic, religious, and sexual minorities are painted with the hypermasculine brush of dangerous masculinity (they are ready to rape and maim the real people and especially the women and children of the real people). This, of course, was the aim of Trump's attack on illegal immigrants from Mexico.

Putin has made common cause with the Russian Orthodox Church headed by Patriarch Kirill who has said that same-sex marriage is "a very dangerous sign of the Apocalypse."[296] Trump has made common cause with evangelicals whose opposition to same-sex marriage is infamous. Putin made a special effort to reach out to others who were more conservative. Trump has embraced white supremacists, biker groups, neo-Nazis, and QAnon adherents.

Putin has undermined and appropriated formal democratic institutions through constitutional changes, limiting the freedom of the media, influencing the judiciary, and imprisoning opponents. Trump has indicated his fondness for such power but has been somewhat stifled by democracy, however ailing. Like Putin, Trump does everything in his power to limit criticism, accountability, and transparency. While lacking the ability to imprison dissenters, Trump enjoys the power of

---

294. Eksil and Wood, "Right-Wing Populism as Gendered Performance," 9.
295. Eksil and Wood, "Right-Wing Populism as Gendered Performance," 10.
296. Radio Free Europe, "Russian Patriarch."

excommunication of his enemies. The Republicans cancel those Trump tells them to cancel. Trump insists that the institutions cannot save the nation but only him as the strong-willed, powerful leader. Trump has slandered the free press, attacked the courts, demeaned military generals, belittled Congress, science, the academy, and anyone who dares disagree with him.

Two Putin advisors quipped, "There is no Russia today if there is no Putin," and "any attack on Putin is an attack on Russia."[297] Trump has convinced us there is no Republican Party today if there is no Trump. And any attack on Trump is an attack on the Republican Party and the nation. The list of Trump enemies, including critical journalists, late-night comedians, movie stars, academics, scientists, Democrats, ordinary citizens, NATO, international financial institutions, and anyone who disagrees is so exhaustive that one is tempted to believe Trump is engaged in constant political warfare. Trump has sought to undermine democratic institutions, encroach on civil rights and liberties, including freedom of speech, and rule the country with executive orders. Trump manages to demonize everyone but his supporters and this reinforces his image as the strongman, the ultimate protector of the nation, allowing him to justify his every word and action. Trump has set in motion a political performance that must be continually repeated in order to prove itself. Like a long-running television crime drama, Trump must seek out enemies, internal and external, who can be dominated. He must keep showing that he is the strongman.

The Wise Woman of Proverbs offers unrelenting, constant warnings of the dangers of this way. "Such is the end of everyone who is greedy for gain; it takes away the lives of those who have it."[298] "I will laugh at you in your calamity, and chuckle when terror overtakes you; when terror strikes you like a disaster, and calamity like a whirlwind, when distress and privation alight on you."[299] "The untutored are killed by their indiscipline, and fools are destroyed by their complacency."[300]

The slippery slope of populist authoritarianism "inclines toward death, and tracks toward the shades" (Proverbs 2:17). "The wicked will

---

297. *Moscow Times*, "No Putin, No Russia."
298. Prov 1:19.
299. Prov 1:26–27 (McKane).
300. Prov 1:32 (McKane).

be cut off from the land, and the treacherous will be uprooted from it."[301] "The way of the wicked is black as pitch, they do not know on what they stumble."[302] The slippery slope goes down to death, its steps set course for Sheol. It has no regard for the path of life, its tracks wavers, it is never at rest."[303]

Conclusion

Proverbs lays waste to claims that Trump is a good man. Plato would have labeled him the worst kind of sophist and an evil lover; Trump is the evil rhetor who turns Yahweh's wisdom upside down and who tries to draw others into his wrongheadedness and confusion by creating ethical chaos. He walks along the paths of darkness, himself devoid of all ethical illumination; he deserts straight roads in preference for those paths and tracks that twist and turn. This is a comparison between a man who is so devious and crafty that he loses himself and others in the maze of his cleverness, and the forthright, open man, who means what he says and whose actions are as unequivocal as his words. The good man needs righteousness if he is to match the opponent who regards the spreading of moral confusion and the engaging in sharp practices as a form of enjoyment.

The two ways have been presented in stark contrast by the Wise Woman of Proverbs. The evil lover creates knowledge and power in the effort to gain control over everything around them. By dominating the political arena, they make what they possess a private matter. They have a deep lust for the ownership of everything. They seek to control what they do not yet control. Believing that they are the meaning of life, that they exist to be served by others, they have a "sequestered intimacy"[304]—the sense that what they know, have, control is for their exclusive use. They assume they are masters; all others are mere servants who serve at the whim of the great ones. This defines Trump's motives and values.

I sense that Donald Trump has created the spectacle of his negative brand of politics to distract himself from the loneliness that comes from living only for oneself. The desire to keep things exciting, to do what has

---

301. Prov 2:22.
302. Prov 4:19 (McKane).
303. Prov 5:5–6 (McKane).
304. Griffiths, *Intellectual Appetite*, 21.

not been previously done or said, the desire to create outrage turns out to be emptiness. The restlessness that swirls around Trump is "inflamed rather than assuaged by the spectacles it constructs."[305]

The alternative to such a self-controlled, self-conscious politics, is offered by the Wise Woman of Proverbs. As noted earlier, according to Griffiths the best description for the life of wisdom and well-being is studiousness. The people who walk in the way of truth, light, and goodness do not seek to "sequester, own, possess, or dominate"; instead they want to "participate lovingly" in democracy, to respond to it knowingly, helpfully, "as gift rather than as potential possession, to treat is as icon rather than as spectacle."[306]

When we treat rhetoric with some modicum of reverence and forego notions that it is mere words of artifice, we can appreciate the Wise Woman of Proverbs as she has unfolded for us a mind of the intellectual love for God. It is intellectual because it is also a book that teaches wisdom and prudence and the virtues of a true and good rhetoric. Weaver was content with the "Intellectual Love of the Good," but I am committed to the intellectual love of God. The good lover, the Wise Woman, the good rhetor wishes to shape the beloved according to the principles of wisdom. She wants to perfect and protect her students. The road to perfection is mapped clearly in that chain that extends upward toward the ideal. The protection is from the Loose Woman, evil lover, and evil rhetor. It is of the essence that we have affection for the Wise Woman of Proverbs and of this no one should be ashamed.

Weaver warns against coupling rhetoric with democracy, meaning the deceptive and dangerous rhetoric of Trump. "It is something that has virtues and limitations, and I think it is very dubious to set it up as a be-all, end-all . . . My point is that I cannot see democracy as the object of all rhetorical endeavor . . . To do so subjects rhetoric to something that is an instrument in itself, and I see rhetoric as serving the highest goals in life, which are expressible only through the profounder ideas of freedom, justice, and order."[307]

I would complicate Weaver's warning with the hypothesis that Trump has exchanged his evil rhetoric for democracy. He has demonized the "god" terms of democracy and put them to his own selfish usages.

---

305. Griffiths, *Intellectual Appetite*, 201–2.
306. Griffiths, *Intellectual Appetite*, 21.
307. Weaver, *Language Is Sermonic*, 86.

He has canonized that what he says is good for democracy is good for democracy. In making this strategic move, he has done democracy more harm than good. His mistake in equating his rhetoric to democracy may lead to the loss of it.

The duty of rhetoric is to bring together action and understanding and here Proverbs has proven to be an excellent guide. Proverbs insists on a certain strenuosity in life, especially the life of the mind. Weaver says, "All things considered, rhetoric, noble or base, is a great power in the world; and we note accordingly that at the center of the public life . . . there is a fierce struggle over who shall control the means of rhetorical propagation."[308] This cosmic war between good and evil has found paradigmatic expression in Donald Trump.

---

308. Weaver, *Language Is Sermonic*, 80.

CHAPTER 2

Biblical Good and Evil

A Picture of the Evil One from the Psalms

IN MY IMAGINED INTERACTION with my assumed universal audience, a question surfaced: What does the Psalms have to do with our politics? "We are born with this book in the depths of our being. A little book: a hundred and fifty poems; a hundred-fifty steps set between death and life; a hundred and fifty mirrors of our rebellions and our fidelities, of our agonies and resurrections."[1] The Psalms is not just a book; it is the way of life between good and evil. Here is the family picture album of all of creation for all of time. Chouraqui reminds us of the historical power of Psalms. Here is the "passing parade of the whole of history—emperors and kings; generals and soldiers; men from the East, men from the West; saints and reformers, nations and churches, poets and scholars, victories, and defeats."[2]

Why turn to this biblical text that on first glance seems to be a collection of hymns, poems, and songs? Like treating Proverbs as a collection of "bumper sticker" aphorisms, the psalter can be dismissed as a collection of prayers and hymns. Yet the depth of human experience oozes from every word of the Psalms. "In this book the world has come to know and recognize itself."[3] The Psalms "belongs to all times of mourning, to all times of celebration in almost every nation."[4] The words of the

---

1. Chouraqui, "Introduction," 3.
2. Chouraqui, "Introduction," 3.
3. Chouraqui, "Introduction," 3.
4. Chouraqui, "Introduction," 3.

Psalms have passed through all the nights, come through all the wars, moved by the mad hope of one day seeing, when night is at an end and darkness is no more, a child rise upon the holy hills to sing before the ark. The Jews carried this book with them into exile; they experienced each and every of its verses in their own flesh, in their own blood. These were not only written words but lived words, the speech acts of a people. This book was their own drama, their own hope.

For this little band, the Psalms lived on as true, authentic language. The Hebrews used praise as primary weapon against evil. Israel's praise burst forth in the dark shadows of evil that was unable to overcome God's people. At times there was intense singing; at other times, there was screaming; then there was even silence. Psalm 137 recounts the lament of not having the spirit to sing another note. "By the rivers of Babylon— there we sat down and there we wept when we remembered Zion. On the willows there we hung up our harps. For there our captors asked us for songs, and our tormentors asked for mirth, saying, 'Sing us one of the songs of Zion!' How could we sing the Lord's song in a foreign land?"[5]

This is lived experience, embodied, flesh and blood human reality. In the words of theologian James McClendon, the Baptist vision is encountered when words are as real now as when they were written: "This is now."[6] Psalms incorporates the messiness, ambiguities, violence, the horrors, and the joys of real life. In the Psalms we have a narrative of what it looks like to choose between good and evil, between light and dark. Metaphorically, that's as archetypal as it gets.

The Psalms offer a battle plan in the war against evil. "The mystics of Israel were enabled to read the psalms as the apocalypse of the future eschatological upheavals and messianic liberation. In the struggle against the Beast, the Psalter constituted the source of supply for the real combat-weapons."[7] Each word, each verse, each image or picture deals out death to demons like the weapons being poured into Ukraine by the United States and NATO.

There are only two ways: evil and good. "Happy are those who do not follow the advice of the wicked, or take the path that sinners tread, or sit in the seat of scoffers."[8] We must choose between these two options.

---

5. Ps 137:1–4.
6. McClendon, *Ethics*, 30–32.
7. Chouraqui, "Introduction," 6.
8. Ps 1:1.

The path or track of evil and the way of the good are the sum total of reality. "The two principles in this duel waged at the frontiers of life and death, and who confront each other from beginning to end, are the good and the evil. The conflict between these two contradictory negations defines the line of axis where horror assaults and murders joy."[9] What then does the Psalms have to do with our politics? In short, everything.

Evil receives a "fleshing out," an incarnating, in the Psalms. Evil is fleshly, physical, material, emotional, bodily. The psalter depicts the faces of evil that seem much like those grinning faces staring back at us in those grainy photographs of southern lynch mobs. In a cinematic expression of the Psalter's pictures of evil, the movie *Catch Me If You Can* came out in 2002. The film is based on the life of Frank Abagnale, who, before his nineteenth birthday, successfully performed cons worth millions of dollars by posing as a Pan American World Airways pilot, a Georgia doctor, and a Louisiana parish prosecutor. He became one of the most notorious impostors, claiming to have assumed no fewer than eight identities. Abagnale escaped from police custody twice (once from a taxiing airliner and once from a US federal penitentiary) before turning twenty-two years old. *Catch Me If You Can*, in typical Hollywood bluster, entices us into liking Abagnale, making him an ally. The face of evil mixed with goodness haunts us.

Here we encounter the struggle of humanity against the beast, what Daniel will later call "the beast kings,"[10] and St. Paul the "cosmic powers of this present darkness."[11] "In the struggle against the beast, the Psalter constituted the source of supply for the real combat weapons. "Each verse, each word was a sword; and each sword could deal out death to demons."[12] There are two ways, and only two ways in the Psalms. The choice is between light and darkness, good and evil. The primordial, archetypal metaphor of light and dark hangs over the entire book. Here we participate in the effort of the darkness to overcome the light. As Hauerwas insists, "Christians need protection because the world is ruled by beast-kings who want to destroy all those who are witnesses to Jesus' triumph over the powers that would falsely rule the cosmos."[13] The

---

9. Chouraqui, "Introduction," 7.
10. Dan 7:3.
11. Eph 6:12.
12. Chouraqui, "Introduction," 6.
13. Hauerwas, *Unleashing the Scripture*, 101.

Psalms, with more efficiency and less fanaticism, are more apocalyptic than Daniel. The Psalms read like the diary of a warrior who is always on his way to exile, fighting to avoid exile, living in exile, or returning from exile. The images of all the Pharaoh's of history lurk behind the Psalms. There's a cosmic, apocalyptic nature to these ancient songs.

Christianity has a cosmic character—there's a cosmic war between good and evil. "Perhaps that is why we are so starved for movies like *Star Wars*."[14] As David Bentley Hart says, "It is as if the entire cosmos were somehow predatory, a single great organism nourishing itself upon the death of everything to which it gives birth, creating and devouring all things with a terrifying and impassive majesty." There is within the world we inhabit the forces that are parasitic—"urged always upward by a blind, thrusting idiotic heliotropism—climbing toward the light of the sun by choking the life from the trees around which it grows, constantly struggling out of the shadows in its thirst for the light, until its burgeons forth at the last in such gorgeous and copious flowers that one might forget what had to perish to make such a triumph of beauty possible."[15] It is this parasitical pretension of righteousness that can attach itself to us so that we imbibe it, and because it still bears the vestiges and language of faith, we are hesitant to see it now as evil. But like Salieri arguing with God, over his disgust of Mozart, we must now declare, "So be it! From time, we are enemies, You and I. I'll not accept it from you—do you hear? . . . They say God is not mocked. I tell you, Man is not blocked! . . . You are the Enemy!: I name thee now . . . And this I swear: To my last breath I shall block You on earth, as far as I am able! What use, after all, is Man, if not to teach God his lessons?"[16] Trump imbibes the sheer antagonism of Salieri in his attempt to undo the legacy of Barack Obama. It is not enough for Trump that he was elected president. He needed, deep in his soul, to destroy Obama by any means necessary. He started his campaign for president by denying that Obama was a citizen of the USA. I can see Trump's face twisted in agony when Salieri expresses anger at hearing the voice of God: "And now I do hear it—and it says only one name: Mozart! . . . Spiteful, sniggering, conceited, infantine Mozart—who has never worked one minute to help another man."[17]

14. Hauerwas, *Unleashing the Scripture*, 110.
15. Hart, *Doors of the Sea*, 50–51.
16. Shaffer, *Amadeus*, 59.
17. Shaffer, *Amadeus*, 58.

Our meeting with the Prince of Darkness on the path starts in Psalm 1 and continues for the entire journey, what John Bunyan called "pilgrim's progress." In the first psalm the prince is shown as a windblown tuft of straw ("The wicked are not so, but are like chaff that the wind drives away"). The Psalter paints an entire landscape portrait of the Evil One—large enough to fill an entire wall in the Art Institute of Chicago:

> The psalmist shows him to us in these roles: the Adam of Evil, the enemy, the liar, the madman, the powerful, the bull of Bashan, the man of violence, the man of deceit, the man of iniquity, the devourer of people, the traitor, the perfidious, the son of the barbarian, the man of blood, the stupid fellow, the profiteer, the proud man, the haughty eye, the thief, the braggart, the assassin, the land-grabber, the boaster, the vainglorious, the prostitute, the dreadful, the sinner, the harsh, the malicious, the greedy, the bearer of infamy, the trouble-forger, the worker of iniquity, the trapper, the flame-thrower, the warrior, the scoffer, the blasphemer, the treacherous tongue, the one on the prowl for souls, the king of the earth, the crooked, the exterminator, the executioner, the rebel, the vindictive, the adversary, the fool, the great man of this world, the bent one, the heritage of the destroyer. He is the soul, the very center of the assembly of the violent, of the horrible, of the eyes that dart destruction, of the senseless people, of the council of scoffers, of the crafty, of the wicked, of the band of malefactors, of the destroyers. He is the opulent, the wealthy, the despoiler, the worker of sin, the man with heart puffed up, the one whom earth holds reprobate, the ferocious, the dog, the forger of nothingness . . . as we know so well. He is the enemy of justice, the man oblivious to God, the oppressor, the adversary of peace. He wields the Scepter of evil; he is the Accuser, so styled by his name in Hebrew: Satan.[18]

Norman Fischer in his translation of Psalm 1 uses the word "heedless" instead of the word "wicked." "Happy is the one who walks otherwise / Than in the manner of the heedless." "The heedless . . . are like chaff scattered by the wind / Endlessly driven, they cannot occupy their place / And so can never be seen or embraced / And they can never be joined." "The way of heedlessness is oblivion."[19] The Wise Woman of Proverbs described these workers of iniquity as "sinners," "scorners," "mockers," and [persons] "whose speech is twisted." This is the community of the

---

18. Chouraqui, "Introduction," 7–8.
19. Fischer, *Opening to You*, 3.

heedless. "The heedless take counsel of the heedless / And in their heedlessness think to flee from you, saying 'Let us break apart the ties and throw away the cords.'"[20] Heedless means "showing a reckless lack of care or attention, paying no heed to, inattentive, and oblivious to." Examples of heedlessness abound in our nation. A guy drives 110 mph on I-890, cutting off other drivers, endangering lives, because he's late for dinner. Heedless. The third guy in the turn lane runs the red light because he can. Heedless. A woman takes a private jet to DC on January 6 and wanders into the Capitol with the crowd. Heedless, but now she's doing ten months to four years in federal prison. A protestor throws a rock through a store window. Heedless. A mother in Virginia threatens the local school board on mask mandates: "I will bring every gun loaded." Heedless. Airline passengers attack flight attendants over mask mandates. Heedless. Multiply the ways that we are a physically heedless people.

The heedless, like the metal orb in an old-fashioned pinball machine, ricochet from cause to cause in fear, outrage, and a sense of "I'm not going to take it anymore." The Wise Woman of Proverbs observes, "By insolence the heedless make strife" (Pro 13:10). The heedless are thrown about by every wind of emotion, rumor, and conspiracy, the mistrust of the government, the whims and fads of the moment. I am convinced that much of our violence is related to becoming a "heedless" people. January 6, 2021, was a national act of heedlessness by a mob taking counsel of madness and evil.

The heedless are inattentive to realities, facts, even truth itself. They are unwilling to be bound by anything, even truth. The battle here is against a certain kind of ignorance of the interconnectedness of all beings. People act heedlessly when they pit themselves, unnecessarily, against others. This is not a denial of people being evil, but a realization that heedlessness can be corrected.

The ancient church had a word that suggests heedlessness: *acedia/sloth*. One of the seven cardinal sins, acedia/sloth means "not caring." Chaucer says that sloth "makes [us] brooding and fretful." It "severs a man from all love." "Sloth does all things with vexation, fretfulness, slackness, excusing, idleness, and reluctance." Perhaps the most telling explanation of sloth in *The Canterbury Tales* are these words: "Sloth will not abide hardship nor Penance." Chaucer shows that sloth, refusing repentance

---

20. Fischer, *Opening to You*, 3.

or change, becomes sluggish, and then, reacting against being shamed, it becomes angry and "is soon inclined to hate and to envy."

A more modern poet, Walt Whitman, lifts up the Psalms' lament of the danger of heedlessness. Whitman says, "Of all the dangers . . . there can be no greater one than having certain portions of the people set off from the rest by a line drawn—they are not privileged as others, but degraded, humiliated, made of no account."[21] Whitman, like Chouraqui, gathers a plethora of powerful metaphors—the "tyrant,"[22] the "menacing one," and the "scorner,"[23] to depict the figure who cannot be tolerated and is always the person who dehumanizes, degrades, and diminishes others with scoffing and mocking, making them of no account by denying their inherent dignity and worth.

Heedlessness defines the Age of Trump and those who walk in its dark paths. American historian David Blight muses:

> The lies have now crept into a Trumpian Lost Cause ideology, building its monuments in ludicrous stories that millions believe, and codifying them in laws to make the next elections easier to pilfer. If you repeat the terms "voter fraud" and "election integrity" enough times on the right networks you have a movement. And "replacement theory" works well alongside a thousand repetitions of "critical race theory," both disembodied of definition or meaning, but both scary. Liberals sometimes invite scorn with their devotion to diversity training and insistence on fighting over words rather than genuine inequality."[24]

Is this the root of our political disorder? Heedlessness. Ignoring injustice piled up at our door for more than four hundred years. Inattentive to the needs of African Americans. Intoxicated by our own imperialism and consumerism and greed. Refusing to even entertain the idea that repentance may be the necessary step forward for us all. Rage may be more emotionally satisfying to people who have been shamed by liberal pedagogy. Resisting the need for seeing clearly the past and present flaws of America. There may have never been a more heedless politician that Donald Trump.

The question is not one of rationality or civility. Everyone claims to be rational, pretends to be civil. The question is who is heedful, and who

21. Whitman, *Democratic Vistas*, 949.
22. Whitman, "By Blue Ontario's Shore," 479.
23. Whitman, "By Blue Ontario's Shore," 479.
24. Blight, "Trump Has Birthed a New 'Lost Cause' Myth."

is heedless. Both Proverbs and the Psalms indict the heedless as those who refuse to recognize human dignity. The enemy is the one who is heedless of the value of other humans, the scorner who divides the nation in order to exclude and humiliate, the tyrant who degrades in order to dominate and destroy. Trump and company out themselves by speaking heedlessly in the language of domination and disrespect and this is the heedlessness that defines evil.

The psalmist, not content with naming the Evil One, also equates the names of evil with the works of evil:

> His name defines his works to good effect. The psalter describes them to us in minute detail. The father of nothingness incarnates a radical inadequacy, an emptiness; and his works are the perfect likeness of the one who fathers them. His every word consummates a lie; his every action, a deed of violence. He is presented from the very first psalm as a wind-blown tuft of straw—with all the weightlessness, instability, dryness, and sterility of straw. Without roots, without weight, he hems himself within the horizon of the merely temporal which becomes his captor. The sum-total of his knowledge finds its resume in the negation of God. "God does not exist." This, then, is the source of his mind's dissatisfaction, of his lust's insatiability, of his anguish. He is a wounded creature; nothing can fill it. His reality, his truth *has* accordingly got to be co-terminous with the radical inadequacy which he incarnates. He utterly refuses as impossible *and* deceitful all resignation such as is imposed by the very nature of the way which leads through time and the temporal. His highest peak of lucidity consists in his seeing himself condemned to live and die in anxiety and in the dark. He passes his life behind closed doors. He has to refuse as illusory a repose such as his accursed horizon prevents him from obtaining. He is acting in keeping with his own kind of reality, his own kind of truth, when he opts for the world; and the choice he makes takes from him any chance of rest. The psalmist makes us see the grimacing of his mouth and lips; makes us see his tongue working up illusion and torment. He denies and calumniates; he lies and insinuates. His justice is robbery; turpitude his pride. His enjoyment is held prisoner within the confines of his horizon. He is nothing more than mockery and gnashing of teeth. Insatiable as he is, he heaps up for pleasure, and is powerless to stop heaping up for pleasure: his torture becomes his pleasure, his captivity his freedom, his darkness his light, his death the measure of all life. His will to power unfurls without rule or measure within

the horizon which keeps him captive. In his hands, however, power and justice become instruments of oppression and subjugation. He perverts justice, declares false what is true, and calls true what is a lie. He is himself his own measure, and he casts on everything he approaches the dark shadow which made him prisoner. Incarnation of evil as he is, whose works sprout like a luxuriant head of black hair on the beings whan he seduces and subjugates, the *Racha'* [the evil one] is stopped short at the one barrier which can refuse him entry: the innocent person reveals to him the non-temporal which he himself refuses, the non-temporal whose reality and truth overthrew his own blind horizons.[25]

"How long will scoffers delight in their scoffing and fools hate knowledge?"[26] is a question that can only be answered by the citizens who finally determine they have heard enough. "Happy is the one . . . Who does not sit in the seat of the scornful / But finds delight in the loveliness of things / And lives by that pattern all day and all night."[27]

Cornel West shakes the rafters of our minds with these searing words: "The black prophetic tradition has been the leaven in the American democratic loaf. What has kept American democracy from going fascist or authoritarian or autocratic has been the legacy of Frederick Douglass, Harriet Tubman, Sojourner Truth, Martin King, Fannie Lou Hamer. This is not because black people have a monopoly on truth, goodness or beauty. It is because the black freedom movement puts pressure on the American empire in the name of integrity, decency, honesty, and virtue."[28]

There needs to be an appropriation of the African American prophetic tradition as one way to save us from heedlessness in the facing of our race problem. Again, it is West sounding the alarm: "It may very well be that black people will never be free in America. But I believe, and the black prophetic tradition believes, that we proceed because black people are worthy of being free, just as poor people of all colors are worthy of being free, even if they never will be free. That is the existential leap of faith."[29]

25. Chouraqui, "Introduction," 8–9.
26. Prov 1:22.
27. Fischer, *Opening to You*, 1.
28. Hedges, "Cornel West and the Fight."
29. Hedges, "Cornel West and the Fight."

I have confidence that such Americans willing to take the leap of faith still exist. In the streets of America, I still see faithful citizens leaping and dancing like King David as racism folds it tent and comes nearer to extinction. By God's help, Americans can learn to "leap over all walls" constructed to keep Others apart. In the day of joyous Jubilee, we will cry out, "The voice of my beloved! Look, he comes, leaping upon the mountains, bounding over the hills."[30] As the prophet Malachi put it, "For you who revere my name the sun of righteousness shall rise, with healing in its wings. You shall go out leaping like calves from the stall."[31] With St. Luke we shall "rejoice in that day and leap for joy."[32] This is the vision of wisdom. This is the 20/20 insight that can stop heedlessness. We will see with the eyes of the heart the day of redemption of the land. With confidence in the American people, I believe that the day of politicians spouting hatred and division and humbug will soon be replaced by the poet worthy of that name of the true sons and daughters of God, and that people of all colors, all ethnicities, all sexual orientations, shall come singing their songs, as Whitman put it.

The rhetoric of heedlessness that produces hatred has been normalized as legitimate political speech, but this will not be the final word. Even as this evil speech has its moment in the sun, already the sun is setting on those who insist on such rhetorical strategies. People will finally suffer exhaustion from the pains of evil inflicted upon the body of democracy. Once again, they shall heed the advice of historian David Blight and

> pick up Whitman's *Song of Myself*, all 51 pages, from the opening line, "celebrate myself, and sing myself," to his musings on the luck of merely being alive. Keep going to a few pages later when a "runaway slave" enters Whitman's home and the poet gazes into his "revolving eyes," and nurses "the galls of his neck and ankles," and then to his embrace of "primeval" complete democracy midway in the song, where he accepts "nothing which all cannot have." Finally read to the ending, where the poet finds blissful oblivion, bequeathing himself "to the dirt to grow from the grass I love." Whitman's "sign of democracy" is everywhere and in everything. The democratic and the authoritarian instinct are both deep within us, forever at war.[33]

30. Song 2:8.
31. Mal 4:2.
32. Luke 6:23.
33. Blight, "Trump Has Birthed a Dangerous New 'Lost Cause' Myth."

In the movie *Wall Street*, tycoon Gordon Gekko, as he takes over Teldar Paper, declares, "Greed, for lack of a better word, is good. Greed is right. Greed works. Greed clarifies, cuts through, and captures the essence of the evolutionary spirit. Greed in all its forms, greed for life, money, love, knowledge has marked the upward surge of mankind, and greed will not only save Teldar Paper but that other malfunctioning corporation called the USA."[34] Evil speaks well and turns vice into virtue.

Evil stares back at us from the pages of the psalter, as if it were the *New York Times* on any given morning, in vivid, dark colors. There is more to the look of evil than we know, especially since he can pass himself off as an angel of light. The psalmist declares that the evil one has a "haughty eye."[35] A later biblical contributor will state, "And the tongue is a fire. The tongue is placed among our members as a world of iniquity; it stains the whole body, sets on fire the cycle of nature, and is itself set on fire by hell."[36] "From the same mouth come blessing and cursing. My brothers and sisters, this ought not to be so."[37] Jesus will say, "You brood of vipers! How can you speak good things, when you are evil? For out of the abundance of the heart the mouth speaks."[38] "It is what comes out of the mouth that defiles."[39] "The good person out of the good treasure of the heart produces good, and the evil person out of evil treasure produces evil; for it is out of the abundance of the heart that the mouth speaks."[40] The apostle Paul had much to say about what comes out of the mouth: "Let no evil talk come out of your mouths."[41] "But now you must get rid of all such things—anger, wrath, malice, slander, and abusive language from your mouth."[42]

"We see round about the Reprobate the wild agitations he stirs up among those who reflect his image."[43] In the Psalter all the visages of the enemy empires of this world are set loose: Edom, Moab, Ammon, Amalech, the sons of Lot, the Philistines, Babel, Tyre, Meshesch, and Kedar.

34. Hauerwas, *Working with Words*, 131.
35. Ps 101:5.
36. Jas 3:6.
37. Jas 3:10.
38. Matt 12:34.
39. Matt 15:11.
40. Luke 6:45.
41. Eph 4:29.
42. Col 3:8.
43. Chouraqui, "Introduction," 10.

Think of this list of enemies as a biblical version of the Southern Poverty Law Center's list of hate groups. "They snarl and menace and slaughter all along the journey's path where Egypt—'the land of two-fold anguish'—seems to be the incarnation of the original homeland of the Rebel."[44] The house of bondage, where Joseph and Israel were held captive, a people struck by all the plagues, prison which must be escaped from in order to attain the liberty of the children of God, the kingdom of Pharaoh—it represents the symbolic place for each and every exile. And Pharaoh represents the power of evil in every age and in every evil ruler. There is one primordial evil ruler in Israel's story and he is known as "the Pharaoh."

Walter Brueggemann says, "There is Pharaoh, always Pharaoh, at the center of the world of power."[45] He is not given a name because he could have been any one or all of the rulers of Egypt. "Because if you have seen one pharaoh, you have seen them all."[46] Pharaoh functions as the dark metaphorical shadow of evil in the Psalms. Into the face of Pharaoh, God's suffering people are always singing, "Set my people free," and "This little light of mine let it shine, let it shine."

The way of evil is made clear in the Psalms. Narrow places, closed round about, darksome, muck, the snare, waters of destruction, ferocious beasts, death. This is the way of the Reprobate. "His every gesture is sketched from life, thanks to the trained eye of a contemplative who never loses sight of him: the hand that strikes and kills, the thrashing arm, the foot that crushes, the heel in flight, the gritted jaws; the cortege of pain and all its weapons; the threats hurled from high towers, walled fortifications, the wild abandoned howls, the look that burns with hatred."[47] The Reprobate would never dream of surrender; still less would he think in terms of the institutions of government. He will never repent, say he's sorry, or admit to wrong. He will never accept responsibility. He will always blame others. He will attack all deemed enemies.

Do what he may, the Racha (the evil one) is incapable of undertaking a lasting, permanent work. His sense of policy is defeated by a short attention span. While he thinks there are none worthy to oppose him, it is at last the Reprobate who is vanquished. Meanwhile, his every move is that of a demolition expert. He destroys all in his path.

44. Chouraqui, "Introduction," 10.
45. Brueggemann, *Truth Speaks to Power*, 15.
46. Brueggemann, *Truth Speaks to Power*, 17.
47. Chouraqui, "Introduction," 10.

The evil person meets fierce resistance from the Psalter: "He loves to curse, let curses come on him! He did not like blessing; may it be far from him! He clothed himself with cursing as his coat; may it soak into his body like water."[48] He has lived in the absurd and perishes in the absurd. While he has seemed to prosper, triumph, lord it over everyone, make his point, mock, demean, and overcome, it is an illusion. He will finally be left with nothing—not even the bitterness of all the trouble he has had. He is the prisoner of nothingness; the tool of incisive justice imprisons him within himself; he is caught in the net he thought he could use to catch others. His negation brings him to naught; his hatred, his greasy fat suffocates him. The Rebel hands out contempt; contempt is what he gets. Cut off from love, he obtains only what emanates from himself. "He amasses wealth: the result will be nakedness, hunger, thirst. He believes only in himself."[49] He is left with the judgment of Psalm 49:

> Mortals cannot abide in their pomp; they are like the animals that perish. Such is the fate of the foolhardy, the end of those who are pleased with their lot. Selah. Like sheep they are appointed for Sheol; Death shall be their shepherd; straight to the grave they descend, and their form shall waste away; Sheol shall be their home. But God will ransom my soul from the power of Sheol, for he will receive me. Selah. Do not be afraid when some become rich, when the wealth of their houses increases.[50]

Whitman warns against this evil obsession with wealth. If life becomes about wealth, if a person devotes everything to accumulation of money, if everything becomes about profit, persons and the earth become expendable and exploitable. Profits trumps persons. "Devotion to money turns a person's vision green. Whitman counters the materialism . . . [b]y modeling total devotion to kosmos, pursuing it at every corner, worshipping it at every opportunity, praising it without qualification. For Whitman, by devoting themselves to kosmos, Americans will begin to see the world as kosmos [rather than as an object of profit], as an interconnected whole animated by divinity."[51]

The Psalter shows no mercy for the Reprobate. The metaphors beat against the doors of the kingdom of evil, unrelenting in their terror. God

---

48. Ps 109:17–18.
49. Chouraqui, "Introduction," 13.
50. Ps 49.
51. Engels, "Kosmic Rhetoric," 73.

appears to exercise justice on behalf of the widow and the orphan, to liberate those who love him from the kingdom of darkness. The earth trembles, the mountains quake, the waters swirl and foam, the skies part asunder, fire from heaven comes down to punish iniquity. Hierarchies of angels come brandishing the sword. The wild forest boar, the beats of reeds and rushes, the buffalo, the fabled Hydra, the frightful Leviathan—all perish when God gives his verdict. Confronted by the real order of the world, the Reprobate is taken back to his pit for an eternity of turpitude.

Conclusion

The Psalms defines, describes, and dispenses with the persona of evil. Here is the evil rhetor who turns Yahweh's wisdom upside down and who tries to draw others into his wrongheadedness and confusion by creating ethical chaos. He walks along the paths of darkness himself devoid of all ethical illumination; he deserts straight roads in preference for those paths and tracks which twist and turn. This is a comparison between a man who is so devious and crafty that he loses himself and others in the maze of his cleverness, and the forthright, open man, who means what he says and whose actions are as unequivocal as his words. The good man needs righteousness if he is to match the opponent who regards the spreading of moral confusion and the engaging in sharp practices as a form of enjoyment—jouissance.

When we treat evil as a way of knowing, it becomes an epistemic rhetoric rather than mere words of artifice. Weaver says, "All things considered, rhetoric, noble or base, is a great power in the world; and we note accordingly that at the center of the public life . . . . there is a fierce struggle over who shall control the means of rhetorical propagation."[52] To utilize the power of rhetoric requires a wisdom rooted in the love of God.

---

52. Weaver, *Language Is Sermonic*, 80.

CHAPTER 3

Rhetorical Evil

Trump's Evil in Starkest Terms—"Hitler's 'Battle'"

TO MENTION THE NAME of Hitler raises red flags of difficult rhetorical challenges. These challenges function like a gas explosion in the basement of a valuable old home that be cleared away before the home can even be entered again. This is only partly about Hitler; it's really about Trump, and it's mostly about us. Roderick Hart in *Trump and Us* argues that its more about us than Trump. Hart says, "I will treat Trump as an emotional revolutionary, a person (1) who is proud of the feelings coursing within him, (2) who is unafraid to display them in public, (3) who treats his supporters' feelings with special reverence, and (4) who regards an unemotional politics as no politics at all."[1]

The evil lurking in the Trump orbit pulls an entire people in its track. Proverbs warns frequently of the danger of the tracks of evil: do not walk in their way, keep your foot from their paths; "for their feet run to evil, and they hurry to shed blood."[2] Hart says, "Trump may not be the best of us, but he is one of us and we need to know what that means. Toggling back and forth between what Trump says and how he is received gets us beyond the story of one election. It tells us who we are as a people and why US politics have become so clamorous."[3]

Patricia Roberts-Miller offers sage advice for those who dare to argue with Hitler as comparative trope: "Hitler does seem an inevitable topos

---

1. Hart, *Trump and Us*. 18.
2. Prov 1:15.
3. Hart, *Trump and Us*, 18.

in arguments about politics. Yet in the ways that we argue, 'HITLER DID THAT TOO' indicates that disagreement has been drowned in anger and contempt. Argumentation theorists call it the fallacy of *argumentum ad Hiterlerum*, when someone tries to discredit a policy, argument, or opponent by accusing them of being just like Hitler."[4] It's not so much that someone becomes like Hitler; it is that he was so awful, that having some of his notions are dangerous to the community of humanity. There is no suggestion here that Trump is Hitler. The issue is how the rhetoric of Hitler has the seeds that produce fascism. My analysis is concerned with Hitler before he became Hitler and thus with Trump as he mirrors the making of Hitler. This is not about the final actions of Hitler's unparalleled evil; it is the story of how one becomes a kind of "Hitler."

This is as much about us as it is about Hitler or Trump. Hitler's rise to power depended upon a large number of Germans already thinking like Hitler. For much of Hitler's audience, he had them at the point that he insisted they were the real victims. The German people had been mistreated. Roberts-Miller offers a helpful critique:

> What he said was: you're in a bad situation; it can't be your fault. You're a German, so it can't be Germany's fault. IT'S THE LIBERALS. Who are Jews. And Bolsheviks. And international financiers. ALL TRUE GERMANS AGREE. Our government sucks because it isn't giving you the things you know you deserve, and it isn't dominating every other country, and GOD WANTS US TO BE THE BEST, and democracy involves letting other people argue and they're all wrong and so it's a waste of time because the true course of action is obvious to every reasonable person and so ELECT SOMEONE WHO CARES ABOUT PEOPLE LIKE YOU. And who will insist that GERMANY IS THE BEST. A strong man who will just walk into every international negotiation and dominate everyone and insist that they submit to Germany and send our kickass military into any country or region that disagrees is the right person for foreign policy. As far as domestic policies, we need someone who gets people like us, who cares about us. Politicians who say it's complicated are just trying to line their own pockets. Democratic deliberation is a waste of time—just hand over all the power to a guy who can get things done. And that's me.[5]

4. Roberts-Miller, "Rhetoric and Hitler."
5. Roberts-Miller, "Rhetoric and Hitler."

This is how good people are drawn into a political rhetoric that promises victory but never works out in the end. Good people like us support what seems like good from the demagogue. This is what was truthful in Trump's remarks after Charlottesville's racial riot: "Good people on both sides."[6]

If one powerful politician appears with remarkable similarities to the rhetoric of Hitler, it would be useful to try to figure out if that politician really is like Hitler. Roberts-Miller argues, "It's important, therefore, to see if there really is another Hitler goosestepping toward us, and not just fling that accusation at any politician we dislike."[7]

Steven Levitsky and Daniel Ziblatt argue that democracies are usually undone by authoritarian leaders like Hitler. Trump deserves treatment in the league of authoritarian and unaccountable leaders like Adolf Hitler, Benito Mussolini, and Vladimir Putin, because these are all dangerous demagogues "who: (1) rejected or showed a weak commitment to democratic rules; (2) denied the legitimacy of political opponents; (3) tolerated or encouraged violence; and (4) were ready to curtail the civil liberties of opponents and the media."[8] "The essential or defining feature of a demagogue as an 'unaccountable leader' is useful for understanding who a dangerous demagogue is and who is a heroic or true demagogue because only dangerous demagogues would seek power as an unaccountable or authoritarian leader."[9] Trump scores a perfect score on all four of these traits of dangerous demagogues and he is off the charts in terms of feeling that he should not be accountable for, well, anything.

Roberts-Miller notes: "Trump supporters have spent years drinking deep from the Flavor-Aid of the pro-GOP Outrage Machine, and so they believe a lot of things. They believe they're the real victims here, that the media is against them, that white people are about to be persecuted, that there is no legitimate criticism of their position, that libruls have nothing but contempt for them and think they're racist, that they are so threatened with extermination that anything done on their behalf is justified."[10]

As a preacher and a poet, I am attempting to engage in an act of imagination. As Robert Duncan put it, "The poet's role is not to oppose

6. Marshall, "Full Transcript."
7. Marshall, "Full Transcript."
8. Levitsky and Ziblatt, *How Democracies Die*, 23–24.
9. Mercieca, "Dangerous Demagogues and Weaponized Communication," 269.
10. Roberts-Miller, "On Being Nice to Trump Supporters."

evil but to imagine it."[11] In my case I will oppose evil, dissent from evil, and imagine it. In the case of Trump and Hitler there is more of an imagined interaction with the historical realities.

My final justification for this chapter comes from words of Burke. He urged writers "to find all available ways of making the Hitlerite distortions of religion apparent, in order that politicians of his kind in America be unable to perform a similar swindle."[12] Burke's analysis of Hitler's "Battle" emphasized that people must inspect Hitler's words in order to prevent the rise of fascism in America. Now, to the battle.

The Rhetoric of Hitler and Trump

Assessing the rhetoric of a Hitler and a Trump requires a more detailed consideration of their goals. If the goals of Hitler and Trump align with one another, there is evidence that Trump's rhetoric may be as evil as that of Hitler. Patricia Roberts-Miller, in her study of Hitler, delineates Hitler's goals as follows:

- Aryans/Germans were entitled to political, economic, military, and cultural dominance of Europe.
- Germany must become purely German.
- Germans were victimized by anything that didn't allow them such dominance.
- Germany had been about to achieve dominance in World War I but was prevented from victory by a "stab in the back" on the part of Jews—who, he said, controlled the media, and caused Germans to give up.
- The historical moment was a battle between fascism and Jewish Bolshevism.
- Germany could not achieve its divinely determined end of a master race that dominated Europe as long as there were any Jews in Germany, so Germany must become "free" of any Jews (or other genetically tainted groups).
- Democracy, with the attendant notions of human rights (including an apolitical judicial system, free speech, freedom of religion) and

---

11. Duncan et al., *Letters of Robert Duncan and Denise Levertov*, 669.
12. Burke, "Rhetoric of Hitler's 'Battle,'" 49.

the benefits of public multi-party debate over policies, was a Jewish plot.

- The New Germany would not have class conflict, although it would still have classes, because it would not have a rigid and snobbish hierarchy in which Aryans looked down on other Aryans—it would instead have a rigid and snobbish hierarchy grounded in race (this is what was meant by "national socialism")—equal opportunity for members of the same race, with all members of that race fully committed to the German nation.
- Hitler was destined by God to lead Germany to its victory over Jewish-Bolshevism and had been given almost supernaturally good judgment (on any topic), stamina, will, and luck.
- Because Hitler's end goals were so good, any means that he used to achieve those ends were good. He was, therefore, entitled to lie, embezzle, attempt a coup, or anything else to get himself to a position where he could lead Germany to its destiny, and Germany was, therefore, entitled to exterminate any people, peoples, or nations that might inhibit (let alone stop) Germany's attainment of its goals. Hitler, the Nazis, and Germany were exceptions to the normal rules of ethics and behavior. Germany's exceptionalism was a necessary consequence of fascist eschatology.[13]

If Trump's goals parallel those of Hitler, then we have a beginning point for the claim that Trump's rhetoric suggests a Hitler-like fascism. Long before he ever ran for president, Trump had certain well-defined and frequently declared goals. In my investigation of the goals of Hitler and Trump, I found that Trump resonates with eight of Hitler's nine primary goals. Considering the summary of Hitler's platform, here are ways that Trump parallels Hitler: In Trump's eyes, Americans, especially white males, are victimized by a liberal elite. White males are persecuted by a liberal pedagogy of shame. White males, in their dreams, had once enjoyed hegemonic control and privilege. This illusion projects an America that never existed. We are engaged in a great battle between the will of one man and the future of democracy.

The United States can't achieve its divinely determined end as a great nation if there are illegal immigrants in the country, if evangelicals are not allowed to teach intelligent design, and unless America is a Christian

13. Roberts-Miller, "Rhetoric and Hitler."

nation. And slavery was not that bad. The liberals are destroying the nation and only Trump can save it.

Democracy, with its notions of human rights (including an apolitical judicial system, free speech, freedom of religion) and the benefits of public multiparty debate over policies was a Democratic plot to drive the nation into socialism. Trump is destined by God to lead America to greatness again by restoring a heteronormative reality to the detriment of all others. Because Trump's goals are so good, in the eyes of his followers, any means that he used to achieve those ends were good. He was, therefore, entitled to lie, embezzle, order murders, attempt a coup, or anything else to get himself to a position where he could lead the United States to greatness.

Like Hitler, Trump didn't have to persuade a large body of people to believe or to accept his goals. Such a body already existed. Miller-Roberts: "Lots of people (especially but not exclusively Germans) believed many or all of these things before Hitler rose to power—he rose to power *because* so many people believed enough of them. Many people believed in Hitler because they already believed in what he said."[14] "If Hitler's rhetorical strategies were essentially damaging to his community—if they ensured that people made decisions badly; if that kind of rhetoric is likely to end badly—then we should be teaching students to avoid and suspect any rhetoric that relies on those strategies. Rhetoric, in this view, isn't a morally neutral set of moves, but itself has a moral valence."[15] This is the turn to ethos that has driven my study. Trump's rhetoric damages democracy, damages the anchor institutions of democracy, and damages the positive aspects of our civil religion that have previously given us a moral compass. This really is about evil and good. Morality matters. Democracy matters. Ethics matter.

Kenneth Burke's "The Rhetoric of Hitler's 'Battle'"

"The Rhetoric of Hitler's 'Battle'" is an influential essay written by Kenneth Burke in 1939, which offered a rhetorical analysis of Adolf Hitler's rise to power in Germany. His prescient warning still has the ring of truth: "Let us try also to discover what kind of 'medicine' this medicine-man has concocted, that we may know, with greater accuracy, exactly what to

---

14. Roberts-Miller, "Rhetoric and Hitler."
15. Roberts-Miller, "Rhetoric and Hitler."

guard against, if we are to forestall the concocting of similar medicine in America."[16]

Burke urged writers "to find all available ways of making the Hitlerite distortions of religion apparent, in order that politicians of his kind in America be unable to perform a similar swindle."[17] Burke's analysis of Hitler's "Battle" emphasized that people must inspect Hitler's words to prevent the rise of fascism in America. Again, I'm not saying Trump is Hitler. I'm saying we shouldn't judge rhetoric by whether we like its outcome or its advocates—it has its own consequences. Bad rhetoric in favor of a cause we like is, I'm saying, still bad rhetoric in that it legitimates what others might do with it.[18]

"The appearance of Hitler, in all his evil rhetorical genius," said Burke, "has called forth far too many vandalistic comments. There are other ways of dealing with such rhetoric than on the pyre—and the favorite method of the hasty reviewer is to deprive herself and her readers by inattention."[19] Nor should the critic be content with inflicting a few symbolic wounds upon Donald Trump and his rhetoric. There are too many resources—tweets, speeches, interviews—available to be content with the cursory throwing of "red meat" at the already convinced. Trump's rhetoric is exasperating, even nauseating; yet the necessity of challenging his rhetoric must be unceasing. If a critic only knocks off a few adverse opinions and calls it a day, all that is accomplished is a favorable reception among the decent members of our populations. Such an effort provides gratification but not much enlightenment.

Burke said of Hitler: "Here is the testament of a man who swung a great people."[20] So we may say, similarly, that Trump has swept a great people—in particular, American evangelicals—into his dream of a great America. Let us study it carefully; and let us watch it, not merely to make our own tribe feel better; "let us try to discover what kind of medicine this medicine-man has concocted, that we may know, with greater accuracy, exactly what to guard against," if we are to stop this un-reality show from renewal for a second term.[21]

16. Burke, "Rhetoric of Hitler's 'Battle,'" 33.
17. Burke, "Rhetoric of Hitler's 'Battle,'" 49.
18. Roberts-Miller, "What Putin's Rhetoric Should Tell Us about Ours."
19. Burke, "Rhetoric of Hitler's 'Battle,'" 191.
20. Burke, "Rhetoric of Hitler's 'Battle,'" 33.
21. Burke, "Rhetoric of Hitler's 'Battle,'" 33.

Trump was helpful enough to put all his cards on the table, that we might examine his hands. Let us, then, for God's sake, examine them. This rhetoric is the well of Trump magic, crude but effective. His transparency, his willingness to say everything that is on his mind, may be as much his Achilles' heel as it has been his source of strength among his followers. The evidence lies around, available, easily discoverable.

Trump made the choice to not be a traditional politician in this regard. He was going to say what no one else dared to say. In one sense, it's an old political trope—attack the establishment. But Trump goes much deeper. He attacks the holy of holies of democratic existence. He had no desire to create what Perelman designates as the "universal audience."[22] Perelman says, "Argumentation addressed to the universal audience must convince the reader that the reasons adduced are of a compelling character, that they are self evident, and possess an absolute timeless validity, independent of local or historical contingencies."[23] In Trump's case the universal audience he creates is a particular audience as he makes no attempt to persuade those who dissent from his views. Trump's speeches have two audiences: his adoring fans who understand his coded language and the liberals Trump is deliberately baiting.

Trump's rhetoric mirrors Hitler's rhetorical strategies. One, there's a dominant trope, a unifying visual metaphor. Second, there's the selection of a geographical holy place. Third, there's unification through a common enemy. Fourth, there's scapegoating and projection. Fifth, there's toxic masculinity. Sixth, there's the notion that America is "weak" and only Trump can make it strong again. Seventh, many UK and USA media endorsed and openly admired Hitler's "strongman" image. Trump's appeal as the "strongman" received its most important boost from evangelical supporters.

The Wall

Trump offered his audience one unifying center of reference for all. He decided that this center must be not merely a centralizing hub of ideas, but a material metaphor, geographically located, towards which all his supporter's eyes could turn at the appointed hours of prayer-in-reverse, the hours of vituperation. So, he selected a wall—between the USA and

---

22. Perelman and Olbrechts-Tyteca, *New Rhetoric*, 31.
23. Perelman and Olbrechts-Tyteca, *New Rhetoric*, 32.

Mexico—as the materialization of his unifying panacea. As Trump put it: "We are going to build a magnificent wall, and Mexico is going to pay for it."[24] The wall became the incarnation of how Trump would keep all enemies from the gates of his supporters. But this line, notoriously, became a linchpin of Trump's campaign. Once again, the issue is not the economics, but degradation, humiliation, and bringing back American pride. Mexico has to be humiliated in retaliation for "laughing at us."[25]

And then the defining metaphor of the Age of Trump: "I would build a great wall, and nobody builds walls better than me, believe me, and I'll build them very inexpensively, I will build a great, great wall on our southern border."[26] Those who discount the power of Trump's wall image weren't listening when the Rev. Robert Jeffress gave divine legitimacy to Trump's wall in his sermon on Inaugural Day. Jeffress blessed Trump and Trump's wall in what appears as a divine sanction for walls: "God has raised you . . . up for a great, eternal purpose." Jeffress, with little attention to biblical exegesis, exulted that Trump would rebuild our great nation. Jeffress assumed that Trump was telling the truth when he promised to make America great again. Then Jeffress placed Trump's wall on an equal basis with the wall Nehemiah built around Jerusalem: "And the first step of rebuilding the nation was the building of a great wall. God instructed Nehemiah to build a wall around Jerusalem to protect its citizens from enemy attack. You see, God is *not* against building walls!"[27] Jeffress completed a "royal liturgical performance" that rivals Nathan legitimizing King Solomon at Gihon. Solomon's throne, secured by deception and violence, now receives divine approval.[28]

A Geographical Holy Place: A Mecca

Hitler and Trump had a mecca. A movement must have its center. Hitler considered this matter carefully and decided that this center must be not merely a centralizing hub of ideas, but a mecca geographically located, towards which all eyes could turn at the appointed hours of prayer

---

24. *Time*, "Here's Donald Trump's Presidential Announcement Speech"; McCarthy, "11 Controversial Things Donald Trump Said."
25. Schaefer, "Whiteness and Civilization," 8.
26. Schaefer, "Whiteness and Civilization," 8.
27. *Time*, "Read the Sermon Donald Trump Heard."
28. Brueggemann, *Truth Speaks to Power*, 54.

(or, in this case, the appointed hours of prayer-in-reverse, the hours of vituperation).[29] So he selected Munich, as the materialization of his unifying panacea. Burke comments on the importance of such a center: "The geo-political importance of a center of a movement cannot be overrated. Only the presence of such a center and of a place, bathed in the magic of a Mecca or a Rome, can at length give a movement that force which is rooted in the inner unity and in the recognition of a hand that represents this unity."[30]

Trump selected Trump Tower as his mecca. Jennifer Mercieca says, "Trump is a fan of gilding—of adding a thin layer of gold or gold colored stuff to things to make them appear to be more valuable than they are."[31] Gold gilding is the signature design feature of Trump-branded properties and products worldwide. According to Trump's decorator Angelo Donghia, his New York City apartment was designed as a gilded golden tribute to France's Louis XIV—the Sun King who once (perhaps, but maybe not) declared to his Parliament *"l'état, c'est moi"*—"I am the state"—in defiance of its attempt to restrain him.[32] Trump has lived his life as a Sun King of sorts—he has believed himself to be above the law, never permitting himself to be held accountable for his actions. In fact, Trump takes pride in his Sun King-like ability to decide what is and what is not. "The Golden Rule of Negotiating," Trump once tweeted to his followers, is "he who has the gold makes the rules."[33] Trump's gilded Sun King ethos isn't just for negotiating, politics, or history. It belies his approach to rhetoric as well—instrumental, fake, unaccountable. Trump, believing he has the gold, made his own rules. His presidential campaign used rhetoric strategically—without regard to ethics—to help him to get what he wanted. He used rhetoric to intimidate, to overwhelm, to mock, to threaten, as well as to entertain. Trump weaponized rhetoric to disrupt the liberal consensus, which means that his rhetorical style was anarchic as well. Trump will always attempt to make his own rules or subvert the rules that are in place with lawsuits, rhetorical tricks, or lies. The rules don't apply to Donald Trump and that makes him an anarchist. This also intensifies the loyalty of his followers as they identify with his tough man performance.

29. Burke, "Rhetoric of Hitler's 'Battle,'" 34.
30. Burke, "The Rhetoric of Hitler's 'Battle,'" 34.
31. Mercieca, "Afterword," 185.
32. Mercieca, "Afterword," 185.
33. Tweet, Donald J. Trump (@realDonaldTrump) July 30, 2013.

Trump Tower would now take the place of the Twin Towers as the symbol of American wealth and power. Yes, Genesis 11 screams at me: "And they said to one another, 'Come, let us make bricks, and burn them thoroughly.' And they had brick for stone, and bitumen for mortar. Then they said, 'Come, let us build ourselves a city, and a tower with its top in the heavens, and let us make a name for ourselves.'"[34] Trump, with his tower already finished, now plans to make an even bigger name for himself. For Hitler and Trump, image is everything.

It has even become an argument among the defenders of the "Big Lie," that Biden couldn't have won the election because of the huge crowds that showed up for Trump rallies. Even if we accept Trump's exaggerated crowd estimates, no one can escape the reality that eighty million Americans voted for Biden, and no crowd of this size has ever existed. The comparison is ludicrous but accepted as matter of fact by Trump lovers. Trump pumped the illusion: "This is beyond anybody's expectations. There's been no crowd like this."[35] The exaggerated claims of crowd size have been mostly overlooked as a powerful Trump trope.

Trump Tower announced that Trump's chief qualifications for being president were fame and wealth. It was as if no one was paying attention as Trump laid out his strategy, his rhetorical tropes with bold exaggeration, hyperbole, and humbug. "I'm really rich" and "I will be the greatest jobs president that God has ever created."[36] Everything that would be Trump happened at the Trump Tower in Trump's announcement speech.

In an unusual twist, Trump also managed to convert his rallies across the nation into mini-meccas. Like an evangelist with a tent, Trump tromps around the country and the faithful gather. He promises that he can heal. Trump with his own tent and pulpit and his sermons spit out the resentment, the rage, and the hatred. "Trump's rallies—a bizarre mishmash of numerology, tweetology, and white supremacy—are the rituals by which he stamps his name on the American dream."[37] Trump supporters, often in large groups, travel from rally to rally, to witness "God's anointed"—the wealthy preacher of the prosperity gospel. Trump Tower metamorphizes into a tent so that when the people can't go to the tower the tower comes to them. Behold the Trump mecca! A Trump rally seems

---

34. Gen 11:1–4.
35. Mercieca, *Demagogue for President*, Kindle ed., loc. 154.
36. *Time*, "Here's Donald Trump's Presidential Announcement Speech."
37. Sharlet, "'He's the Chosen One To Run America.'"

to merge a professional wrestling crowd with a faith healer's crowd. A people, convinced they were sick and tired, traveled across the country to cry out to Trump, "Heal us, preacher. Heal us." And Trump delivered.

He was more shaman than evangelist with his medicine-man rhetoric. He offered to heal the afflictions of his victimized, persecuted white followers through myth, hyperbole, exaggeration, lies, and deception. It was as if he was reaching out his "large hands" and placing them on the collective heads of his supporters to give understanding and solace. As shaman he takes on the devils that have deprived his followers of greatness, and he does what ordinary folks can't do: he exorcizes the demons. Behold, the shaman, the healer, the evangelist.

A Universal Devil

If a movement must have its mecca, its garden paradise (note that the garden paradise here is the reverse of the garden of democracy), it must also have its devil. Burke says,

> As a whole, and at all times, the efficiency of the truly national leader consists primarily in preventing the division of the attention of a people, and always in concentrating it on a single enemy. The more uniformly the fighting will of a people is put into action, the greater will be the magnetic force of the movement and the more powerful the impetus of the blow. It is part of the genius of a great leader to make adversaries of different fields appear as always belonging to one category only, because to weak and unstable characters the knowledge that there are various enemies will lead only too easily to incipient doubts as to their own cause.[38]

Burke makes much of the central rhetorical strategy of the enemy.

> "As everyone knows, this policy was exemplified in [Hitler's] selection of an 'international' devil, the 'International Jew' (the Prince was international, universal, "catholic"). This materialization of a religious pattern is, I think, one terrifically effective weapon of propaganda in a period where religion has been progressively weakened by many centuries of capitalist materialism. You need but go back to the sermonizing of centuries to be reminded that religion had a powerful enemy long before organized atheism came upon the scene. Religion is based upon

---

38. Burke, "Rhetoric of Hitler's 'Battle,'" 34–35.

the "prosperity of poverty," upon the use of ways for converting our sufferings and handicaps into a good—but capitalism is based upon the prosperity of acquisitions, the only scheme of value, in fact, by which its proliferating store of gadgets could be sold, assuming for the moment that capitalism had not got so drastically in its own way that it can't sell its gadgets even after it has trained people to feel that human dignity, the "higher standard of living," could be attained only by their vast private accumulation. So, we have the international devil materialized, in the visible, point-to-able form of people with a certain kind of "blood," a burlesque of contemporary neo-positivism's ideal of meaning, which insists upon a material reference.[39]

As soon as people find themselves confronted with too many enemies, objectivity at once steps in, and the question is raised whether actually all the others are wrong and their own nation or their own movement alone is right. This has changed. There's no such thing as too many enemies for Donald Trump. He lives for the antagonism. The thrill of the fight. The rhetorical strategy at work here is association. For example, Jamieson describes the rhetoric of the 2016 pro-Trump trolls: Those who endanger us include Muslims, illegal aliens, Black Lives Matter activists, atheists, demanding women, those who oppose gun rights, and Hillary Clinton, to name a few. Among those cast as "we" were white males, Donald Trump, Christians, veterans, and workers whose jobs are threatened by bad trade deals and job-stealing "illegals." All these are confronted with open hostility, and accented with the highly competitive nature of winning and losing. A telling remark Trump has made as he teased a 2024 run for president: "I think a lot of people are going to be very happy, because it's a little boring now."[40]

Therefore, several different enemies must always be regarded as one in such a way that in the opinion of the mass of one's own adherents the war is being waged against one enemy alone. People who can unite on nothing else can unite on the basis of a foe shared by all. As everyone knows, this policy of identifying the enemy took many forms, but incarnates in liberals—the media, the press, the system, the Democrats, the socialists, minorities, immigrants, and all Others.

Trump's selection of a national devil, the Democratic liberal, drives his entire enterprise. Here is another instance where Trump's strategy

---

39. Burke, "Rhetoric of Hitler's 'Battle,'" 35.
40. Panetta, "Trump Says People Will Be 'Very Happy.'"

mirrors Hitler's. Trump presents, with a huge assist from his evangelical preacher allies, the declension of the nation to a status of not great because of liberal poisoning, visible to all. Lumped under the term "radical liberals" are political correctness, gay marriage, illegal immigration, loss of religious faith and freedom, big urban cities rife with black crime, the weakness of Congress, the corruption of Washington, DC ("Drain the Swamp"), the court system, the "fake news," and ideas like "wokeness" and "Critical Race Theory."

Once Trump has thus essentialized his enemy, all "proof" is henceforth automatic. Trump constantly points, with 100 percent regularity, to the cunning and power of the liberal enemy that is engineering the plot to overthrow America. Trump inherited the "enemy" from his evangelical forebears. These preachers honed the message of liberals to a demonic intensity unrivaled by any propaganda short of the propaganda of a nation at war with an enemy. The ability to paint the liberal as "less than human," as demonic, as a witch, as a powerful and satanic presence, has been the constant playbook of evangelical preachers, especially the televangelists. Jerry Falwell Sr., Robert Jeffress, and Franklin Graham are representative of this approach. The end times preachers have added decades of logs to the burning flames of an apocalyptic scene. This is the perverse religious version of the enemy coming to burn down the house, kidnap your children, and rape your wife trope.

Trump successfully completed the evangelical work of embedding a single trope into the American mind: Democrats are devils. Trump framed Democrats. "A movement must have its devil."[41] "The first unifying step in gaining a huge following is a devil materialized, in a viable, point-to-able people—a material reference."[42]

Evangelical resentment, rage, and disgust as all liberals goes back at least a century. Evangelicals have genuinely suffered at the hands of liberals. This has been the case since at least 1925 and the Scopes trial. They have long been sensitive to the mistreatment, the mocking, the caricatures, the incessant accusations of being a bunch of dumb hicks. Their resentment has burned like the fires of Gehenna. Also, Trump shared a similar fate at the hand of the New York aristocrats.

At this point, Trump is tracing the resentment, the ressentiment, of his hatred for the establishment. He now confronts it with his rhetoric

---

41. Burke, "Rhetoric of Hitler's 'Battle,'" 34.
42. Burke, "Rhetoric of Hitler's 'Battle,'" 34.

of demolition. He connects with his resentful evangelicals and teaches them to stop feeling shame at the political correctness of the liberal. No bowing of the head, no averting of the eyes will be needed. Instead, they could revel in the scene of pushing back at the liberal with overt racism, resentment, and revenge. Shame could be replaced with a sense of dignity. Here his drastic structure of identification is formed. Trump offers an apocalyptic vision of the end of the world if the liberal is allowed to win. With one of his associational tricks that he brings forth at every opportunity, he emerges with his slogan: "Make America Great Again." And he is waging this battle in the name of the Lord. A frequent right-wing post on Facebook shows a picture of President Obama and Jesus with Jesus saying that he had to send Trump because Obama was undoing all of Jesus' work. Similarly, Trump develops his rhetoric of destruction in the name of humility, order, peace, law, and love. Trump so easily manipulates tropes like the Bible, prayer in public schools, and anti-abortion screeds. The patterns of Trump's thought are a caricatured version of religious thought.

By centering his attack on the symptoms of a democracy riddled with gridlock and dysfunction, Trump managed to produce an alleged cause: his medicine, his racial theory by which he could produce a scapegoat for his economically endangered white supporters. Interpreters of Trump's movement went for the illusion that his victory came about because of the resentment and anger of working-class whites. This old charade, as Ta-Nehisi Coates has shown, is trotted out in every era when white privilege seems threatened.[43]

Here again is where Trump's corrupt use of religious patterns comes to the fore. Church thought, being primarily individualistic and concerned with matters of the "personality," with problems of moral betterment, stresses the act of will upon the part of the individual. Hence its resistance to environmental, social, corporate accounts of human ills. Hence its proneness to seek simply noneconomic explanations. In other words, the tendency to scapegoat rises to the top of the religious support of President Trump. There must be an enemy that can be personified. Trump's proposal of a noneconomic cause for the disturbances in our democracy and in our streets was incredibly enticing to an audience already predisposed to berating liberals of all stripes as the incarnation of Satan. Even after almost four years as president and in the midst of a

---

43. Coates, "First White President."

tough reelection campaign against Joe Biden, Trump returned again and again to attacks on Ms. Clinton, insisting that the Justice Department charge her with high crimes and treason: "Lock her up!" Thus, Trump tied his program of a promise to make America great again with sexist, racist, and antisemitic unifiers. Hiding under the gushing praise of "this president's wonderful policies," under the white sheet of invisibility, is the racism that fuels the Trump movement.

Radical liberals, always radical, attach to every Republican criticism. The Green New Deal can't be normal, natural, or necessary but the radical, extreme Democratic Green New Deal. Perhaps Trump's "medicine" would have convinced Americans of an earlier age not to give up smoking. Perhaps he would have inveighed against wearing seat belts and carried the day. Or maybe he could have stopped Martin Luther King Jr.'s dream in its tracks. But I think that is too much conjecture. Also, I think Trump was a man who captured "evangelical/conservative rage" as if it were magic in a bottle and he had his moment in the sun. If we are fortunate, the Age of Trump will have been a chimera and then the last one out could turn out the lights at the Trump Tower of Babel.

The Scapegoating Trope

Closely allied with enemy selection is the use of scapegoating. Hitler used scapegoating as a major trope. "Hitler had two kinds of rhetoric. For his internal audience, it was exactly what the rhetoric scholar Kenneth Burke described in 1939: scapegoating/projection, rebirth, bastardization of religious forms of thought, toxic masculinity (not Burke's term, of course—he talks about the feminization of the masses)."[44]

The scapegoating device has unlimited usage among the religious. Religious authorities used the idea of a scapegoat to justify the crucifixion of Jesus. Christians used Judas to scapegoat all Jews as the "killers of Jesus." The relationship, in terms of consequences, to the rhetoric of Hitler and the words of Matthew 28:18–20—as they have been used in history to justify the killing of Jews—still shocks the sensible. Reynolds Price argues, "The single saying of Jesus which—in the hands of self-blinded followers—has fueled the most tragic effects has been his final words in the Gospel of Matthew 28:18–20. . . . The crusades of the Middle Ages, the European conquest of the Americas and the resulting slaughter and

---

44. Roberts-Miller, "Rhetoric and Hitler."

enslavement of millions of indigenous peoples and a great deal of similar Western triumphalism and murderous anti-Semitism are only the largest of these effects."[45]

The Sexual Symbolism

Burke says,

> The sexual symbolism that runs through Hitler's book, lying in wait to draw upon the responses of contemporary sexual values, is easily characterized: Germany in dispersion is the "dehorned Siegfried." The masses are "feminine." As such, they desire to be led by a dominating male. This male, as orator, woos them—and, when he has won them, he commands them. The rival male, the villainous Jew, would on the contrary "seduce" them. If he succeeds, he poisons their blood by intermingling with them. Whereupon, by purely associative connections of ideas, we are moved into attacks upon syphilis, prostitution, incest, and other similar misfortunes, which are introduced as a kind of "musical" argument when he is on the subject of "blood-poisoning" by intermarriage or, in its "spiritual" equivalent, by the infection of "Jewish" ideas, such as democracy.[46]

In a footnote, Burke adds, "Hitler also strongly insists upon a total identification between leader and people."[47]

The sexual symbolism that runs through Trump's rhetoric mirrors his own convoluted, questionable treatment of women. America, in Trump's rhetoric, is weak and vulnerable. The nation is actually feminine and deep down it desires to be led by a dominating male. This male, as orator, woos them and wins them—and as a result commands them. The rival males, the liberals, are perverts, very sick people, a bunch of losers who only attempt to seduce. Trump plays these twin themes over and over—a feminized weak nation and a virile, powerful male. He positions himself as the only one who can save the nation. Trump casts the nation as "losing" and not "winning." He feminizes the nation as being raped by the other nations of the world, and then projects himself as the only strong male capable of saving the weak, losing, feminine nation. This theme began with Trump's announcement that he was running for president:

45. Price, *Serious Way of Wondering*, 10.
46. Burke, "Rhetoric of Hitler's 'Battle,'" 35.
47. Burke, "Rhetoric of Hitler's 'Battle,'" 35.

Trump paints the nation as weak and feminine, as a loser, as a victim. This is humiliation, but then he promises to deliver dignity. "Our country is in serious trouble," Trump says, as he begins his prepared remarks. "We don't have victories anymore. We used to have victories, but we don't have them. When was the last time anybody saw us beating, let's say, China in a trade deal? They kill us. I beat China all the time. All the time."[48]

Here Trump borrows extensively, whether consciously or unconsciously I can't tell, from Putin's rhetoric. As noted earlier, Putin's speeches insisted that the Motherland was a "man's affair" and rejects women in public debates on the grounds that he did not need to engage in arguments on which was better, "Tampax or Snickers." Putin quoted Stalin: "We showed weakness and the weak get beaten." He projected an air of grandeur as he talked often of the "might" of Russia. He drove home the point that the goal of enemies is "to tear off a fatty piece."

Trump creates an image of America as losing and uncertain. The more America is feminine the more it loses. His use of sexual tropes, especially rape, expose a particular preoccupation Trump has with sex. Referring to a then-recent capture of an American patrol boat by the Iranian government, Trump describes the event as an American confrontation with "images of our sailors being forced to their knees."[49] The sexual imagery emphasizes America's humiliation, which is reinforced as Trump goes on to narrate the consequences of a feminized political apparatus by discussing the time before—and after—Hillary Clinton was in charge at the State Department. Before Hillary Clinton, America could violently humiliate its enemies, as Iran was "choked by sanctions."

Attacks on the Institutions of Democracy

Burke suggests, "From this we may move to another tremendously important aspect of [Hitler's] theory: his attack upon the parliamentary. For it is again, I submit, an important aspect of his medicine, in its function as medicine for him personally and as medicine for those who were later to identify themselves with him."[50] Confer Trump's attack on Congress, the judiciary, and the military.

---

48. *Time*, "Here's Donald Trump's Presidential Announcement Speech."
49. *Politico*, "Donald Trumps's 2016 RNC Draft Speech Transcript."
50. Burke, "Rhetoric of Hitler's 'Battle,'" 38.

Hitler insisted there was a "problem" in the parliament"—and nowhere was this problem more acutely in evidence than in the pre-war Vienna that was to serve as Hitler's political schooling. For the parliament, at its best, is a "Babel" of voices.[51] So, Hitler saw this parliament as the basic symbol of all that he would move away from. He damned the tottering Habsburg Empire as a "State of Nationalities."[52] The many conflicting voices of the spokesmen of the many political blocs arose from the fact that various separationist movements of a nationalistic sort had arisen within a Catholic imperial structure formed prior to the nationalistic emphasis and slowly breaking apart under its development. So, you had this Babel of voices; and, by the method of associative mergers, using ideas as imagery, it became tied up, in the Hitler rhetoric, with "Babylon,"[53] Vienna as the city of poverty, prostitution, immorality, coalitions, half-measures, incest, democracy (i.e., majority rule leading to "lack of personal responsibility"), death, internationalism, seduction, and anything else of the thumbs-down sort the associative enterprise cared to add on this side of the balance.[54]

Hitler's attack on the parliament is mirrored in Trump's relentless attacks on the foundational institutions of democracy. Trump's fury at the dialectics of those who oppose him is unleashed indiscriminately on Republicans and Democrats, on the living and the dead. This leads to another of his blatant attacks: his attack on the foundational institutions of the democracy: free press, the courts, and Congress. It is an important aspect of his medicine, in its function as medicine for him personally and as medicine for the evangelicals who helped create him. Trump's attack on the parliamentary makes up a large portion of his authoritarian vision. His hatred of democracy is an important aspect of his medicine, in its function as medicine for him personally and as medicine for those who identify with him.

There is a problem in Congress. Trump repeats this message with as much regularity as he attacks the press. Congress and the press represent the "Babel" of voices—the demonic infiltration of the government. Trump personalizes his attacks on Congress by concentrating his venom on Nancy Pelosi, Speaker of the House, and a quartet of young American

---

51. Burke, "Rhetoric of Hitler's 'Battle,'" 38.
52. Burke, "Rhetoric of Hitler's 'Battle,'" 38.
53. Burke, "Rhetoric of Hitler's 'Battle,'" 200.
54. Burke, "Rhetoric of Hitler's 'Battle,'" 37–38.

members of Congress, some Muslim: "Send them back." After all, according to Trump, "They hate America."⁵⁵ These women are an especially drastic instance of the disruption and corruption of Congress. So, we have this Babel of voices; and using ideas as imagery, it became tied up, in Trump's rhetoric with large cities, liberal cities, immorality, poverty, rank democracy, violence, and anything else of the thumbs-down sort of associative enterprise Trump cared to add on this side of the balance.

For Trump, Congress was a woman split into several sub-personalities at odds with one another, variously combining under hypnosis, and frequently in turmoil. This represents his allegory of a democracy fallen upon evil days—an evil produced by a person of color, President Barack Obama; a notorious witch who represented the system, Hillary Clinton; persons of color; liberals; socialists; immigrants; and foreigners. Trump rolled all these enemies into this paranoia of the "deep state."

When a judge of Hispanic descent was put in charge of the Trump University fraud case, Trump said the judge could not be objective because he was "Mexican." The judge was born in Indiana. Trump went on to claim that a Muslim judge could not be objective if ruling on his case.⁵⁶ "The opinion of this so-called judge, which essentially takes law-enforcement away from our country, is ridiculous and will be overturned!"⁵⁷ The president said the "courts seem to be so political" and called the hearing "disgraceful."⁵⁸

In February 2020, Trump attacked Amy Berman Jackson, the judge who presided over his former adviser Roger Stone's pending criminal case in the US District Court for the District of Columbia. Stone was convicted of lying to Congress, witness tampering, and obstructing an investigation by the US House of Representatives. Trump's attacks came after the Department of Justice recommended a sentence of seven to nine years for Stone. In a series of tweets published in February, Trump criticized this recommendation, and as a result, the Department of Justice indicated it would seek a shorter sentence for Stone, prompting four career prosecutors to withdraw from the case. Trump texted: "A total miscarriage of justice!"⁵⁹

55. *Middle East Monitor*, "Trump to Muslim Congresswomen."
56. Dickerson, "Interview."
57. Donald J. Trump (@realDonaldTrump) February 4, 2017.
58. *EconoTimes*, "Donald Trump Attacks Judges."
59. Donald J. Trump (@realDonaldTrump) February 25, 2020.

In November 2018, Trump announced new rules that would bar anyone crossing the US-Mexico border not through an official port of entry from receiving asylum. On November 20, Judge Jon Tigar of the US Court of Appeals for the Ninth Circuit ordered the administration to accept asylum claims regardless of where migrants entered the country. Trump called the decision "a disgrace," attacked Tigar as "an Obama judge," and critiqued the Ninth Circuit as "really something we have to take a look at because it's not fair," adding, "That's not law. Every case that gets filed in the Ninth Circuit we get beaten."[60]

In a rare response, Chief Justice John Roberts told the Associated Press that the US doesn't have "Obama judges or Trump judges, Bush judges or Clinton judges. What we have is an extraordinary group of dedicated judges doing their level best to do equal right to those appearing before them." Roberts added that "The independent judiciary is something we should all be thankful for."[61]

Trump wasted no time refuting the Chief Justice: "Sorry Chief Justice John Roberts, but you do indeed have 'Obama judges,' and they have a much different point of view than the people who are charged with the safety of our country. It would be great if the 9th Circuit was indeed an 'independent judiciary,' but if it is why [there] are so many opposing view [on border and safety] cases filed there, and why [there] are a vast number of those cases overturned. Please study the numbers, they are shocking. We need protection and security—these rulings are making our country unsafe! Very dangerous and unwise!"[62]

The anchor institution most frequently assailed by Trump is the press. He attacks the freedom of the press enshrined in the First Amendment as vigorously as the American history "hobbyist," David Barton, and Barton sees the First Amendment as the work of the devil. There's a point in every rally when Trump confronts the enemy directly. Not Hillary Clinton, or Joe Biden, or Mexican immigrants, but a small group of men and women penned in a metal cage on the arena floor. They're "very bad people" and "scum" and "liars." "Look at them!" he cries, pointing. His thousands turn to the cage to scream. Journalist Jeff Sharlet reports:

> If I had thought to bring a sound-level meter to the rallies, I could give you a precise rendering in decibels of the ascending

---

60. Levine, "Trump Administration Calls U.S. Judge's Asylum Ruling 'Absurd.'"
61. Pendleton, "Justice Roberts Says No Such Thing as 'Obama Judge.'"
62. Donald J. Trump (@realDonaldTrump) November 21, 2018.

passions of the Trumpocene: God, guns, and, loudest of all, hating CNN. A cartoon Trump pissing on the CNN logo is a popular T-shirt at rallies; another reads: "Rope. Tree. Journalist. Some assembly required."

"Does *anybody* think the media is honest?" Trump asks the crowd at the third rally I attended, in Hershey, Pennsylvania.

"No!" they cry.

"Does anybody think they're totally corrupt and dishonest?"

"Yes!" they cry. A woman next to me leans back on her heels, lower lip tucked under her teeth, eyes closed, arms outstretched, her two middle fingers raised.[63]

Hitler, Trump, and Victimization

Not content to attack the institutions of democracy, Hitler turned to blaming the government for failure and making the German people victims. Trump has followed this portion of Hitler's playbook religiously. Hitler's rhetorical steps are especially interesting here, in that he begins by seeming to flout the national susceptibilities: "The military defeat of the German people is not an undeserved catastrophe, but rather a deserved punishment by eternal retribution." He then proceeds to present the military collapse as but a "consequence of moral poisoning, visible to all, the consequence of a decrease in the instinct of self-preservation . . . which had already begun to undermine the foundations of the people and the Reich many years before."[64] This moral decay derived from "a sin against the blood and the degradation of the race," so its innerness was an outerness after all: the Jew, who thereupon gets saddled with a vast amalgamation of evils, among them being capitalism, democracy, pacifism, journalism, poor housing, modernism, big cities, loss of religion, half measures, ill health, and the weakness of the monarch.

As Burke points out, "Hitler had here another important psychological ingredient to play upon": restoring national dignity.[65] "A people in collapse, suffering under economic frustration and the defeat of nationalistic aspirations, with the very mid-rib of their integrative efforts (the army) in a state of dispersion, have little other than some 'spiritual' basis to which they could refer their nationalistic dignity. Hence, the

63. Sharlet, "He's the Chosen One To Run America."
64. Quoted in Burke, "Rhetoric of Hitler's 'Battle,'" 40–41.
65. Burke, "Rhetoric of Hitler's 'Battle,'" 40–41.

categorical dignity of superior race was a perfect recipe for the situation. It was 'spiritual' in so far as it was 'above' crude economic 'interests,' but it was 'materialized' at the psychologically 'right' spot in that 'the enemy' was something you could see."[66]

For Trump this was a major rhetorical challenge. His followers had been shamed. Trump had to concoct a medicine that would cure the sense of shame developed by the liberal pedagogy of shame. He did this by transforming shame into dignity. Trump supporters were despondent until Trump made his appearance on the political stage. Trump gave them a way to furiously deny culpability. Lauren Berlant writes, "Trump's people want fairness of a sort, but mainly they seek freedom from shame."[67] To a humiliated people Trump promised to deliver dignity. Trump's presidential campaign announcement on June 16, 2015, is an early indicator of the driving dynamic of Trump's rhetoric. It offers a dyad of shame and dignity, often organized around race. "Our country is in serious trouble," Trump says, as he begins his prepared remarks. "We don't have victories anymore. We used to have victories, but we don't have them. When was the last time anybody saw us beating, let's say, China in a trade deal? They kill us. I beat China all the time. All the time."[68] "When do we beat Mexico at the border?" Trump continued. "They're laughing at us, at our stupidity . . . The US has become a dumping ground for everybody else's problems."[69]

One would be tempted to think that Trump, a notorious nonreader, must have read Hitler for his bedtime reading material. Ivana Trump once told her lawyer Michael Kennedy that her husband, real-estate mogul Donald Trump, kept a book of Hitler's speeches near his bed.[70]

Violence and the Threat of Violence

"Hitler also tells of his technique in speaking, once the Nazi party had become effectively organized, and had its army of guards, or bouncers, to maltreat hecklers and throw them from the hall. He would, he

66. Burke, "Rhetoric of Hitler's *Battle*," 41.
67. Berlant, "Trump, or Political Emotions."
68. *Time*, "Here's Donald Trump's Presidential Announcement Speech."
69. *Time*, "Here's Donald Trump's Presidential Announcement Speech."
70. *Business Insider*, "Donald Trump's Ex-wife."

recounts, fill his speech with provocative remarks, whereat his bouncers would promptly swoop down in flying formation, with swinging fists, upon anyone whom these provocative remarks provoked to answer."[71] The efficiency of Hitlerism is the efficiency of the one voice, implemented throughout a total organization. The trinity of government which he finally offers is: popularity of the leader, force to back the popularity, and popularity and force maintained together long enough to become backed by a tradition.[72]

Jennifer Mercieca helpfully reminds,

> Obviously not all dangerous demagogues will use physical force like Hitler did; however, all ad baculum attacks—whether or not they invoke actual physical violence—have the same end: to use coercion and intimidation to gain compliance. The fact that physical violence is possible makes ad baculum that much more powerful and that much more difficult to argue against. If rhetoric is a method of arriving at phronesis via consent in the absence of sophia, then weaponized communication is an anti-rhetorical method of gaining compliance characterized by aggression, disregarding ethics, and instrumentality.[73]

Ad baculum arguments are used by demagogues to attack opponents. The Latin refers to "appeal to the stick."[74]

Trump must love this explanation of Hitler. After all, Trump often suggests that he would love to have bouncers throw out dissenters. Donald Trump encouraged supporters to rough up potential protesters at a pre-Iowa caucus rally. "If you see somebody getting ready to throw a tomato, knock the crap out of them," Trump said after warning of possible rabble-rousers. "I'll pay the legal fees," he added. This came before Trump told the crowd that "You're going to say please ,please Mr. President, we're winning too much" and reminding the crowd that Vladimir Putin had called him a "genius."[75] He also told security to eject a protester at an event in Vermont, and to confiscate the heckler's coat, sending him into the Vermont winter without protection. "You know it's about ten degrees below zero outside," he enthused at the time.[76] "When the looting starts,

71. Burke, "Rhetoric of Hitler's 'Battle,'" 45.
72. Burke, "Rhetoric of Hitler's 'Battle,'" 45.
73. Mercieca, "Dangerous Demagogues and Weaponized Communication," 271.
74. Mercieca, "Dangerous Demagogues and Weaponized Communication," 271.
75. Reisman, "Trump."
76. Reisman, "Trump."

the shooting starts," Trump tweeted on Floyd protests. "These THUGS are dishonoring the memory of George Floyd, and I won't let that happen. Just spoke to Governor Tim Walz and told him that the Military is with him all the way. Any difficulty and we will assume control but, when the looting starts, the shooting starts. Thank you!" Trump tweeted.[77] What always seemed hyperbolic, exaggerated macho bluster in Trump's longing for violence, changed to stark reality on January 6, 2021. The question I kept asking of that horrific day was, "How has this happened?" How do good people engage in evil conduct?

The question of how normal people, often good Christian people, came to justify the rhetoric and actions of Donald Trump receives a more detailed review in the work of rhetorical scholar Patricia Roberts-Miller. She offers four explanations: 1) They decided it was okay to violate their basic ethical system . . . because it was a matter of us versus them. Either the in-group would lose power, lose the nation, and lose the church or they would control all aspects of the nation's life; 2) They were just trying to survive, stay in good standing with their fellow church members, be thankful for a good life, and not say or do anything that would get them excluded from the in-group; 3) That strategy, like working as an undercover agent for the FBI, meant they would find themselves being cruel to a minority, or shouting racist slogans, or despising and demonizing liberals and other dissenters. This is a matter of doing wrong and persuading oneself that it was actually the right thing. Once we have been cruel there's a cognitive dissonance of our sense of ourselves as good Christians, and the bad and unkind thing we have done. For Christians unwilling, like Trump, to repent, the only track to take becomes rationalization. This kind of behavior will make it more likely for one to find Trump's racist rhetoric persuasive; 4) Believing, as most good people do, that we live in a just world where people get what they deserve, it becomes easy to believe that people suffering from economic precarity have done something to cause it. The minorities are seen as lazy, less deserving of goods, and more deserving of punishment.[78]

This can be seen as playing out along the parameters of a principle of process theology. The more often a person resists and rejects the good, the easier it becomes to do the evil. What starts as a seemingly almost innocent act will be repeated over and over, and the evil will

---

77. Cathey and Keneally, "Look Back at Trump Comments."
78. Roberts-Miller, "Rhetoric and Hitler."

intensify in unconscious ways. This may account for how a good person can insist, "I'm not a racist" on the day after engaging in an overt act of discrimination.

A crucial move here is to see how Trump evolved to his own explicit racist approach to his campaign. Trump's campaign appealed to the racist history of our nation from the beginning. He began his political career with a racist claim that Obama was not born in the USA. He moved from "birtherism" to attacking the "swamp"—his preferred trope for the political establishment in Washington, DC. Trump constantly harps on the problem in Congress. At its best the Congress was a "Babel" of voices. There is the infighting of mostly men representing the interests of the elitists, the liberals, and even the Jews. Patriotism, nationalism, white nationalism, and antisemitism mix seamlessly in Trump's world. MAGA hats and Seig Heil salutes keep company with one another. What I am addressing is the rise of antisemitism in explicit identification with the rise of Trump. This is a way of being together in language that is also physical and material. It is about being both joined and separate, at once a distinct substance and a total identification with each other. Racialized hate and Trumpism are different, but they are together.

The Strong Man Trope

This one strongman, this one authoritarian demagogue, this one united voice was to be made uniform throughout the land, as leader and people were completely identified with one another. In sum: Trump's inner voice equals leader-people identification, equals the mecca of the evangelical garden of Eden, equals military might, equals war against terrorists ("Unite the civilized world against Radical Islamist Terrorism, which we will eradicate completely from the face of the earth"), equals the sole, superior responsibility of the chosen leader. Trump accepts the mantle of the "anointed one" and accepts responsibility for making his people safe and in return demands absolute obedience in exchange for his sacrifice, which equals love (with the nation as feminine), equals idealism, equals obedience to nature, equals race, equals nation (with his patriarchal patriotism).

The "strongman" trope has been repeated so often by tyrants, fascists, and dictators as to seem commonplace. For instance, a lot of UK media—specifically "conservative"—endorsed and openly admired

Hitler's "strongman" crushing of liberal democratic practices and leftist policies, since they hated those policies and practices. They were also antisemitic, anti-Slav, and believed in the Aryan bullshit behind Nazi policies, as did many people in the US. In both the UK and US, many major political figures were sympathetic to thinking of Jews as "a problem" who should be denied immigration. Hitler, Trump, Putin, and Erdogan and the "strongman" metaphor is a key part of the evil rhetoric.

Nazi typology regarding Hitler made him religious and historical: he was Charlemagne, Frederick Barbarossa, Frederick the Great, Napoleon, Jesus. Trump has been made religious and historical by his followers: Cyrus, David, Solomon, Samson, Jesus. As things got materially worse for the Nazis and Germany was clearly losing the war, Hitler seems to have started believing that the comparison to Frederick the Great was not just an analogy, or even metaphor, but a matter of fact—so true that Hitler could make plans based on Frederick the Great's military career being a perfect prediction of his own. Because the Russian Empress Elizabeth's death in 1761 caused the coalition of allies to fracture as they were advancing on Berlin (as part of what is commonly known as the Seven Years' War), thereby saving Frederick from defeat, Hitler's strategies for the war in 1945 were to hold out until Roosevelt's death would cause the same fragmenting of the allies.

Hitler's obsession with believing he would win the war finds resonance in Trump's ongoing insistence that he did not lose the 2020 election. Nazi confidant Albert Speer describes the scene in Hitler's bunker April 12, 1945 (less than a month before Berlin was overrun) when Hitler got news that Roosevelt had died:

> Hitler caught sight of me and rushed toward me with a degree of animation rare in him these days. He held a newspaper clipping in his hand. "Here, read it! Here! You never wanted to believe it! Here it is!" His words came in a great rush. "Here we have the miracle I always predicted. Who was right? The war isn't lost! Read it! Roosevelt is dead!"
>
> He could not calm down. He thought this was proof of the infallible Providence watching over him. Goebbels and many others were bubbling over with delight as they exclaimed how right he had been in his reiterated conviction that the tide would turn. Now history was repeating itself, just as history had given a hopelessly beaten Frederick the Great victory at the last moment. The miracle of the House of Brandenburg! Once again the

Tsarina had died, the historic turning point had come, Goebbels repeated again and again and again.[79]

It's as though they lost track of the comparison to Frederick the Great being a typological interpretation—an idea—and saw it instead as a material fact.

In a stunning reversal of tropes, Trump also presents himself as a suffering savior to his followers. He laments that he has been treated worse than any president in history, even worse than Abraham Lincoln. Yet he insists that he is strong enough to take it. In Trump's logic he and his followers merge into one entity, his blandishments so integrate leader and people, commingling them so inextricably, that the politician does not even present himself as the candidate. Somehow the two have become one. Does this mean that Trump is sincere or deliberate? Does his vision of the omnipotent conspirator have the drastic honesty of paranoia or the sheer shrewdness of a demagogue trained in Machiavellian politics? Perhaps he should be perceived as both/and. Have we not by now offered grounds enough for our contention that Trump's sinister powers of persuasion derive from the fact that he spontaneously evolved his "cure-all" in response to inner necessities?

The Nazis' persistent propensity to feel sorry for themselves provide a rhetorical backdrop to the whining of Trump and his evangelical followers. Eichmann, the Nazis on trial in Nuremberg, the generals in their self-serving and fundamentally dishonest postwar memoirs, Goebbels in his diaries, and Hitler at every opportunity—they all whined. Even Albert Speer, who at least had the grace to be genuinely shocked at the films of concentration camps shown at his trial, whined during his sentence in Spandau Prison, without ever acknowledging that, as boring as his incarceration was, no matter how bad the Russian food, how ugly the paint on the walls, or how petty the rules, it was worlds better than the conditions under which the slave laborers in his factories lived, let alone the conditions of victims in the concentration camps he helped to build.

Hannah Arendt remarked on that same "trick" (her term): "So that instead of saying: What horrible things I did to people, the murderers would be able to say: What horrible things I had to watch in the pursuance of my duties, how heavily the task weighed upon my shoulders!"[80] White evangelicals have learned the same magical trick of turning shame into

---

79. Speer, *Inside the Third Reich*, 463.
80. Arendt, *Eichmann in Jerusalem*, 103.

dignity, of turning racism into "I'm not racist," of claiming victimhood and precarity far greater than minorities who actually endure victimhood and precarity. The rhetorical move producing this turn (ironically the meaning of repentance) consists of making issues about rights rather than race. Thomas Nakayama and Robert Krizek observe that whiteness functions as a privileged and unmarked center—a position from which all other identities are marked as different. Whiteness, they write, "occupies a more universal discursive space."[81] Trump lays claim to a "coveted position of universality for whites without sacrificing the opportunity to reap the benefits of the politics of victimhood: whiteness as neutrality and whiteness as property. Neutrality names how whiteness operates within colorblind principles, legal statutes, and institutional frameworks that are nominally accessible to all, but historically and structurally speaking, tend to privilege white identities and interests."[82]

Trump positions himself and his followers as victims of political correctness, but he is the greatest victim, the most mistreated of all. He takes the blows for his people, endures the punishment for them, and then he gives it back to the hateful enemy in spades. The rhetoric of reversal plays a particularly potent role in Trump's appeals to law and order. He insists that his followers are being persecuted with a form of unfair defamation and vilification. Being accused of racism is, Trump suggests, worse than being subjected to it. Political correctness is, in Trump's rhetoric, an evil teacher. It is a pedagogy of shame, and he uses the resentment of his followers to make this a vital part of his medicine. Political correctness creates a false shame, Trump claims. His followers should be proud, and he promises to restore their dignity.

The Power of Repetition

What do we learn from Trump's rhetoric? For one thing, I believe that he has shown, to a very disturbing degree, the power of endless repetition. Burke says of Hitler, "I believe that he has shown, to a disturbing degree, the power of repetition."[83] Hitler used repetition as a major rhetorical strategy—a strategy that defines propaganda. Hitler was notorious for repeating himself in his meetings and speeches. Every Nazi circular

---

81. Nakayama and Martin, *Whiteness*, 291.
82. Kelly, "Whiteness, Repressive Victimhood," 61.
83. Burke, "Rhetoric of Hitler's 'Battle,'" 48.

repeated two slogans: "Jews not admitted" and "War victims free."[84] Hitler repeatedly drives home the message of the power of spectacle and insists that "mass meetings are the fundamental way of giving the individual a sense of being protectively surrounded by a movement, the sense of 'community.'"[85]

One of the more alarming trends in the USA is the drawing power of Nazi ideology. Young men hungry for a sense of meaning and belonging are signing up to give Nazism a second chance. And this is coupled with a complementary danger: young people on the right and the left are losing faith in democracy. The Age of Trump suggests a sinister presence.

Trump uses repetition in his tweets and his slogans and nicknames. "Lock her up!" "Send her back!" "Build the wall!" "Make America Great Again!" The substance of Trump propaganda is bumper sticker philosophy. He is a spectacle, and his rallies are spectacles. His mass meetings are a fundamental way of giving the individual a sense of being protectively surrounded by a movement, the sense of community. The rally is where Trump supporters meet to reassure one another that what they believe is what all smart people believe. It is a fellowship of the depraved, but its ties are deep. They love Trump because he makes them feel like insiders even as they imagine him their outsider champion. Trump's tough-guy routine, his bravado, his violent rhetoric is of great importance in building up in his followers a willingness to place center of authority in Trump and Trump alone.

Trump also offers his followers a worldview because they had previously only seen the world piecemeal. Much of his lure derives from the bad filling of a good need. Trump's followers are suffering from the mocking of the left, from economic hardships, and from being out of step with the modern world. Hart says that Trump supporters feel trapped, conflicted, ignored, and besieged.[86] They are ready for any rationales that will offer them some felt dignity, some universal explanation.

The Power of the Symbolic and Visual

Burke points out that for Hitler, the presence of a special Nazi guard in Nazi uniforms was of great importance in building up a tendency to put

---

84. Burke, "Rhetoric of Hitler's 'Battle,'" 48.
85. Burke, "Rhetoric of Hitler's 'Battle,'" 48.
86. Hart, *Trump and Us*, 4–5.

the center of authority in Hitler. Never lose sight of the reality that for Trump, the visuals, the appearances, and the symbols matter most of all. Hitler paid careful attention to uniforms. I think he really liked uniforms. During his January 27, 1945 meeting with his generals—a time when the Soviets were rolling over German forces in the East and Anglo-American forces were rolling over them in the West, a time when careful thinking was desperately necessary—General Alfred Jodl mentions that Cossacks would participate in an action in the Papuk mountains (in Croatia), and Hitler responds:

> *The Cossacks are good. But why do we have to put them in German uniforms? Why don't we have those beautiful Cossack uniforms?*
>
> Jodl: *Most of them have Cossack uniforms.*
> Guderian [German General]: *Red fur hats.*
> [Hitler]: *Do they still have those?*
> Jodl: *They have red trousers with silver stripes.*
> [Hitler]: *We have to leave that. It's wonderful.*[87]

Trump too loves pomp and circumstance. He has publicly dreamed of having people snap to attention for him. He has kidded about wanting to be president for life. As a television creature, he makes maximum use of the symbolic. Think of Trump's love for military parades. This is not a trivial concern given Trump's visual world—the world of television. Trump wanted a fourth of July military parade in DC. "The marching orders were, 'I want a parade like the one in France.'"[88] The US traditionally has not embraced showy displays of raw military power, such as North Korea's parading of ballistic missiles as a claim of international prestige and influence.

But above all, I believe we must make it apparent that Trump appeals by relying upon a "bastardization of fundamentally religious forms of thought. There is nothing in religion proper that requires a fascist state. There is, however, much in religion, when misused by evangelicals, that does lead to a fascist state: "Corruptio optimi pessimal, 'the corruption of the best is the worst.'"[89] And it is the evangelical corruptors of religion who are the Trump enablers today in giving the profound patterns of religious thought a crude and sinister distortion. I have no doubt that when

---

87. Heiber and Glantz, eds., *Hitler and His Generals*, 650.
88. Blumberg, "Trump Saw A Military Parade."
89. Burke, "Rhetoric of Hitler's 'Battle,'" 49.

Trump falls, like Humpty Dumpty from his wall, the evangelicals will line up to decry and deny him. Even kings fail in contests with nature.

Our job, then, our anti-Trump battle, is to find all available ways of making the Trump distortions of religion apparent, in order that politicians of his kind are unable to perform a similar swindle. Our ongoing task is to make clear that Trump's "hyperpolarizing misdirection of public discontent subverts democratic values and processes. His rhetoric of antagonism alienates the polity from democracy, deflects politics away from deliberating the inequities of neoliberal globalization, and thereby sustains the reigning system of economic privilege."[90] The entire nation loses some of its soul with each day of the Trump trickery, but the evangelicals are the ones with the most to lose. They have allowed President Trump to back a group of gangsters to protect him from the necessary demands of the law. His gangsters, from Attorney General Barr in DC and the Proud Boys in the street ("Stand down and stand by"), will also turn on him in defeat. Who will be his insurance against his own gangsters? Burke first asked this question of Hitler: "His gangster then, would be his insurance against his workers. But who would be his insurance against his gangsters?"[91]

How did Trump take a nation that prided itself on being tolerant and turn so many millions of them into racists? He did four things. First, he rode the wave of white resentment about Barack Obama being president for eight years. Second, he gained almost complete control of the Republican Party. He convinced a lot of people that he could make things better, that he would shake things up, and that they would be safer under his administration. He made his authoritarianism look like freedom by reframing it as strength and decisiveness. He carefully controlled his public image and rhetoric. He set a low bar yet people felt they could trust him. I believe that Trump is playing the last act of the world's most ancient tragedy:

> How you are fallen from heaven, O Day Star, son of Dawn! How you are cut down to the ground, you who laid the nations low! You said in your heart, "I will ascend to heaven; I will raise my throne above the stars of God; I will sit on the mount of assembly on the heights of Zaphon; I will ascend to the tops of the clouds, I will make myself like the Most High." But you are brought down to Sheol, to the depths of the Pit. Those who see

---

90. Ivie, "Trump's Unwitting Prophecy," 708.
91. Burke, "Rhetoric of Hitler's 'Battle,'" 50.

you will stare at you and ponder over you: "Is this the man who made the earth tremble, who shook kingdoms, who made the world like a desert and overthrew its cities, who would not let his prisoners go home?"[92]

Babel, Babylon, Trump's Tower, Trump's Wall—and it all comes tumbling down. And all the Trump supporters in the world will not be able to put the evil one back together again.

---

92. Isa 14:12–17.

CHAPTER 4

The Rhetorical Good

Vaclav Havel

THE RHETORICAL GOOD FINDS a portrait in Vaclav Havel, the poet who became president of Czechoslovakia. While Havel died in 2011, his philosophy of democracy still shines as a beacon of light in our current darkness. Havel made a statement that is the most diametrically opposite of the mindset of Donald Trump: "Truth must be integrated with love; morality is not whole without it."[1] Historian James Miller reminds us, "Democracy amazingly enough survives—at least as an article of faith or a figment of modern ideology."[2] He also adds that "in the end, via examples like Václav Havel in the Czech Republic, the 'ideal survives.' Democracy does require the 'best laws,' Havel intoned, but it must also manifest as 'humane, moral, intellectual, and spiritual, and cultural.'" Miller does the history to show that democracy is almost always a "riddle, not a recipe. Democracy is much harder than autocracy to sustain. But renew it we must."[3]

Havel noted that democracies always face temptation. There will be those who conclude that political life "is the manipulation of power and public opinion, and that morality has no place in it."[4] This amoral concept of politics dominates Trump's view. Havel suggested that the world was losing "the idea that the world might actually be changed by the

---

1. Havel, *Power of the Powerless*, 214.
2. Miller, *Can Democracy Work?*, 4.
3. Miller, *Can Democracy Work?*, 244.
4. Havel, "Politics, Morals, and Civility," 5–6.

force of truth, the power of a truthful word, the strength of a free spirit, conscience and responsibility—no guns, no lust for power, no political wheeling and dealing." To abandon truthfulness for lies, deception, and the vague notion of freedom puts the public sphere at risk. Havel said, "I am convinced that we will never build a democratic state based on the rule of law if we do not at the same time build a state that is . . . humane, moral, intellectual and spiritual, cultural."[5] Havel's poetic expressions of the power of moral democracy resound as an orchestra filled with trumpets drowning out the cacophonous sounds of Trump.

Havel offered a rhetoric of folly that stands in stark contrast to the evil rhetoric of Donald Trump. The folly of Havel resides in the spirit of St. Paul in 1 Corinthians: "For God's foolishness is wiser than human wisdom, and God's weakness is stronger than human strength."[6] The theological implication of what Paul was saying was that knowledge of God is not obtained through wisdom but through faith in the saving action of Christ on the cross. Here, the move to faith, which, philosophically speaking, was seen as foolish, was really wisdom. In 1 Corinthians 1:20, Paul wrote, "Has God not made foolish the wisdom of the world?" He meant the "foolishness" of what was preached, and that is (verse 23) "Christ crucified." Thus, Paul was using folly as the great reversal mentioned above, as an irony. Those who entered Christ's death knew that what appeared to outsiders as foolishness was really God's wisdom. They also knew—since everything is reversed in irony—that it was those who rejected Christ who were genuinely foolish. Richard Brown defines irony as "a metaphor of opposites, a point of view that distances and de-realizes what is taken as real in order to permit the realization of new meanings."[7] The worldly think that human wisdom can obtain God, but if they were truly wise, they would recognize the logical impossibility of this. The word of the cross is folly but ironically it became the power and wisdom of God, and this is fundamentally "critical for human knowledge and expectations; in this word an alternative humanistic rhetoric is offered as hope of survival."[8]

Havel's rhetoric originates from the lowly position of the fool, not from the bluster, bar talk, branding, braggadocio, and deception of

---

5. Havel, "Politics, Morals, and Civility," 18.
6. 1 Cor 1:25.
7. Brown, *Society as Text*, 3–4.
8. Kennedy, *Creative Power of Metaphor*, 36.

Trump.[9] Havel showed that folly is a kind of lived wisdom, a source of strength, motivation for overcoming despair and moving toward hopeful human action. As Karen Foss says, "The effectiveness of the fool depends on the ability to hold a mirror up to the traditional social order . . . showing that reality as it is experienced could very well be different."[10] Havel sang the primal song of democracy. He reached a high note here: "The salvation of this human world lies nowhere else than in the human heart, in the human power to reflect, in human meekness, and human responsibility."[11]

Communication scholar Kenneth Zagacki sets the historical background for Havel's song and his embodiment of a rhetoric of folly: "Post-cold war Eastern and Central Europe was racked by the transition from totalitarianism to democracy, the struggle of moral conscience over political opportunism, and the tension between national civility and violent nationalism."[12] In other words, a scene that sounds familiar to what now plays out in the democracy of the United States. For we are presently engaged in the declension of democracy by those favoring totalitarianism. The contrast between Havel and Putin and Turkey's Erdogan (not to mention between France's Macron and Le Pen), for example, shows the great gulf that exists between democracy and totalitarianism. Democracy always contains the seeds of potential destruction. "One of the great challenges of democracy, Jeremy David Engels says, "is to keep this contestation from spiraling out of control into fascism, schism, and hateful, resentful violence."[13] The problem in the USA is that it is spiraling out of control. One has only to take a cursory glance at the burgeoning research on the devastating impact of social media on democracy as one example of the problem. Whether the rise of a destructive anti-social media can be attributed to Trump may not be self-evident, but Trump has been the drum major for the rapid decline of social trust due to the use of anti-social media.

Jonathan Haidt declares that we are living in a new Babel: fragmented, polarized, fractionalized, and angry. He says, "Social scientists have identified at least three major forces that collectively bind together

9. Smith, "Ronald Reagan's Rhetorical Re-invention of Conservatism," 52.
10. Foss, "Logic of Folly," 10.
11. Havel, "Address by his Excellency Vaclav Havel," 394.
12. Zagacki, "Vaclav Havel and the Rhetoric of Folly," 17.
13. Engels, "Kosmic Rhetoric," 67.

successful democracies: social capital (extensive social networks with high levels of trust), strong institutions, and shared stories."[14] Haidt argues that "social media has weakened all three."[15] While Haidt sees Donald Trump as only one among many threats, I think that Trump is the primary devil in social media and elsewhere, as he has steadfastly attacked all the major forces that make democracy strong. Babel is a metaphor for what Trump and his personal mecca—Trump Tower—have done to nearly all the institutions most important to the country's future—and to our democracy.

Havel's goal was idealistic, to establish a new post-Cold War world, a sort of "one democratic family."[16] Whitman's dream of an "us without a them" places two poets on the same rhetorical plane across time and space.[17] In a footnote, Engels elaborates on Whitman's vision as "a truly universal community unbounded by any borders."[18]

Zagacki notes, "The rise of Havel to the Presidency of Czechoslovakia represents an astonishing ascent to political authority. Beginning as a rather self-effacing playwright, Havel became a vocal, if at times soft-spoken opponent of communist oppression during the 1960s and 1970s, a position for which he was constantly harassed and eventually imprisoned in 1979."[19] Quickly pushed to the forefront of Czech politics, Havel was asked to be a candidate for the presidency on the platform of the Civic Forum, a Czech oppositional group he had helped to form. He was elected in a landslide. "Havel 'enacted' history's 'central interpretive part' by offering a bold and profound 'rhetoric of folly.'"[20] According to Zagacki, Havel's rhetoric was bold because he assumed the difficult task of defining, to both Czechs and Westerners in general, the direction of the post-Cold War world in a way that avoided the realpolitik of many political spokespersons. It was profound because Havel encouraged an unusual reversal of thinking about the new world order and the role of citizens within it. Rather than boasting about the achievements of his people or his own administration, Havel was first and foremost concerned with the folly of the human endeavor, with people, nations, and governments in

---

14. Haidt and Rose-Stockwell, "Why the Past 10 Years."
15. Haidt and Rose-Stockwell, "Why the Past 10 Years."
16. Zagacki, "Vaclav Havel and the Rhetoric of Folly," 17.
17. Engels, "Kosmic Rhetoric," 80.
18. Engels, "Kosmic Rhetoric," 94.
19. Zagacki, "Vaclav Havel and the Rhetoric of Folly," 17.
20. Farrell, *Norms of Rhetorical Culture*, 267.

their human state, restrained and frequently made ridiculous by their limitations or attempts to overcome them.[21] While Trump brags about being a stable genius or the smartest man in the world, Havel expressed humility. Folly was a way of transforming commonsense assumptions. As Foss says, to quote her again, "The effectiveness of the fool depends on the ability to hold a mirror up to the traditional social order . . . showing that reality as it is experienced could very well be different."[22]

In line with the trope of singing democracy, Havel located the beginning of end for the post-totalitarianism in his country in an underground rock-and-roll group that was arrested and put on trial: "The Plastic People of the Universe." Havel explains that "their trial was not a confrontation of two differing forces or conceptions, but two differing conceptions of life . . . There was the sterile puritanism of the post-totalitarian establishment and . . . unknown young people who wanted to live within the truth, to play music, and to live freely in dignity and partnership."[23]

Folly

Living in a world turned upside down by a demolition of democratic values, as we surely do, our nation stands in need of a reversal of Trump's values, since he seems to have turned the seven cardinal sins into the seven lively and highly profitable seven virtues. The reversal I find so necessary belongs to the religious realm. In particular, it resides in the concept of folly. What the world calls folly, God has defined as wisdom. What the world deems weakness, God has presented as strength. There is a sense of comedy involved in any celebration of human weakness, fragility, and precarity. Havel's rhetoric "illustrates how the comic mode of discourse might encourage peaceful persuasive practice, especially during periods of great social or historical turmoil."[24]

Comedy rather than tragedy dominates the concept of folly. Human failure, frailty, and weakness are seen as strengths. Listen to any of Trump's speeches and the idea of "folly" never appears. Trump is all about winning, so much so that he can't tolerate losing. He often refers to others as "losers." He has called more than one hundred people "loser," "moron,"

---

21. Zagacki, "Vaclav Havel and the Rhetoric of Folly," 17.
22. Foss, "Logic of Folly," 10.
23. Havel, *Power of the Powerless*, 45.
24. Zagacki, "Vaclav Havel and the Rhetoric of Folly," 18.

"dummy," "fool," "stone cold loser," "idiot," "failure," "joke," and "a zero."[25] His inability to fathom the idea of losing energizes his ongoing promotion of the idea that he won the 2020 election. Now, the test of loyalty to Trump is whether you are willing to support Trump's insistence that he won the election. "He will not acknowledge truths that everyone else sees. His lies are transparent: he does not expect you to believe them, but he wants you to display your loyalty by affirming them."[26] As Jeffrey Robert Wilson describes Trump, "He wrongly accuses family members of betrayal, creates elaborate loyalty tests for friends, turns against his closest advisors and bars them from his presence."[27] At a "cabinet meeting in 2017 Trump asked high-level members of his administration for declarations of loyalty to him. And anyone even a little familiar with Shakespeare immediately thought of the scene in *King Lear* when Lear demands professions of loyalty. Trump isn't Caesar; he's Lear."[28]

The Greek word for folly, *moria*, deals with a physical or intellectual deficiency of persons in their conduct and actions. In the New Testament, St. Paul imbued folly with a metaphorical and metamorphic function.[29] The metaphorical character resulted from an irony, from the transferring of the usual negative meaning of folly to a positive meaning. In 1 Corinthians 4:10, for example, Paul was proud to be "a fool for Christ's sake." The metamorphic transformation took place with Paul's assigning to folly the meaning of true, original knowledge. An example of this transformation and transvaluation occurs in 1 Corinthians 1:18—"For the word of the cross is folly to those who are perishing, but to us who are being saved it is the power of God . . ." Folly, according to Paul, therefore involved a complete reversal of human standards, expectations, and conventional wisdom; it entailed a paradoxical manner of thinking, an irony.

In a bit of delightful irony, Trump's own supporters demonstrate the reversal of folly that their master never gets. When Hillary Clinton referred to Trump followers as "deplorables,"[30] they adopted it as a positive trope. They reveled in it, admitted it, trumpeted it with T-shirts, hats,

---

25. Gilmore, "Definitive List."
26. Wilson, *Shakespeare and Trump*, 199.
27. Wilson, *Shakespeare and Trump*, 204.
28. Roberts-Miller, "Charisma Isn't Leadership," 113.
29. Kennedy, *Creative Power of Metaphor*, 35.
30. Reilly, "Read Hillary Clinton's 'Basket of Deplorables' Remarks."

and mugs: "The Deplorables." A Trump rally resembles a party of joyful people rather than the dark carnage that Trump's rhetoric spouts.

What I have called "Christian humanism" combines the humanistic studies of Ernesto Grassi with the Christian proclamation of the great reversal. A. Cheree Carlson suggests a "comic frame" as an option to the tragic interpretation of movements. She argues that the comic frame enables people to accept their own foibles. A comic movement requires a "spiritual element in its rhetoric that identifies with humanity in a unifying sense; and a comic movement must assume that the individuals in the order are moral beings."[31] The church has a history of embracing a rhetoric of folly. In the rituals of the medieval church there were celebrations such as the Feast of Fools or the Feast of the Ass, during which a carved donkey was carried in procession, and the priest, as representative of ecclesial authority and power, was mocked and ridiculed. Mikhail Bakhtin notes, "Carnival celebrated temporary liberation from the prevailing truth and from the established order; it marked the suspension of all hierarchical rank, norms, and prohibitions. Carnival was the true feast of time, the feast of becoming, change, and renewal."[32] What the church considered a "folly"—a pretension, a comedy to release tension once a year—now becomes the norm, the primary function of a rhetoric of folly.

The irony here is that a Trump rally resembles a churchly "Feast of Fools"—but there's no pretension. The purpose of the celebration of cruelty is to undo the hierarchy of shame that Trump supporters face because of their opposition to gay marriage, immigration, diversity, and Others. The Trump emotion machine pumps out resentment, revenge, and rage all the time. The rally is, in appearance, a joyful event; in substance, it is the perverse carnival, the suspending of the rules of democracy on behalf of a group that feels persecuted and victimized.

In the case of Paul, there was, to use Paul Tournier's phrase, a "great reversal."[33] The world's values were turned upside down since power now resided in weakness, and wisdom came from folly. God's power was not demonstrated with forceful signs from above; it showed its strength in the word of a weak cross. God's wisdom was not displayed with scientific certainty or absolute dogmas; knowledge was now reticent, hesitant, weak in the word of a foolish cross. "Has not God made foolish the wisdom of

---

31. Carlson, "Gandhi and the Comic Frame," 447.
32. Bakhtin, *Rabelais and His World*, 10.
33. Tournier, *Guilt and Grace*, 111.

the world? . . . It pleased God through the folly of what we preach to save those who believe."[34] The cross was a supreme paradox, an objective uncertainty of the greatest magnitude that was an absurdity to reason. The cross is the primordial, archetypal Christian metaphor. When Jesus put that cross on his shoulder and climbed Golgotha's hill, the whole world now knew that was what God was like. It signaled a disjunction between transcendental claims and the exercise of worldly sovereignty, divine manifestation without grandeur. As a result, the world was perishing with its wisdom of proof and rationality.

St. Paul embraced the cross in his very being and embodied its message. He wrote to the Corinthians, "And I came to you in weakness and in fear and in much trembling. My speech and my proclamation were not with plausible words of wisdom, but with a demonstration of the Spirit and of power, so that your faith might rest not on human wisdom but on the power of God."[35] But this world wants nothing to do with a cross. The sin of many conservative evangelicals is their desertion of the cross for the power promised by Trump. Perhaps they are not aware of Trump's goal of reversing the foolishness and weakness of the cross with his strength and power. He doesn't represent a new force in politics. Instead he is the resurrection of any dime-a-dozen autocrat, dictator, or would-be Pharaoh.

Trump, the strongman, the winner, will have nothing to do with a cross though he feigns fidelity to Christianity (in vague, vacuous comments concerning religious freedom) every now and then. Trump and his evangelical followers are like the pastor of a giant church in California who told the architect for his new building, "We do not want any crosses on the church . . . We don't want anyone to think failure and weakness."[36] Given the overt racism of Trump, he would be more at home with the KKK's use of the cross. The Klan knew how to transform that symbol of weakness into a terrifying and vicious power as they burned crosses across the South. The folly of the cross? This may be too much for people intent on winning and gaining power.

What Trump and company fail to recognize is that the "power of moria opens up the immense stage of the world with the unfolding of its paradoxical play of comedy/tragedy. The principal actors are humans;

---

34. 1 Cor 1:20–21.

35. 1 Cor 2:3–5.

36. Craddock, *Cherry Log Sermons*, 80.

folly is the divine director; and the outcome of the play depends upon the actors' willingness to embrace the claim of folly."[37]

Ernesto Grassi argues that two kinds of folly present themselves: one is the folly of insanity, the other folly is viewed as a god. Insanity results when a person loses her sense of the value of life. What is at stake here is the attempt to cope with the ambiguities, the messiness, of democracy. For Grassi, the important move is to remain under the spell of folly. "Only in the word can I find myself again in that I recover my world from nature."[38]

What we are now experiencing is a different kind of play—a reality television show with Trump as the divine director and the result will be insanity. Appearances wipe out reality. Style subverts rational thought. "In other words, from food to home décor, runway shows to reality television, politics to religion, and everywhere in between, style dominates the 21st century as a vehicle for making and understanding meaning. And importantly . . . , our politics are styled."[39] Trump was director and leading character in everyday news discourse in an era in which the distinction between reality TV and news TV seems to have dissolved.[40] Television ethics revolve around what sells and what profits. Television has answered the question, "What does it profit to gain the whole world"[41] with one word: Everything. As the *New York Times* wrote, Trump is "a human breaking-news event," a figure who seemed as if he "had built his entire campaign around nothing so much as his singular ability to fill cable news's endless demand for engaging content."[42] Trump is an automatic news-making machine because his "engaging content" sizzles. His explicit sexism and racism triggers liberals and offers conservatives a sense of jouissance.[43] In the insanity of the Age of Trump (the opposite of folly as wisdom), when Trump insults women, his sexism "sells" and becomes "engaging news content."[44] When Trump attacks people for being losers, it sells. When Trump criticizes people who have died, it makes

37. Zagacki, "Rhetoric of Folly," 20.
38. Grassi quoting Soren Kierkegaard in *Rhetoric as Philosophy*, 112.
39. Young, "Rhetorics of Fear and Loathing," 30.
40. Marche, "Celebrity Warfare."
41. Mark 8:36.
42. Mahler, "CNN Had a Problem."
43. Andrejevic, "Jouissance of Trump," 651.
44. Mahler, "CNN Had a Problem."

the news. Instead of "If it bleeds it leads," during the Trump administration the television mantra was, "If Trump tweets, it leads." Television is not a moral actor in informing viewers of the dangers Trump poses to democracy; television is an ally of Trump's destructive message. What is interesting is that executives from MSNBC and CNN are saying publicly that Trump is a TV character in a story for the ages that they are riding to profit. As Brian Beutler argued, "The press is not a pro-democracy trade, it is a pro-media trade. By and large, it doesn't act as a guardian of civic virtue that can be controlled."[45]

Havel saw folly as the proper function of democracy because democratic deliberation depends on a certain humility and willingness to acknowledge the weaknesses of one's position while not reducing disagreements with others to invective and demonizing. Folly leads to a high view of human existence.[46] Havel claims that folly enables humans to survive, to change, to cope, and to appreciate their existence: "It seems to me that if the world is to change for the better it must start with a change in human consciousness, in the very humanness of modern man."[47] And again: "I see only one way out of this crisis: man must come to a new understanding of himself, of his limitations and his place in the world."[48] Individuals are not, by virtue of their limitations, led to despair, helplessness, or a feeling of being "nobody" in the larger scheme of life. In contrast, the tradition of folly allows that such a change in consciousness affords an opposite interpretation, i.e., an ironic attitude, what Grassi calls an act of ingenium or creative transformation that leads to greater awareness and responsible action.[49] Havel puts it this way: individuals "must discover again, within [themselves], a deeper sense of responsibility toward the world, which means responsibility toward something higher than [themselves]."[50] Havel desired others to see a kind of folly in history, thus opening the human world and looking beyond what had been passed down from the past to an alternative truth or possibility for the future.

45. Beutler, "Why the Media Is Botching the Election."
46. Havel, "On Kafka," 19.
47. Havel, *Disturbing the Peace*, 11.
48. Havel, "Postcommunist Nightmare," 10.
49. Zagacki, "Rhetoric of Folly," 27.
50. Havel, *Disturbing the Peace*, 11–12.

Havel's address to the American Congress, on February 21, 1990, resonated in a way that is clearly ironic. As Zagacki has pointed out, Havel's speech was billed as a request for American aid to the newly liberated Czech nation. It employed irony to caution about the limits of government power.[51] Havel suggested that "attempts by totalitarian governments to maintain power and to impose particular historical inevitabilities, ironically, brought about their demise."[52] As Havel told the "extraordinary" tale, he was arrested and lived in a nation controlled "by the most conservative Communist government in Europe," a nation whose people "slumbered beneath the pall of a totalitarian system. Today, less than 4 months later, I am speaking to you as the representative of a country that has set out on the road to democracy."[53] As Zagacki notes, Havel admonished that no government stands forever, no power is beyond reproach, that even chance may override the best of human intentions. In his speech, Havel expressed the folly, unacknowledged by the Communists, of assuming that history can be completely controlled. John Howard Yoder, in *The Politics of Jesus*, points out that there are always those who live with the illusion they can control the handles of history.[54] Hauerwas notes, "For as Yoder reminds us, Jesus did not promise his followers they would conquer within time if they did things right."[55] There are Christians laboring under the illusion that they can discern, direct, and control history. There's always the temptation to think that we can get exactly the right handle that will give us the control of history. These attempts are usually labeled as various forms of Constantinianism. As Chris Huebner states, "Yoder helps us to envision the church as a counter-political and counter-epistemological interruption of the logic of violence."[56] Havel also employed irony to disclose a new way of thinking about the post-Cold War world. Furthermore, dehumanized by decades of oppression, Havel wished to restore human dignity and trust.

In case we forget, Trump preaches a gospel of revenge including getting even with members of his own political party. Instead of speaking from a note of folly and humility, Trump speaks from foolishness and

---

51. Havel, "Address by His Excellency Vaclav Havel."
52. Zagacki, "Rhetoric of Folly," 21.
53. Yoder, *Politics of Jesus*, 392.
54. Yoder, *Politics of Jesus*, 297.
55. Hauerwas, *Working with Words*, 92.
56. Huebner, *Precarious Peace*, Kindle ed., loc. 1427.

arrogance. Perhaps Trump comes closest to the truth when he claims, at times after the fact, that he is or was joking. When Trump said he wanted to be president for life, he later said he was only joking. When he claimed that he was impressed by how everyone in North Korea stood at attention and saluted the leader, he said he was joking when he said he would like that kind of reverence. When Trump claims the country was doing "too good of a job on Covid testing," his staff said he was joking.[57] Trump said he was joking when he said he was the "chosen one."[58] Trump claims he's the joker, the king's "fool": Havel embraced the rhetoric of folly.

In what sounds prophetic of our present crisis, Havel said, "I feel that this arrogant anthropocentrism of modern man, who is convinced he can know everything and bring everything under his control, is somewhere in the background of the present crisis."[59] In my view, Donald Trump is the first truly postmodern, post-truth human being in all his perverted glory and evil machinations. He is the exact opposite of wisdom and truth. His is a folly that has no relationship with God's wisdom.

Evangelicals have imbibed the Trump post-truth vision and feel such pride in their choice. If only they had the clarity that Salieri revealed in his twisted relationship with Mozart: "Fiasco! . . . Fiasco! . . . The sordidness of it! The sheer sweating sordidness! . . . Worse than if I'd actually done it! . . . To be that much in sin and feel so ridiculous as well! . . . What has he done to me, this Mozart? Before he came, did I behave like this? . . . It was all going—slipping—growing rotten . . . because of him!"[60] Trump has produced a rottenness in democracy that smells of pure evil.

Folly and Irony

Havel's rhetoric of folly relied on a social grammar of dialectical irony. "Through irony, Havel claimed that power was obtained through weakness, strength through vulnerability, wisdom through ignorance. Havel proposed irony as a means of easing the passage to an uncertain geopolitical future."[61] To the rich mix to the tune of irony, Havel would add folly,

---

57. Freking, "Staff Says Trump Is Joking."
58. Singletary, "Trump Says He Was Joking."
59. Havel, *Disturbing the Peace*, 11.
60. Shaffer, *Amadeus*, 56.
61. Zagacki, "Rhetoric of Folly," 18.

empathy, humility, and hope. In contrast, Trump revels in arrogance, revenge, profanity, and insults.

Carolyn Sharp says, "Irony is a performance of misdirection that generates aporetic interactions between an unreliable 'said' and a truer 'unsaid' so as to persuade us of something that is subtler, more complex, and more profound than apparent meaning. Irony disrupts cultural assumptions about the narrative coherence that seems to ground tropological and epistemological transitions, inviting us into an experience of alterity that moves us toward new insight by problematizing false understandings."[62] Irony occupies the space between appearance and reality, between truth and power. Wayne Booth talks about the "secret communion" between author and reader who share an understanding that is not on the surface of the world.[63]

"It may well be," says Walter Brueggemann, "that irony is the vehicle for traducing the unsettled space between truth and power, for truth readily subverts power in the expose of irony."[64] Irony becomes a primary rhetorical strategy in the battle against forces of evil like fascism, authoritarianism, fake populism, and the tsunami of lies flooding America. Irony offers a way of exposing idolatry as well as a method for dethroning idols. In this case, the idol is the totalizing claim to power that Trump keeps pushing. Having previously compared Trump to the infamous biblical idol of the bronze snake, I argue that we should follow the example of King Hezekiah: "He broke in pieces the bronze serpent that Moses had made, for until those days the people of Israel had made offerings to it; it was called Nehushtan."[65]

Trump and his supporters are surface skimmers: simplicity, spontaneity, impulsivity, profanity. There is appearance but not reality. No irony is involved because as Trump supporters like to brag, "Trump says what he thinks, and we like it." He is an unrepentant liar, but to his supporters he is a liar because he is so transparently truthful. Philosopher Rupert Read argues that there is another interpretation available of Trump's followers not caring about his lying:

> One that points disturbingly in the direction of the slippery slope towards fascism that an emotive subjectivism combined

---

62. Sharp, *Irony and Meaning in the Hebrew Bible*, 24.
63. Booth, *Rhetoric of Fiction*, 300.
64. Brueggemann, *Truth Speaks to Power*, 7.
65. 2 Kgs 18:4.

with "populism" have arguably put us on. It is this: Trump's followers are not put off by him lying [because] that they like it. Because being able to do this and not being finished by it are a sign of strength. If that is the reason why, then we are quite close to a neo-fascist situation here.[66]

Trump's followers often say that he should be taken seriously but not literally. In other words, they trust him even when they know he is lying. Trump has bequeathed to his followers a sense of shamelessness. There's no shame in lying if you are "sticking it" to the liberals.

Havel appealed regularly to irony in his speeches. Even President Nixon, until Trump the most notorious of our presidents, regularly used irony to show himself as a reasonable person. Trump's seething resentment and overweening need for revenge are out in the open, up front, close, and personal. There is no irony in the power that Trump grasps for with his blatant appeals to racism, misogyny, cruelty, anti-LGBTQ bigotry, anti-intellectualism, obsession with violence, and anti-human values. "You know exactly what Trump is thinking. You don't have to wonder what's going on."[67]

Roderick Hart treats Trump as "an emotional revolutionary, a person (1) who is proud of the feelings coursing through him (a sort of perverse Walt Whitman's "Song of Myself"), (2) who is unafraid to display them in public, (3) who treats his supporters' feelings with special reverence, and (4) who regards an unemotional politics as no politics at all."[68] "[Trump] says what some people say only in private and, for other Americans, he is their unspoken voice."[69]

An enlightening trope for grasping Trump's demolition rhetoric is called "hush harbors." The phrase is from Vorris Hunley's "From the Harbor to Da Academic Hood."[70] Hunley defines this trope as the "safe rhetorical space" where African Americans express their anger over segregation and racism. John Pearson, the itinerant preacher in Zora Neale Hurston's *Jonah's Gourd Vine*, refuses to testify in his divorce trial. He offers this reason: "Ah didn't want de White folks tuh hear 'bout nothin' lak that. Dey knows too much 'bout us as it is . . . Dey's some strings

---

66. Read, "What is New in Our Time," 84.
67. Hart, *Trump and Us*, 17.
68. Hart, *Trump and Us*, 18.
69. Hart, *Trump and Us*, 19.
70. Nunley, "From the Harbor to Da Academic Hood," 221.

on our harp fuh us to play on an sing all tuh ourselves."[71] This offers a literary picture of the meaning of the hush harbor. That anger, Obama says, was not expressed in public, but at home, the barbershop, and in church. Obama explains that the anger in Jeremiah Wright's "God Damn America" sermon was not intended for audiences outside their hush harbors. Obama says,

> Even for those blacks who did make it, questions of race and racism continue to define their worldview in fundamental ways. For the men and women of Reverend Wright's generation, the memories of humiliation and doubt and fear have not gone away nor has the anger and the bitterness of those years. That anger may not get expressed in public, in front of white co-workers or white friends. But it does find voice in the barbershop or the beauty shop or around the kitchen table. At times that anger is exploited by politicians, to gin up votes along racial lines, or to make up for a politician's own failings. And occasionally it finds voice in the church on Sunday morning, in the pulpit and in the pews.[72]

Obama suggested that whites also have their "hush harbors." White anger is not always expressed in polite company. "Even the indirect referencing of racism continues to traumatize many white Americans, and it is their trauma that must be addressed if we are to consider seriously the possibility of coherent racial reconciliation."[73]

Trump, in the rage of his impolite rhetoric, burned down the hush harbors of white America and made public all the previously private communication. Trump made Twitter, Fox News, the networks, and all social media the new universal "hush harbor," except now there was no hush—only rancor and revenge and resentment publicly declared.[74] Trump demolished the "hush harbor" of white males. The simmering resentment that had been squelched by a civic moral consciousness during the civil rights movement had not ended; it had been silenced. The resentment, with Trump as drum major, now came back through the sewage and out into the public arena. The new litany of white men was to shout, protest, and sling racist tropes and statements on one day, and deny they were racists the next day.

71. Hurston, *Jonah's Gourd Vine*, 169.
72. Obama, "More Perfect Union" Speech Transcript.
73. Frank and McPhail, "Barack Obama's Address," 266–67.
74. Frank, "Prophetic Voice and the Face of the Other."

The revenge of the previously shamed white males has become the right to say anything. Foucault, in *The Order of Discourse*, says, "In a society like ours . . . we know quite well that we do not have the right to say everything, that we cannot speak of just anything in any circumstances whatever, and that not everyone has the right to speak of anything."[75] Foucault also argues that the "'will to truth" is the major system of exclusion that forges discourse and which "tends to exert a sort of pressure and something like a power of constraint on other discourses," and goes on further to ask the question "what is at stake in the will to truth, in the will to utter this 'true' discourse, if not desire and power?"[76] The "will to truth" has been deconstructed by Trump and company.

Foucault never encountered Donald Trump, who utters words in public that should never be uttered. He speaks words no other president has ever dared utter in the public space. Trump has made his political career endlessly repeating incendiary language. He does it because it works. His rhetoric does offend, it does widen the racial divide, it does threaten democracy, but bulls his way forward with weaponized words. The folly of Trump exhibits the opposite traits of folly in Havel. Trump embodies the bitter statement of H. L. Mencken: "No one in this world . . . has ever lost money by underestimating the intelligence of the great masses of the plain people. Nor has anyone ever lost public office thereby."[77]

Folly and Humility in Havel

Essential for Havel was humility, a constant awareness of the frailties of the human condition and the desire to work with rather than ignore those vulnerabilities. Zagacki argues that in Havel's rhetoric, humility, and the mindful moral action it engenders, overcame the political paralysis caused by communist oppression, along with the political opportunism that frequently attends political revolution. He quotes Timothy Garton Ash, who cautioned that in the post-communist environment, humility was a necessary public virtue: "the drumbeat" of political opportunism could drown "the whisper" of moral conscience.[78]

---

75. Foucault, *Order of Discourse*, 1460–70.
76. Shapiro, *Archaeologies of Vision*, 113–14.
77. Mencken, "As H. L. Sees It."
78. Ash, *Uses of Adversity*, 12.

For Havel, humility represents meekness. Jesus said that the "meek shall inherit the earth."[79] The word rhymes with weak but means the opposite of weak—folly and irony. The Greek term translated as "meek" speaks of a wild stallion's power coming under control through discipline and training. The meek person turns out to be an incredibly strong person who is not filled with braggadocio and exaggeration of his own value. As St. Paul puts it, "I say to everyone among you not to think of yourself more highly than you ought to think, but to think with sober judgement."[80] As Zagacki shows, Havel, in his address to Congress, made humility a major theme of his rhetoric. "The salvation of this human world lies nowhere else than in the human heart, in the human power to reflect, in human meekness and human responsibility."[81] The theme recurs in Havel's speeches and writings: "I must admit that if I am a better president than many others would be in my place, then it is precisely because somewhere in the deepest substratum of my work lies this constant doubt about myself and my right to hold office."[82]

Havel's commitment to folly, weakness as strength, expressed itself in humility. Any Sunday school Bible veteran will hear echoes of John the Baptist: "He must increase, but I must decrease."[83]

In direct contrast, Trump tweeted: "How do you impeach a president who has won perhaps the greatest election of all time, done nothing wrong (no Collusion with Russia, it was the Dems that Colluded), had the most successful first two years of any president, and is the most popular Republican in party history 93%?"[84] This is one of many examples of how Trump likes to define his presidency as an exercise in self-promotion, a reality show in which he claims to be better in every way—smarter, better looking, more successful, a better dealmaker—than his opponents, his allies, his generals, his staff, and everyone else in the world. This is one of the ways that Trump shatters everything Americans have ever expected or thought of their presidents—as men of humility. Trump's story is about shattering every tradition, expectation, decorum, and decency that has ever existed in the office of the president.

79. Matt 5:5.
80. Rom 12:3.
81. Havel, "Address by His Excellency Vaclav Havel," 394.
82. Havel, "On Kafka," 19.
83. John 3:30.
84. Ross, "Trump Says He's Unimpeachable."

This expression of folly as humility by Havel appears out of place (even as it is desperately needed) in the Age of Trump—an unpretentious democratic leader who fades into the background away from the cameras of an excitement-seeking media. There's no time for reflection as only instant rebuttal takes center stage for politicians. There's no reticence in the remarks of our politicians, only a sense of divine certainty. The confidence, bordering on cockiness, refuses to see even the possibility of downfall. There is no moral strength or moral action in the off-the-cuff remarks that criticize, demean, or puff up the speaker. Jesus' usage of "blessed are the humble" and the reflective president Abraham Lincoln appear in my imagination here.

One could not imagine Trump admitting what Havel said: "If I've accomplished anything good, then it's mainly because I've been driven by the need to know whether I can accomplish the things I'm not sure I have the capability for."[85] Perhaps Havel comes as close as any democratic leader in modeling the religious nature of humility. Zagacki explores Havel's April 26, 1990 speech at Hebrew University, in Jerusalem, where the he said: "It's a paradox, but I must admit that if I am a better president than many others would have been in my place, then it is precisely because somewhere in the deepest substratum of my work lies this constant doubt about myself and my right to hold office."[86] According to Zagacki, here Havel modeled the biblical pattern that weakness was strength. From this ironic reversal his humility shines. Havel put it this way: "The lower I am, the more proper my place seems; and the higher I am, the stronger my suspicion is that there has been some mistake. And every step of the way, I feel what a great advantage it is for me as president to know that I can at any moment, and justifiably, be removed from the position."[87] In a conversation with Karel Hvizdala, Havel's humility sparkles brightly as he expresses concern about the "arrogant anthropocentricism of modern man, who is convinced he can know everything and bring everything under his control."[88] Haley Britzky has documented Trump's willingness to claim he knows everything about everything.[89] Havel's humility divulges from politicians who matriculated at the school of power, opportunism,

---

85. Havel, *Disturbing the Peace*, 6.
86. Havel, "On Kafka."
87. Havel, "On Kafka."
88. Havel, *Disturbing the Peace*, 11–12.
89. Britzky, "Everything Trump Says He Knows."

pragmatism, and Machiavellianism. With no sense of self-importance, Havel willingly accepted the role of the clown, the fool at king's court, the lowest of the low. Instead of acting the role of the clown, Havel's reversal issues in actual wisdom. Humility ruled Havel; hubris controls Trump. Drawing upon the literary critic Kenneth Burke, Zagacki argues that for Havel, "identification" with the audience—assuming their perspective—depends on mutual humility. After all, humility from the leader "engenders the sort of moral reflection and responsible moral activity that liberates the actor from the numbness imposed by totalitarian rule."[90] Havel invited his audience to accept the humility of human precarity, to transcend themselves for a cause greater than themselves, and to act in responsible ways for the sake of democracy.

Humility struggles to find her footing in the Age of Trump, but that doesn't mean that the possibilities for humility to bloom again have been totally quelled. Abraham Joshua Heschel reminds us that humility and awe made Old Testament characters receptive to the workings of the world and to God's purpose.[91] Moses expressed to God his inability to speak to Pharaoh. Yet God called Moses and placed on his mouth the words, "Let my people go." Jeremiah pleaded with God that he was too young to be a prophet, and God inspired Jeremiah to take up the prophet's mantle. Havel appears to use humility to open a heretofore impossible realm of political possibility. In his vision, the post-Cold War could "escape from the rather antiquated straitjacket of this bipolar view of the world, and to enter at last into an era of multipolarity."[92]

Folly and Empathy

Folly encourages speakers to imagine a connection with all of suffering humanity. The person of empathy is the first to hear the cries of the oppressed. By *empathy* I mean the ability to understand and integrate our basic nature as humans. As historian Lynn Hunt notes, "Democracy is rooted in empathy, in connecting viscerally with others . . . and therefore, to comprehend a common humanity as a basis of equality."[93] Richard Harvey Brown interprets the need for emphatic discourse as a result

90. Zagacki, "Rhetoric of Folly," 24.
91. Heschel, *God in Search of Man*, 73.
92. Zagacki, "Rhetoric of Folly," 25.
93. Hunt, *Inventing Human Rights*, quoted in Lakoff, *Political Mind*, 57.

of the bifurcation of the private sphere of the individual and the public sphere of society. He laments the lack of bridges between groups and the lack of communication. Brown also argues that we have failed to figure out how to communicate with people who have different understandings.[94] Empathy allows one to assume the perspective of those who might otherwise be neglected from (or persecuted by) the observer's allegedly superior vantage point.

Empathy sets aside the sociological tent poles of sex, family, race, region, religion, class, and economics. The compassion of empathy puts every one of these old tent poles under judgment to "bless or damn each, on the basis of what faithful service does to persons."[95] The speaker of empathy revels in the offering of compassion without any sense of certainty. The speaker risks everything to care for others. What the empathic speaker has at her disposal is the experience of a common humanity and a rhetoric of folly: pathetic, indirect, metaphorical, and always and everywhere empathic, intimate, loving, trusting, and personal.

In the context of democracy, it is important to realize that empathy formed the basis for a union of states. The revolutionary changes that led to the establishment of democracy in the eighteenth century and the USA were "propelled by empathy, by identification with the problems and plights of ordinary citizens . . . By 1776, human rights became 'self-evident' via the development of empathy for one's fellow citizens."[96]

Havel's song of democracy rings with the affirmation of folly as wisdom, humility, and empathy. It would be hard to imagine a politician less like Donald Trump. Havel's words are music to the ears of those sick and tired of the rantings of Trump. In what could stand at the chorus of a song for democracy, Havel insisted:

> I feel that the dormant goodwill in people needs to be stirred. People need to hear that it makes sense to behave decently or to help others, to place common interests above their own, to respect the elementary rules of human coexistence. They want to be told about this publicly. They want to know that those "at the top" are on their side. They feel strengthened, confirmed, hopeful. Goodwill longs to be recognized and cultivated. For it

---

94. Brown, *Society as Text*.
95. Marney, "Fundaments of Competent Ministry," 8.
96. Lakoff, *Don't Think of an Elephant*, 47.

to develop and have an impact it must hear that the world does not ridicule it.[97]

Havel argued that folly allowed humans to change and to appreciate their existence as a mirror that shows them observing themselves as actors.

George Lakoff argues, "Behind every progressive policy lies a single moral value: empathy, together with the responsibility and strength to act on that empathy."[98] Lakoff links responsibility with empathy so completely that there is no way of interpreting empathy as merely feeling sympathy for people. In fact, for Lakoff, "American democracy was founded on the politics of empathy and responsibility, with the role of government being protection and empowerment. From these flow the progressive ideals of equality, freedom, fairness, opportunity, general prosperity, accountability and so on."[99]

Empathy empowers the moral capacities of democracy. Once again, the contrast glares at us because in Trump's reign of rage, there is an empathy deficit—a lack of caring for all persons. There's an accountability deficit as Trump always seeks to deflect blame. Senator Mitch McConnell offers a revealing insight into Trump in comments about Trump's involvement in the Georgia senate races after the 2020 election: "What it looks to me like he's doing is setting this up so he can blame the governor and the secretary of state if we lose. He's always setting up somebody to blame it on."[100] There's an ethical deficit as Trump continues to praise Putin in the face of the horrific invasion of Ukraine. On February 23, Trump issued a written statement: "Putin is playing Biden like a drum. It is not a pretty thing to watch!"[101] Trump appeared at the Conservative Political Action Conference (CPAC), reiterated his belief that Putin is "smart," and denounced his own country's leaders as "so dumb."[102]

Folly aligns naturally with empathy. Grassi observes that in the absence of folly, contemporary lives become divorced from their social, corporate selves: "Contemporary men feel the need for values that can unify their lives. But the source of this need lies in man's original nature

97. Havel, "Politics, Morals, and Civility," 28.
98. Lakoff, *Don't Think of an Elephant*, 47.
99. Lakoff, *Political Mind*, 118–119.
100. Kaufman, "McConnell on Trump."
101. Trump, "Statement by Donald J. Trump."
102. Benen, "Even now, Trump continues to praise Putin's 'intelligence.'"

as a human being and not in his momentary situation."[103] Zagacki argues that "empathy was vitally important for Havel because the dangers of unrestrained nationalism and its resulting ethnic and political divisions were everywhere apparent, especially in Yugoslavia and parts of the former Soviet Union."[104] As Havel consoled those who had suffered the subjugation of communism, he also articulated the virtues necessary to reduce division. Havel's condemnation of antisemitism was one of the ways he created empathy. He presented his empathy as a sense of shared shame. This paralysis "proceeds mainly from a deep—I would even say a metaphysical—feeling of shame. I am ashamed . . . of the human race, of mankind, of man."[105] "I feel that this is his crime and his disgrace, and thus also my crime and my disgrace. It is as if that paralysis suddenly threw me to the very bottom of the perception of human guilt and of my own co-responsibility for human actions and for the condition of the world in which we live and which we build."[106]

Havel's acceptance of accountability "for human actions and for the condition of the world in which we live and which we build"[107] increased his sense of empathy. Unlike Trump, who has given a lack of accountability a new meaning in the USA, Havel embraced his sense of accountability. Havel insisted that the horrors of communist oppression "have given us something positive: a special capacity to look . . . somewhat further than someone who has not undergone this bitter experience."[108] Again, as Zagacki points out, Havel's embodiment of the lowly, persecuted fool suggests that he possesses true wisdom. Havel's own "bitter experiences" placed him in a credible position to understand the suffering of Jews or any other oppressed group which, as a result of its oppression and suffering, felt divided or estranged from other individuals. In this way, Havel identified with and consoled his audiences because he could, in a sense, countenance his own origins. "His public speech was entirely personal, spoken by a man who had come to terms with his difficult history and tradition."[109]

    103. Krois, "Comments on Professor Grassi's Paper," 187.
    104. Zagacki, "Rhetoric of Folly," 25.
    105. Havel, "Message to the International Conference."
    106. Havel, "Message to the International Conference."
    107. Havel, "Message to the International Conference."
    108. Havel, "Address by his Excellency Vaclav Havel," 394.
    109. Zagacki, "Rhetoric of Folly," 26.

Havel identified with his audience because he was willing to accept the reality of his own terrible ordeal, and his personal involvement in all of this precarity. I am reminded of the empathy of Joseph revealing himself to his brothers. "I am your brother Joseph, whom you sold into Egypt. And now do not be distressed, or angry with yourselves, because you sold me here; for God sent me before you to preserve life."[110] Joseph identified with his brothers in the deepest possible empathy, an empathy that included forgiveness and reconciliation. "I am your brother" becomes an act of empathy whereby Joseph assumes the perspective of his brothers.

Havel understood that democratic institutions were fraught with dangers. He was, however, optimistic about the prospects for democracy. He said, "It is extremely dangerous for the new democracies to underestimate the manifestations of anti-Semitism, to play them down, to fail to take action against them and, to remain silent about them."[111] Havel embraced empathy, compassion, and reassurance. Without empathy a leader cannot console his/her people. At some point, a leader has to sing the song of consolation. Perhaps only Abraham Lincoln and Franklin Roosevelt have reached the heights of consolation, Lincoln during the Civil War and Roosevelt during the Great Depression. A leader has to know the words of consolation and they have to be embodied in his life and character. No political leader can give a word of consolation that he/she has not yet heard. Like Ezekiel, the leader must sit on the banks of the river Chebar "among the exiles."[112] Ezekiel writes, "I came to the exiles at Tel-abib, who lived by the river Chebar. And I sat there among them, stunned, for seven days."[113] There's one other vivid illustration of the depth of empathy and the time and investment it requires. After Job lost everything, his friends "sat with him on the ground for seven days and seven nights, and no one spoke a word to him, for they saw that his suffering was very great."[114] Consolation arises in silence, companionship, shared grief.

Empathy possesses a dialogical nature. There is no consolation unless the words spoken are received as such. The problem with the friends of Job is that their proposed consolation ended when they opened their

---

110. Gen 45:4–5.
111. Havel, "Message to the International Conference."
112. Ezek 1:1.
113. Ezek 3:15.
114. Job 2:13.

mouths and blamed Job for his misfortune. There's no empathy in this sort of self-righteousness. Some days I sense that all our debates are attempts to get the other side to admit they are wrong. Have we all become the friends of Job? Trump instinctively, consistently blames all others for whatever is wrong. His own administration's response to the COVID pandemic was to brag on how tremendously they had responded. He took all the credit for any good, deflected all criticism as the fault of others.

In addition, there is no consolation from any leader who cannot bless his/her own origins, suffering, and oppression. The empathic word is always personal, spoken by one who has come to terms with one's history and tradition. The speaker of any word of consolation embodies the suffering of the hearers. This insight lies behind the poem of the servant in Isaiah 53: "Surely, he has borne our griefs and carried our sorrows . . . wounded for our transgressions . . . and with his stripes we are healed."[115] Carl Jung says, "Only the wounded can heal."[116]

Havel risked everything when he spoke from the position of the fool and with the rhetoric of folly. He identified with his people and the two became one in precarity, suffering, and possibility. Here is the embodiment of the rhetoric of folly: Always intimate, loving, trusting, personal, empathic. I think it fitting to hear the words of President Lincoln's beating heart of empathy in his Second Inaugural Address: "With malice toward none with charity for all with firmness in the right as God gives us to see the right let us strive on to finish the work we are in to bind up the nation's wounds, to care for him who shall have borne the battle and for his widow and his orphan—to do all which may achieve and cherish a just and lasting peace among ourselves and with all nations."[117]

The Quest for Hope

Havel said, "Hope is not the conviction that something will turn out well, but the certainty that something makes sense, regardless of how it turns out."[118] After all, the folly of the cross, as Paul would have it, is not a story

---

115. Isaiah 53:4–5.
116. Quoted in Marney, "Fundaments of Competent Ministry," 10.
117. Lincoln, "Second Inaugural Address," https://www.nps.gov/linc/learn/historyculture/lincoln-second-inaugural.htm.
118. Havel, *Disturbing the Peace*, 181–82.

ending on Good Friday, or else the Christians would literally be simple fools. As Zagacki puts it,

> Thus, it could be claimed that Havel's folly fails as a deliberative mode, something required of any political leader, in not offering audiences a grounded choice, other than acquiescence to the folly of history. This is not to underplay the tremendous difficulty, as Havel seemed to see most clearly, of restoring a moral view of the world in the wake of the collapse of a cynical, state-centered ethic. On the other hand, the deeper significance of Havel's rhetoric may lie in its recovery, through ironic and epideictic means, of a discovery of the power of ordinary people to transcend the lies that are so huge they often become believable.

Havel observed, "There are thousands of nameless people who try to live within the truth and millions who want to but cannot, perhaps only because to do so in the circumstances in which they live, they would need ten times the courage of those who have already taken the first step." Havel offers a profound analysis of the direction that life usually moves: "Life in its essence moves toward plurality, diversity, independent self-constitution and self-organization, in short towards the fulfillment of its own freedom."[119] What we see with Trump and company, on the other hand, is a dreary conformity, uniformity, and sameness.

Havel, with prophetic insight, describes the culture we inhabit:

> Human beings are compelled to live within a lie, but they can be compelled to do so only because they are in fact capable of living in this way . . . Alienated humanity supports this system as its own involuntary master plan, as a degenerate image of its own degeneration, as a record of people's own failures as individuals . . . Each person is capable of . . . coming to terms with living within the lie. Each person somehow succumbs to a profane trivialization of his or her inherent humanity, and to utilitarianism. In everyone there is some willingness to merge with the anonymous crowd and to flow comfortably along with it down the river of pseudo-life.[120]

This is the evil that resides in Trump and his followers. The lies, the lies, the lies add up to the evil that most threatens democracy.

Trump and company involve a fantasy of atomism; an unhealthy contrarianism. The crowd at a Trump rally, already programmed to

119. Havel, *Power of the Powerless*, 38.
120. Havel, *Power of the Powerless*, 38.

repent Trumpian litanies, could easily be imagined chanting, "We are all individuals." The acolytes entertain the notion that they are radical and different but they are exactly the same. This is especially the case with white males within the Trump orbit: dogmatic, certain, contrarian "worker bees" with a fixed set of beliefs resistant to fact, reason, or truth.

In Havel's turn toward folly—the wisdom that is divine—we can find true identity as humans not controlled by evil. Indeed, the move toward folly must always acknowledge "that no individual can soar above the crowd for very long. With our reconciliation to the worldly order of necessity, is our reconciliation to the crowd as well."[121]

Havel's democracy song heralds the ring of truth, a truth rooted in Hebrew Scripture (especially Psalms, Proverbs, Song of Solomon, and the prophets) and the politics of Jesus. Here is the trumpet blast of folly as wisdom. Here is the resounding theme that weakness is strength. Here is the reality that humility and not arrogance is the way of hope. Here is the gift of irony and empathy coupled with accountability and responsibility. Here is the song that dares lift its tune in the Age of Trump.

---

121. Farrell, *Norms of Rhetorical Culture*, 16.

CHAPTER 5

Singing for Democracy

Like a Southern Baptist evangelist announcing, "Let's stand for the closing hymn, 'Just As I Am,'" the preacher determined to save souls from hell would have the congregation sing all the stanzas, and then start over again. The heartfelt plea would become almost desperate after twenty verses: "If no one comes on this verse, we will be closing out the invitation, shutting the door to heaven, and leaving some lost soul in danger of hell." Having no love for the theology, I am feeling the preacher's plea in my song for democracy. We need to keep singing the verses, and now we come to the closing song.

We take our deep desire to sing the songs of democracy from Walt Whitman's "For You, O Democracy."

> Come, I will make the continent indissoluble,
> I will make the most splendid race the sun ever shone upon,
> I will make divine magnetic lands,
> With the love of comrades,
> With the life-long love of comrades.
> I will plant companionship thick as trees along all the rivers of America,
>   and along the shores of the great lakes, and all over the prairies,
> I will make inseparable cities with their arms about each other's necks,
> By the love of comrades,
> By the manly love of comrades.
> For you these from me, O Democracy, to serve you ma femme!
> For you, for you I am trilling these songs.[1]

---

1. Whitman, "For You, O Democracy," 1892 ed.

Joshua Gunn reminds us, "Friedrich Nietzsche argues that the stuff of rhetoric is gestural and rhythmic, a bodily act, a kind of singing and dancing that is perhaps most familiar to us as music or poesy."[2] Gunn also expresses the idea poetically, "But the ancients also taught us that persuasive speech is not only to be understood as bodied forth because it also sends forth bodies, like so many lovely lips setting off a thousand scripts."[3] The choir that sings of democracy contains "the voice of many angels surrounding the throne and the living creatures and the elders; they numbered myriads of myriads and thousands of thousands."[4] Many singers of democracy could be profitably studied, but then this discussion would become unwieldy. Instead, I have selected the Song of Solomon, companion volume to Proverbs in the wisdom literature of the Hebrews, Isaiah's Suffering Servant song (Isa 53), and Walt Whitman. The Song of Solomon will lift solo renditions that will go largely unremarked upon because the odes to love are so powerful and so pungent with meaning. The use of the analogy of democracy in the Song of Solomon has no biblical warrant but is a matter of my own biblical imagination. Just as the Song has nothing to do with Jesus and the church in any literal sense, it has nothing to do with democracy except in the context of this political discussion.

Can Rhetoricians Speak of the Good?

The discussion of the good creates rhetorical difficulties. According to Charles Taylor, "We cannot do without some orientation to the good ... we each essentially are (i.e., define ourselves at least inter alia by) where we stand on this."[5] Jeremy Engels says, "What we assume to be the point of life—to be good—shapes our hopes, our dreams, our fears, and our habits."[6] Talk of the good is foundational to democratic politics. Of course, philosophers disagree about the origin of the good: does it come from God, from the stars or the social world into which we are thrown? This was a particularly contentious debate during the nineteenth century. "For Whitman, the poets, bards, and orators must awaken Americans to

   2. Gunn, *Political Perversion*, Kindle ed., loc. 714–15.
   3. Gunn, *Political Perversion*, Kindle ed., loc. 714–15.
   4. Rev 5:11.
   5. Taylor, *Sources of the Self*, 33.
   6. Engels, "Kosmic Rhetoric," 76.

the true meaning of democracy by setting aside trivial things and talking 'first principles,' namely, what is good."[7] Whitman's conception of the good is based on the ontology of the All (the cosmos)—to experience the All is the good that should guide democratic life.

In *Phaedrus* Plato argues that it is necessary to invoke the good in moments when truth alone is not enough to persuade.[8] For Plato there is a mysticism associated with the good. Whitman writes from within this mystical tradition of rhetoric, in which reason can only take us so far and there is more to the world than our representations and formulas can capture. Ernesto Grassi makes much the same point in warning against humanity giving over all of life to technology. He calls this an act of ingenium or creative transformation that leads to greater awareness and responsible action.

However, as Plato recognizes, the truth alone does not always have the power to set us free. It is often necessary to create an appetite for the truth by framing it as good. Whitman does just this in his poetry. For him, champions of democracy should not privilege the *how* over the *what*, because it is the *what*, and specifically the *so what*, that keeps democracy's heart beating.

Plato's Socrates argued, repeatedly, that the good life could be found by imitating the divine order of the universe, of the kosmos.[9]

With those parameters in mind, I argue that a pathos of the good has to be wed to democracy in every possible way. A moral vision of the good offers a way out of the stultifying pathos of conservative politics. My concern is for emotional arguments that inspire us to want to be better and to do better. If the right word for the state of democracy is that it is in danger of dying, then we have no choice but to engage in soteriology and say out loud, "Democracy needs to be saved," as in made whole or rescued from the affects of revenge, retaliation, and rage. Ott and Dickinson's *The Twitter Presidency* reminds us of the horrors that imperil democracy and call it by one name: white rage.[10] They locate white rage in "the fear and anxiety surrounding the social decentering of white privilege and hegemonic masculinity."[11] A pathos of the good challenges

---

7. Engels, "Kosmic Rhetoric," 74–75.
8. Weaver, *Ethics of Rhetoric*, 15, 18.
9. Brague, *Wisdom of the World*, 33.
10. Ott and Dickinson, *Twitter Presidency*, 3.
11. Ott and Dickinson, *Twitter Presidency*, 29.

the reigning affects of rage, disgust, shame, revenge, resentment, anger, cruelty, and violence. It calls us instead to the opposite of rage: peace, happiness, calmness, patience. And the opposite of disgust: attraction, pleasure, acceptance. It calls us to the opposite of revenge: forgiveness. And the opposite of resentment: cheerfulness, friendliness, contentment, delight. And, finally, to the opposite of cruelty: empathy, compassion, mercy. Democracy, rooted in the good and empathy, gives us a whole new world in which all humans may flourish.

For the rhetorical scholar to invest in a pathos of the good has a psychological analogy. The study of psychology historically concentrated on what was bad in humans, the diseases, the neuroses. This was the case because no one seemed to have interest in identifying the good. Such an endeavor would have seemed to smack of feel-good positive thinking related in Christian circles to the purposes of God.

In psychology, the affects of good were not even considered until Martin Seligman opened the door. What if, he began to wonder, he studied well-being instead of unhappiness, accomplishment instead of failure, strength instead of sickness? Perhaps psychology could become less fixated on neuroses, less dependent on Prozac, and, altogether, more useful. Perhaps he could improve his life and redirect the profession: "Positive psychology called to me just as the burning bush called to Moses."[12]

Rhetorical critique, like psychology, thrives on the ills, the neuroses, the transgressive nature of our politics. The premise of positive psychology is that well-being can be defined, measured, and taught. Well-being includes positive emotions, intense engagement, good relationships, meaning, and accomplishment. Questionnaires can measure it. Trainers can teach it. Achieving it not only makes people more fulfilled but makes corporations more productive, soldiers more resilient, students more engaged, marriages happier. Can there be a positive politics for the sake of democracy?

While rhetoric and psychology share this reluctance to consider the good, these two actually start to look the same the more you keep digging. This study is an argument from definition, suggesting that once we name and describe the nature and qualities of the good, we are better able to offer it as a model for politics. In a sense this is a work of psychoanalytic rhetorical criticism set to the music of democracy.

---

12. Gibbon, "Martin Seligman and the Rise of Positive Psychology."

Talking about questions of soteriology, ontology, and the good creates epistemic pressure for a rhetorical critic. The answers often given to define the good are the usual problem because they can sound so moralizing. Rather than a lofty discussion of the good worthy of Plato the critic ends up sounding like an eighteenth-century English boy's school headmaster handing down the laws of behavior. Every effort has been made to avoid the fundamentalistic heresy of insisting on dogmas that have to be defended at all costs. The move toward a pathos of the good doesn't indicate all the answers have been carved in stone and sent down from heaven. Even the good is contestable in a post-truth age.

So let the singing begin in a paraphrased springtime rhapsody:

> Democracy, o democracy, "my love."
> "As a lily among brambles,
> so is my love among maidens.
> As an apple tree among the trees of the wood,
> so is my beloved among young men.
> With great delight I sat in his shadow,
> and his fruit was sweet to my taste.
> He brought me to the banqueting house,
> and his intention towards me was love."[13]

> Democracy your kisses are better than wine,
> your anointing oils are fragrant;
> your name is perfume poured out.
> Draw me after you, the people wait for you,
> We will exult and rejoice in you
> We will extol your love more than wine;
> Rightly do we love you.
> I am black and beautiful,
> O daughters of Jerusalem,
> like the tents of Kedar,
> like the curtains of Solomon.[14]

The African American Prophetic Tradition

This has been a book about good and evil—about the politics of good and evil. My hope is that the politics of life will not allow the politics of death

---

13. Song 2:2–4.
14. Song 1:1–5.

to dominate the American political landscape on a permanent basis. Gardner Taylor has a powerful sermon about communities of darkness and death versus light and life. In that sense this is a hopeful book. Some American prophet, if we can magnify the good of democracy, will not be required to ask, "Can these bones live?"[15] There is the possibility that the question already presents as a live option. Can the bones of democracy—now fractured by evil, fakery, lies, and deception—live again? I believe that the prophetic realism of the African American prophetic tradition represents our best hope for a living democracy. The Song of Solomon celebrates the "black and beautiful."[16] The African American prophetic tradition has wrestled with the promises and perils of radical democracy from the beginning. "Radical democracy names the intermittent and dispersed traditions of witnessing, resisting, and seeking alternatives to the politics of death wrought by those bent on myriad forms of immortality-as-conquest."[17] As noted earlier, Cornel West argues: "The black prophetic tradition has been the leaven in the American democratic loaf. What has kept American democracy from going fascist or authoritarian or autocratic has been the legacy of Frederick Douglass, Harriet Tubman, Sojourner Truth, Martin King, Fannie Lou Hamer. This is not because black people have a monopoly on truth, goodness, or beauty. It is because the black freedom movement puts pressure on the American empire in the name of integrity, decency, honesty and virtue."[18] The leaven in the African American prophetic tradition is good. This is not the leaven of the Pharisees. This is the good leaven like the "yeast that a woman took and mixed in with three measures of flour until all of it was leavened."[19]

Like the lover in the Song of Solomon, democracy disappears from the world.

> Upon my bed at night
> I sought him whom my soul loves;
> I sought him, but found him not;
> I called him, but he gave no answer.
> I will rise now and go about the city,
> in the streets and in the squares;
> I will seek him whom my soul loves.

15. Ezek 37:3.
16. Song 1:5.
17. Hauerwas and Coles, *Christianity, Democracy, and the Radical Ordinary,* 3.
18. Hedges, "Cornel West and the Fight to Save the Black Prophetic Tradition."
19. Matt 13:33.

> I sought him, but found him not.
> The sentinels found me,
> as they went about in the city.
> Have you seen him whom my soul loves?[20]

Democracy fades as she goes. "The American public doesn't understand that democracy is a fragile system that can wither away if you don't take care of it."[21] Democracy wilts and withers. A book waits to be written that chronicles the recession of democracy in the USA. Working from the post-World War II confidence in the glory of democracy, a picture forms of a democracy that fades as it goes. Characteristics, virtues, practices, decorum, traditions, goodness that were strong and vital for more than two centuries grow blurry as anti-democratic forces step forward with beguiling promises. Cornel West asks penetrating questions:

> Do we now live in a postdemocratic age in which the very "democratic" rhetoric of an imperial America hides the waning of a democratic America? Are there enough democratic energies here and abroad to fight for and win back our democracy given the undeniable power of the three dominant dogmas that fuel imperial America [free market fundamentalism, aggressive militarism, and escalating authoritarianism]? Or will the American empire go the way of the Leviathans of the past—the Roman, Ottoman, Soviet, and British empires? Can any empire resist the temptation to become drunk with the wine of world power or become intoxicated with the hubris and greed of imperial possibilities? Has not every major empire pursued quixotic dreams of global domination—of shaping the world in its image and for its interest—that resulted in internal decay and doom? Can we committed democrats avert this world-historical pattern and possible fate?[22]

Unless we love democracy more than political party, West's questions will be answered in the negative and to the detriment of democracy.

The foreboding of these questions and their potentially horrific answers pleads for a solo from a voice from the past. From the nineteenth-century social gospel movement, here is a song of democracy by Katherine Lee Bates:

---

20. Song 3:1–3.
21. Cited in Chirindo, "Precarious Publics," 430.
22. West, *Democracy Matters*, 8.

> O beautiful for spacious skies, For amber waves of grain, For purple mountain majesties Above the fruited plain! America! America! God shed his grace on thee And crown thy good with brotherhood From sea to shining sea! O beautiful for pilgrim feet Whose stern impassioned stress A thoroughfare of freedom beat Across the wilderness! America! America! God mend thine every flaw, Confirm thy soul in self-control, Thy liberty in law! O beautiful for heroes proved In liberating strife. Who more than self their country loved And mercy more than life! America! America! May God thy gold refine Till all success be nobleness And every gain divine! O beautiful for patriot dream That sees beyond the years Thine alabaster cities gleam Undimmed by human tears! America! America! God shed his grace on thee and crown thy good with brotherhood From sea to shining sea![23]

Bates possessed a realistic optimism that there were Americans who loved their country more than themselves. She saw clearly that America's got flaws, but persisted in the paean of praiseworthiness for America. This moment allows us to catch our breath as we descend into the darkness of the precarity now facing our democracy.

Yet West refuses to let us off the hook as he evaluates our current malaise. The black prophetic tradition "no longer has a legitimacy or significant foothold in the minds of the black masses," West said.

> With corporate media and the narrowing of the imagination of all Americans, including black people, there is an erasure of memory. This is the near death of the black prophetic tradition. It is a grave issue. It is a matter of life and death. It means that the major roadblock to American fascism, which has been the black prophetic tradition, is gone. To imagine America without the black prophetic tradition, from Frederick Douglass to Fannie Lou Hamer, means an American authoritarian regime, American fascism. We already have the infrastructure in place for the police state.[24]

Freedom House, in its *Freedom in the World 2021* report, shared the growing pessimism about democracy's prospects around the world. "Even before 2020," they wrote, "Trump had presided over an accelerating decline in U.S. freedom scores, driven in part by corruption and

---

23. Bates, "America the Beautiful," *Hymns for the Living Church* 520.
24. Hedges, "Cornel West and the Fight to Save the Black Prophetic Tradition."

conflicts of interest in the administration."[25] Moreover, around the world more countries had performed worse on various measures of freedom than had improved compared to any other point since 2005. "The expansion of authoritarian rule, combined with fading and inconsistent presence of major democracies on the international stage, has had tangible effects on human life and security."[26]

In *Precarious Rhetorics*, Wendy Hesford, Adela Licona, and Christa Teston suggest that one cause of the growing sense of precarity felt around the world is the growth of right-wing nationalist populism in nations of the North Atlantic. The rise of "hard-right populism," they note, "is cultivated through the sowing of fear and suspicion."[27] Politicians in the West have exploited feelings of disaffection among those who believe globalization has left them behind—white, American blue-collar workers, for example. These leaders have amplified appeals that blame the global and cultural Other for the vulnerability those who were previously privileged may now face. Whether it be immigrants that allegedly "take our jobs"; corporations who are perceived to enjoy unfair competitive advantages because the countries in which they operate extend financial, legal, or other subsidies; or those whose cultural practices seem otherworldly when compared to received wisdom relative to, say, gender, this scapegoating of the cultural and foreign Other evokes inchoate feelings some have associated with "tribalism" both positively and negatively.[28] That affective register of precarity—feeling at once exposed to, vulnerable to, dependent upon, and impinged upon by others—is itself a function of a sociability Judith Butler recognizes as a condition of living. "One's life," Butler observes, "is always in some sense, in the hands of the other."[29] This cultural or socialized precarity, in other words, is an inescapable fact of being human and of the publics humans constitute.

The precarity glares back at the African American community. West speaks hard truth:

> That has always been a skeleton in the closet, the fundamental challenge to the black prophetic tradition. It may very well be that black people will never be free in America. But I believe,

---

25. Cited in Chirindo, "Precarious Publics," 431.
26. Repucci and Slipowitz, *Freedom in the World*, 2.
27. Hesford et al., *Precarious Rhetorics*, 1.
28. Chua, *Political Tribes*.
29. Butler, *Frames of War*, 14.

and the black prophetic tradition believes, that we proceed because black people are worthy of being free, just as poor people of all colors are worthy of being free, even if they never will be free. That is the existential leap of faith. There is no doubt that with a black president the black masses are still treated unfairly, from stop and frisk to high unemployment, indecent housing and decrepit education."[30]

Eddie Glaude believes "a revolution of value could change the current course of this nation." His revisioning of the black prophetic tradition insists that "we have to break loose from the straitjacket of race that confines how African Americans live and how democracy is imagined in this country. That will mean ... letting a thousand flowers of black political expression bloom (we need more than black liberals arguing among themselves), and burying, once and for all, 'Negroes,' 'niggers,' their cousins (thugs, welfare queens, absent fathers, and all the other ugly names and stereotypes), and the white people who invented them."[31]

A revolution of value stands a real chance in assisting the revival of democracy. As Glaude implores, "But we, black folk, have to change our habits too."[32] Charlene Carruthers, national coordinator of the Black Youth Project 100 puts the point powerfully:

> Until we really, really go beyond the respectable black people or the young black man and woman who is a college graduate [we will not succeed] ... So, we're going to lift them up because they were an A student, but also have to care about the ones who never graduated from high school or the one who was incarcerated or the one who doesn't speak well or isn't particularly eloquent or the one who doesn't follow along some gender binary ... Until we are able to do that, how we see justice is limited.[33]

Glaude connects African American oppression at home with US foreign policy. Sounding like the Rev. Martin Luther King Jr. challenging the Vietnam War, Glaude argues that the heart of democracy in black lies in imagining a democratic way of life without the burden of the value gap. "We have to do better ... Illusions will not save us; they have to be smashed. We have to change fundamentally, and that will require

---

30. Hedges, "Cornel West and the Fight to Save the Black Prophetic Tradition."
31. Glaude, *Democracy in Black*, 232.
32. Glaude, *Democracy in Black*, 232.
33. Glaude, *Democracy in Black*, 234.

uprooting the racial habits that are the lifeblood of the value gap.... We must close the value gap and uproot racial habits by doing democracy, once again, in black. If we fail this time—and if there is a God I pray that we don't—this grand experiment in democracy will be no more."[34]

I believe that Eddie Glaude Jr. hits exactly the right note in *Democracy in Black*, with the agricultural metaphor: uprooting. He acknowledges the long-standing and dangerous racial habits lurking beneath our politics. "And Barack Obama's election did little, if anything, to uproot them. In fact, he conceded to their terms."[35] The fact of a black man in the White House made the historical habits more difficult to uproot. The white evangelicals applied a chemical for strengthening the root system of racism. They learned to deny the existence of racism. They found African American spokespersons to give presentations insisting that racism no longer existed in America. They unleashed a withering attack on "political correctness" and Critical Race Theory. The historical habits are now more entrenched, the roots are stronger, deeper, more intractable.

White evangelicals, the one-time masters of shame, refuse to be shamed by the historical realities of slavery, lynching, and segregation and instead fight back with fierce denials. It is an odd culture where a person can shout from the rooftop "I am not a racist" after engaging in racist rhetoric and actions.

Glaude suggests we need to listen to Malcom X: "Stop sweet talking them. Tell them how you really feel. Tell them what kind of hell you've been catching. And let him know that if he's not ready to clean up his house—if he's not ready to clean up his house, he shouldn't have a house. It should catch on fire and burn down." As Glaude concludes, "In other words, we should remind America that chickens do, in fact, come home to roost."[36] Today, Republican Representative Marjorie Taylor Green would probably file a complaint with the Capitol police accusing Malcom of violence.

The Rev. Dr. Martin Luther King Jr. knew the difficulty of uprooting racial habits. He saw clearly that the habits of racism were worldwide, and his condemnation of the war in Vietnam demonstrated how far he had come in his understanding and revealed the wrath of white America against the great preacher. King: "The fact is that the ultimate logic of

---

34. Glaude, *Democracy in Black*, 49.
35. Glaude, *Democracy in Black*, 91.
36. Glaude, *Democracy in Black*, 91.

racism is genocide. If you say that I am not good enough to live next door to you ... because of the color of my skin or my ethnic origins, then you are saying in substance that I do not deserve to exist."[37]

The attempt to uproot racial habits also faces the unrelenting framing of whites to mark all the people and movements attempting to uproot white supremacy as radical and violent. All attempts to protest white supremacy get reduced to an orgy of violence or a simple demand for black cultural recognition. The "bloody heirloom," Coates's phrase for ingrained racial habits, remains intact to this day.

There's an illusion in many local churches that if people would just try to get along, all the problems would disappear. Somehow this illusion has managed to sneak into the racial habits of our nation. This is an attempt to protect American innocence as if slavery never happened and segregation was good for African Americans. Glaude argues, "'Getting along' does not measure up to a more fundamental concern about racial justice or get at how we are all complicit in racial injustice. The illusion hides the rot. A revolution of value would seek to uproot those ways of seeing and living that allow Americans to support racial equality and yet live in ways that suggest they believe otherwise."[38]

Uprooting the racial habits of America would require bulldozers and backhoes to attack the roots. The plant, freshly green and shining with examples of black success, looks fine, but the rot is below in the roots. In order to get at the roots, to change the value system will require a change in how we view the government, a change in how we view black people—and a change in how we see what ultimately matters to us as Americans.[39] Current ways of doing things make it hard to "uproot the racial habits that are choking the life out of democracy."[40]

Democracy in black has received no more powerful expression than that of the Mississippi Freedom Riders and the heroine of that movement, Mrs. Fannie Lou Hamer. On August 22, 1964, Mrs. Hamer, who was a co-founder of the Mississippi Freedom Democratic Party, spoke before the Credentials Committee of the Democratic National Convention in Atlantic City. In this speech that addressed voter suppression and state-sanctioned violence, she uttered the famous quote "I'm sick and

---

37. Glaude, *Democracy in Black*, 99–100.
38. Glaude, *Democracy in Black*, 184.
39. Glaude, *Democracy in Black*, 184.
40. Glaude, *Democracy in Black*, 221.

tired of being sick and tired." Her closing words still ring with truth: "I was in jail when Medgar Evers was murdered. All of this is on account of we want to register, to become first-class citizens. And if the Freedom Democratic Party is not seated now, I question America. Is this America, the land of the free and the home of the brave, where we have to sleep with our telephones off the hooks because our lives be threatened daily, because we want to live as decent human beings, in America?"[41]

The tragedies embodied in the life of Fannie Lou Hamer would become the celebration of new life. As a people who believe in the goodness, the generosity, the graciousness of an abundant God, we dare, in the face of a culture and philosophy of scarcity, to proclaim the gospel of abundance and plenty. Otis Moss III says, "Blue note preaching . . . is prophetic preaching—preaching about tragedy but refusing to fall into despair."[42] The sense of precarity will yield to no voice but the poetic.

In the face of such precarity, the paraphrased singer of the Song of Solomon returns to center stage for a solo:

> You have ravished my heart, democracy, my bride,
> you have ravished my heart with a glance of your eyes,
> with one jewel of your necklace.
> How sweet is your love, my sister, my bride!
> how much better is your love than wine,
> and the fragrance of your oils than any spice.[43]

> Set me as a seal upon your heart,
> as a seal upon your arm;
> for love is strong as death,
> passion fierce as the grave.
> Its flashes are flashes of fire,
> a raging flame.
> Many waters cannot quench love,
> neither can floods drown it.
> If one offered for love
> all the wealth of one's house,
> it would be utterly scorned.[44]

---

41. Hamer, "Testimony Before the Credentials Committee."
42. Moss, *Blue Note Preaching in a Post-Soul World*, 6.
43. Song 4:9–10.
44. Song 8:6–7.

Walt Whitman: The Bard of Democracy

After the seas are all cross'd, (as them seem already cross'd)
After the great captains and engineers have accomplish'd their work,
After the inventors, after the scientists, the chemist, the geologist,
 the ethnologist,
Finally shall come the poet worthy of that name,
The true son of God shall come singing his songs.[45]

For Walt Whitman, the choicest fruits of democracy were government of the people, by the people, and for the people. For Whitman there could only be one possibility: Freedom across the board. His love of diversity posited no "us" versus "them." Let Whitman sing his poems. At last, the true child of democracy has come singing his poems. According to Robert L. Ivie, "democracy exists only in the presence of dissent,"[46] and as such nothing could be more important than to sing, to scream, and to fight for it.[47] Dissent is one of the musical scores for democracy's lyrics. In Walt Whitman we get a different song of democracy. "Democracy has its seer in Whitman."[48] For Whitman, democracy is not dissent but a deep spirituality. In *Democratic Vistas*, Whitman goes so far as to say, "For I say at the core of democracy, finally, is the religious element."[49] The religious element in democracy alludes to what rhetoric, since Aristotle, has defined as ethos. This means that character and issues of good and evil are integral to democracy. Whitman also says, "I say that the real and permanent grandeur of these States must be their religion, Otherwise there is no real and permanent grandeur; (Nor character nor life worthy the name without religion, Nor land nor man or woman without religion)."[50]

Theologian Cornel West lauds Whitman's "impassioned odes to democratic possibility,"[51] "his penetrating visions and truth telling."[52] "Walt Whitman became the American bard Ralph Waldo Emerson called for. From *Leaves of Grass* to *Democratic Vistas*, he expressed a vision of

---

45. Whitman, *Leaves of Grass*, 833.
46. Ivie, "Enabling Democratic Dissent," 49, 46.
47. Blight, "Trump Has Birthed a Dangerous New 'Lost Cause' Myth."
48. Dewey and Rogers, *Public and Its Problems*, 184.
49. Whitman, *Democratic Vistas*, 949.
50. Whitman, *Democratic Vistas*, 180.
51. West, *Democracy Matters*, 21.
52. West, *Democracy Matters*, 67.

democratic individuality, community, and society with an unprecedented passion."[53] Is democracy future-oriented as Whitman prophesied?[54] "Whether democracy in America can flourish . . . Only its citizens can resolve . . . and only they can decide if its vistas remain as 'enchantingly' democratic as Walt Whitman once hoped—or if democracy comes to stand for something much narrower, even mean."[55]

Love / Companionship / Fellowship / Whitman

What we need are prophets, poets, and rhapsodes for democracy. Somehow, we must rediscover what President Lincoln referred to as "the better angels of our nature."[56] In the destruction and death of the Civil War, dying soldiers renewed Whitman's faith in democracy. We may see these Civil War soldiers as "suffering servants."[57] Consider Whitman's poem, "Vigil Strange I Kept on the Field One Night." Here is the key to democracy for Whitman. What a constraint we find in the vigil of the dead soldier with Trump's violation of all human decency in his attacks on the dead. "Think about the corpse in the 'Vigil Strange I Kept on the Field One Night.' It no longer needs to survive, yet it still deserves the dignity and respect offered by the surviving soldier."[58] John Marsh points in the direction democracy needs to go. "We might also draw comfort from the fact that, thanks in part to Whitman, we know where democracy in the United States must head: toward affection, toward friendship, toward a nation founded on care . . . We might also draw comfort, as Whitman did, from the fact that though much of our politics and culture conspires against it, somewhere within them Americans have sufficient reserves of affection to get them there."[59]

Whitman sings his song to offer consolation and healing to a nation so deeply divided. He sings his faith in ordinary people and their ability to care for themselves and for one another as a prerequisite to survival. Our future doesn't depend on how many billionaires the USA produces

53. Engels, "Kosmic Rhetoric," 77.
54. Miller, *Can Democracy Work?*, 9.
55. Miller, *Can Democracy Work?*, 18.
56. Lincoln, "First Inaugural Address."
57. Marsh, *In Walt We Trust*, 196–98.
58. Marsh, *In Walt We Trust*, 200.
59. Marsh, *In Walt We Trust*, 202.

or how many flights they take to space, but on the millions upon millions of ordinary Americans who keep singing the song of democracy at the top of their lungs. "Whoever you are," Whitman exults, "to you endless announcements! Daughters of the land did you wait for your poet? Did you wait for one with a flowing mouth and indicative hand? Toward the male of the States, and toward the female of the States, Exulting words, words to democracy lands."[60] Add to this faith in the ordinary ones a deeper faith in the religious faith of citizens.

Whitman's words have never had more urgency: "I say we had best look our times and lands searchingly in the face, like a physician diagnosing some deep disease. Never was there, perhaps, more hollowness at heart than at present, and here in the United States. Genuine belief seems to have left us. The underlying principles of the States not believ'd in, (for all this hectic glow, and these melodramatic screamings), nor is humanity itself believ'd in. What penetrating eye does not everywhere see through the mask? The spectacle is appalling."[61]

Song of Solomon / The Suffering Servant Song / Whitman's Care of Dying Soldiers

Whitman's deep love for democracy and her citizens brings into focus the Hebrew Scripture—especially the Song of Solomon and the suffering servant poems of Isaiah. The Song of Solomon celebrates deep love. Analogically, we encounter the beating heart of democracy—a commitment to maintaining democracy through all the vagaries and vulgarities of our politics. "Set me as a seal upon your heart, O democracy, as a seal upon your arm; for love is strong as death, passion fierce as the grave. Its flashes are flashes of fire, a raging flame. Many waters cannot quench love, neither can floods drown it. If one offered for love all the wealth of one's house, it would be utterly scorned."[62]

Add the suffering servant song of Isaiah 53 and there we see Isaiah as a physician diagnosing the deep disease of the servant. In a merging act of compassion, place Whitman's poem "Vigil Strange I Kept on the Field One Night" beside Isaiah's suffering servant poem. Marsh argues that Whitman's syntax offers an ethics. Instead of the subject, verb, object

60. Whitman, *Leaves of Grass*, 235.
61. Whitman, *Democratic Vistas*, 937.
62. Song 8:6–7.

structure, Whitman employs object, subject, verb. The title serves as example: "Vigil Strange I Kept on the Field One Night." "My comrade I wrapt in his blanket." Marsh says, "The shift makes Whitman's point about affection. Instead of occupying the position of authority, bodily commanding the world and its objects, . . . the subject in the sentences of Whitman's poem subordinates itself to the object. . . . Grammar becomes ethics. . . . So, what Whitman says matters, but so does how he says it."[63] This is what "Whitman means by affection, manly love, adhesiveness, comradeliness, and what makes the virtue by whatever name so crucial to his notion of democracy. In affectionate relationships you subordinate yourself to others. You put their interests above your own. In short, you care for them. That is what Whitman did for soldiers . . . For Whitman, that affection, and only that sort of affection, would form the basis of any democracy worth the name."[64] The same love shines brightly from the Song of Solomon and from the song of Isaiah.

The metaphors pile up around the deep spiritual resonance produced by Whitman. Otis Moss III joins Isaiah with the prophetic voice of Billie Holiday singing, "Southern trees bear strange fruit."[65] James Cone complicates the anguish in *The Cross and the Lynching Tree* with a theme verse—"The put him to death by hanging him on a tree."[66] Isaiah laments the policies of those in power who "make widows their prey" and rob the fatherless.[67] Isaiah sees the precarity induced by those who create a top-heavy world of male power—"the patriarchy of political power—who view women as objects for sport."[68]

One venue for democracy's survival might be taking the role of the suffering servant of Isaiah. I tend toward the opposite of the dog-eat-dog capitalism that fuels our national greed, in the direction of a more religious expression of servanthood and stewardship. Unless someone carries the water and hews the wood and keeps the fires of democracy blazing, there will be only darkness. The suffering servant is a major theme of Second Isaiah, as articulated in the servant poems. These are extensive theological commentaries on Israel as God's servant. The poems, especially Isaiah

---

63. Marsh, *In Walt We Trust*, 198.

64. Marsh, *In Walt We Trust*, 198.

65. Moss, *Blue Note Preaching*, 10. For a deeper discussion of lynching see Cone, *Cross and the Lynching Tree*.

66. Acts 10:39.

67. Isa 10:1–2.

68. Moss, *Blue Note Preaching*, 10.

53, embrace pain and suffering as the necessary experiences of life. Such willingness of sacrifice and suffer are exceedingly rare in our day. During wars of a previous century, America rallied to protect democracy.

American historian Robert S. McElvaine made a similar argument about the centrality of religion to democracy during the Great Depression. McElvaine reflects, "It was in this book that I first began to identify the values of cooperation and community that enjoyed a brief renaissance in the Depression years as attitudes that have usually been more associated with women than men . . . Men began to move toward values more often linked with women when they found themselves in the position society traditionally assigned to women."[69] Tocqueville also believed that Christianity was necessary to restrain democracy's excesses, especially its tendency toward a brutal dog-eat-dog capitalism. McElvaine elaborates on Tocqueville's theme: "The system that had failed in the thirties, that of every-man-for-himself, the-devil-take-the-hindmost, competition, and acquisitive individualism . . . tended to discredit the more male approach to the world and open men, as well as women, more to the possibility of restoring values of mutualism."[70] Now, we are drowning in individualism, escalating authoritarianism, and rampant greed. The poet of Isaiah likens the path to well-being as "walking without fainting."[71]

While the capacity for this sacrificial life is available to everyone, it is rare, but fortunately it doesn't require everyone to ensure the ongoing existence of democracy. As in the day of Sodom, if ten righteous people were found, the city would be saved. There is a deep mystic insight at the heart of democracy. Whitman: "A highest widest aim of democratic literature may well be to bring forth, cultivate, brace, and strengthen this sense in individuals and society."[72] Democracy demands and is immersed in suffering and sacrifice, a deep willingness to love and give for others. Without this desire, there is no democratic polis.

Our current state suggests a lack of faith in democracy and so many citizens locked in their "frivolous sullen moping angry affected disheartened atheistical ways."[73] Whitman's description parallels Ott and Dickinson's *The Twitter Presidency* discussion of white rage in the Age

69. McElvaine, *Great Depression*, xxxvii.
70. McElvaine, *Great Depression*, xxxvii–xxxviii.
71. Isa 40:31.
72. Whitman, *Democratic Vistas*, 989.
73. Whitman, "Song of Myself," 178.

of Trump.[74] They locate white rage in "the fear and anxiety surrounding the social decentering of white privilege and hegemonic masculinity."[75] Trump, they propose, is effective as a communicator precisely by virtue of his ability to ignite this latent fund of frustration. But rage is no facilitator of democracy.

The gross performative nature of political rhetoric now obscures who people really are as each character speaks the "lines" dictated by the gross drama of the anti-democratic spirit. Appearance replaces reality. A political playbook, from which lines are repeated, replaces authentic political deliberation. As Engels puts it,

> For much of Western history, rhetoric has been concerned with more than amassing technical knowledge. The study of rhetoric encompasses more than learning how to turn a phrase or discover the available means of persuasion in any given case. Rhetoric is an 'art of living' and 'care of the self' that teaches people how to be in the world, especially in public. I understand rhetoric to be ethical to its core, for its practice and serious study demand that people change who they are (and not just who they appear to be to the audience).[76]

I am convinced that we can speak to one another and interact with the other side to create a new sense of democracy—including the suffering servant of Isaiah as paradigm for a thriving democracy. This model of life multiplies the possibilities of all persons cooperating in a shared mutualism. If we choose to engage in the servant mode, democracy can become a polis in which citizens practice the ethics of oneness as they promote freedom for all.

West calls this movement the Socratic questioning mode. "The Greek creation of the Socratic commitment to questioning—questioning of ourselves, of authority, of dogma, of parochialism, and of fundamentalism."[77] I earlier developed the thesis that Proverbs is a rhetorical textbook whose purpose is to train young men in the art of rhetoric, especially ethos. West says, "The Socratic commitment to questioning requires a relentless self-examination and critique of institutions of authority, motivated by an endless quest for intellectual integrity and moral consistency. . . . We

---

74. Ott and Dickinson, *Twitter Presidency*, 1.
75. Ott and Dickinson, *Twitter Presidency*, 29.
76. Engels, "Kosmic Rhetoric," 54.
77. West, *Democracy Matters*, 15.

desperately need the deep democratic energy of this Socratic questioning in these times of rampant sophistry on the part of our political elites and their media pundits."[78] A similar argument is made by Foucault when he points out that in the Hellenistic and Roman periods (classical rhetoric), rhetoric "teaches [the student] how to be a public man."[79]

This amounts, on my part, to a soteriological goal (wrapped in a theology of suffering inspired by the Wise Woman of Proverbs and the Hebrew prophetic tradition of Isaiah). I frame democracy as a religious enterprise (whether it is Christian or not is irrelevant) as a means to a higher end. Democracy is the path toward freedom and liberation for all if we embrace the suffering servant trope. Though we are rich, for the sake of democracy, we will become less rich. Though we are powerful, we will put down all power and privilege, for the sake of democracy. We will humble ourselves and become obedient servants to the cause of freedom and liberty especially for the oppressed. Does democracy have any magic left to inspire us to be better than we are today? My answer is yes.

If citizens are not working toward a common good for all it is doubtful that we will put in the work required to sustain democracy and questionable if we will sacrifice much if anything. Given our usual mistrust of all forms of authority, we are reluctant to give any effort to a political community that embodies practical agreements based on a conception of the human or common good. Such a self-centered philosophy, indeed an evil philosophy, arises from what has become of the nation in its democratic malaise. Alasdair MacIntyre argues, "The modern nation-state, in whatever guise, is a dangerous and unmanageable institution, presenting itself on the one hand as a bureaucratic supplier of goods and services, which is always about to, but never actually does, give its clients value for money, and on the other as a repository of sacred values, which from time to time invites one to lay down one's life on its behalf. . . . It is like being asked to die for the telephone company."[80]

Democracy, for Whitman, seems to "mean the creative power of a multitude of people, thrown together by circumstance, to create unique patterns, communities, and ways of being that are contingent, unpredictable, and often beautiful in their own way."[81] Democracy requires

---

78. West, *Democracy Matters*, 16.
79. Foucault, *Subjectivity and Truth*, 30.
80. MacIntyre, "A Partial Response to My Critics," 302.
81. Engels, "Kosmic Rhetoric," 57.

individuals to develop the "suffering servant" mentality that facilitates good for others, a religious experience of being at one with God's purpose in creation. This shatters the illusion that the individual can be isolated from the world. This is the opposite of the individualism of liberalism and much of Protestant Christianity.

Nothing in our current democratic malaise makes room for suffering servants. American ingenuity, hard work, positive thinking, and advertising are not enough to achieve it. We cannot talk our way or fake our way into this condition. The idea is not in any political manual. It doesn't find utterance in either political party's platform. Suffering for others is based on a religious commitment that is beyond language, political strategy, argument, rhetoric, or deceptive words.

Who among us has approached this description? The American prophet, Martin Luther King Jr., may be the closest America has come to producing a suffering servant. Embracing Isaiah's original corporate meaning of the servant as the people of Israel raised up out of slavery to Egypt, the entire African American people—the oppressed ones of slavery and segregation and racism—may be our suffering servant. Are they our suffering servants? Does our salvation depend on their suffering? West says of the black prophetic tradition, "This tradition, which stretches back to Sojourner Truth and Frederick Douglass, has consistently named and damned the cruelty of imperialism and white supremacy."[82]

Many of the public speakers of our day are numbered with the cowards and the liars. They traffic in fear, violence, demagoguery, rage, shame, and lies. Whitman insists that how we talk, judge, and argue reveals the truth of who we are. It is democracy's job and the job of all the singers of democracy's song to cultivate the possibility that anyone of us or all of us collectively can be the suffering servants of God.

We are yet to unlock the secrets of democracy. It's great spirit "still sleeps, quite unawaken'd."[83] Our task, as singers, rhapsodes, poets, prophets, storytellers, orators, preachers is to awaken the song of democracy and place its tune on every lip so that all the world may dance in utter joy of freedom and liberation. Suffering for others represents democratic spirituality. Here our love for democracy enables us to surpass what Foucault calls "the art of living" and "the care of the self." Now, with a new politics—dare I say the politics of Jesus—we replace the politics of

---

82. Hedges, "Cornel West and the Fight to Save the Black Prophetic Tradition."

83. Whitman, *Democratic Vistas*, 960.

selfishness with caring for others, because to care for others is to be willing to die for the others—all the Others in the world. This resonates with Whitman's pleas for "kosmic democracy," the all as one. And what else could Jesus mean when he says, "If any want to become my followers, let them deny themselves and take up their cross and follow me.[84] And: "No one has greater love than this, to lay down one's life for one's friends."[85] Linger in the company of the suffering servant to note the required sacrifice: "Do nothing from selfish ambition or conceit, but in humility regard others as better than yourselves. Let each of you look not to your own interests, but to the interests of others."[86] In the Age of Trump these words seem like the talk of a crazy person, but they remain at the heart of democracy's future.

One doesn't embrace the suffering servant motif for its own sake. This experience is the means for the salvation of all others. The promise of liberation gives suffering servanthood its meaning. People embrace the suffering servant theme because they believe this will bring the most happiness, joy, tranquility, and liberation to the most people. This is soteriological and deeply religious. This is the essence of democracy. The lovers of democracy, put down whatever power they possess, reject the power they are offered, to serve the needs of the many.

Those willing to suffer for the common good experience a union with God's love that sets people free from pain, desire, and worry. It marks the end of living in fear and rage because it demonstrates that the world is enfolded by the presence of God. There is an interconnected "oneness." The result is an explosion of ethical behavior that multiplies empathy, compassion, sympathy, and love for all our fellow citizens and a sense of solidarity with one another. In the moment of recognizing that we are part of God's eternal purposes we become one with Joseph, who setting aside the privileges of Pharaoh, spoke to his estranged brothers, in his native tongue. "Then Joseph could no longer control himself before all those who stood by him, and he cried out, 'Send everyone away from me.' So no one stayed with him when Joseph made himself known to his brothers. And he wept so loudly that the Egyptians heard it, and the household of Pharaoh heard it. Joseph said to his brothers, 'I am Joseph.'"[87]

---

84. Mark 8:34.
85. John 15:13.
86. Phil 2:3–4.
87. Gen 45:1–4.

Isaiah's song gives us a map of how an individual might attain to suffering servanthood. I understand this as a spiritual and rhetorical experience, a spiritual exercise and an art of living. The suffering servant disengages from egocentric patterns and econocentric goals and produces the experience of empathy. Here is where goodness enters the arena. "What we assume to be the point of life—to be good—shapes our hopes, our dreams, our fears, and our habits. Though certain theorists of 'public reason' attempt to disallow it, talk of the good is foundational to democratic politics."[88]

Until we once again focus on what is good, we will continue to do business with evil. The good demands sacrifice, suffering, love. The good demands sacrifice of time, money, energy and at times, life itself. Take this orientation to democracy away, and we wander in the wilderness with no way out. In *Phaedrus* Plato argues that it is essential to produce the good when truth alone is not enough to persuade.[89] Reason can only take us so far. The truth alone does not have the power to set us free. This is even more urgent in our postmodern, post-truth, alternative-truth society.

Whitman imagines a universal community without division, a solidarity that does not exclude, an us without a them. Such a vision finds little expression in our political drama. Instead of addressing one another personally, we attack one another impersonally. Whether it's a Judiciary Committee interrogating a Supreme Court nominee or a member of Congress attacking Black Lives Matter, there's no conversation. Historian David Blight asks,

> Who on the left will volunteer to be part of a delegation to go discuss the fate of democracy with Mitch McConnell, Kevin McCarthy or the foghorns of Fox News? Who on the right will come to a symposium with 10 of the finest writers on democracy, its history and its philosophy, and help create a blueprint for American renewal? As a culture we are not in the mood for such reason and comity; we are in a fight, and it needs to happen in politics. Otherwise it may be 1861 again in some very new form. Unfortunately, it is likely to take events even more shocking than 6 January to move our political culture through and beyond our current crisis.[90]

---

88. Engels, "Kosmic Rhetoric," 60.
89. Weaver, *Ethics of Rhetoric*, 15, 18.
90. Blight, "Trump Has Birthed a New 'Lost Cause' Myth."

Whitman conceives of a community that involves everyone, a community without walls. The experience of being one united people—an actual "united" States of America is the ground on which we can stand together as we argue, judge, evaluate, deliberate, discern, and draw the lines that make politics work. In a thriving democracy, everyone knows that politics is the conversation that people have to discover the goods we have in common. This contrasts with our current obsession with placating the base (an intended double meaning as in partisans on one side and base as in base or lower-grade rhetoric designed for emotional proofs only). The ascendant "base" rhetoric led by the lead "Trump-et" in the orchestra is not helping democracy but hurting it.

Conclusion

GOOD AND EVIL IN Proverbs, Psalms, and the Song of Solomon have been traced. Good and evil in rhetoric has been explored—the singers of democracy and Hitler. The good has been celebrated. Democracy has been defended.

The Song of Solomon, the songs of Isaiah, Whitman, West, Blight, Socrates, Glaude, and all the poets of democracy sing of the ties that bind people together. This is not about blood, tradition, or ancestry. This is not engaged in privilege, standing, or wealth. None are excluded. "Not until the sun excludes you do I exclude you."[1] There's a dignity and decorum here that flings open the doors, knocks down all the walls, and makes all into a cosmic one. This is democracy's last great hope.

Progressives struggle with producing emotional arguments that have the same power and impact of the emotion-laden proofs of conservatives. George Lakoff argues that conservatives have won the communication wars as a result. Progressives are almost allergic to emotion. They still think people are convinced by facts. If progressives could find an emotional voice, a lilting song that touches the heart, there's a chance for democracy. Lakoff argues that the most needed emotion for progressives is empathy.[2]

Jeremy David Engels suggests that the emotion needed is "gratefulness."[3] In his book *The Art of Gratitude*, Engels argues that the reciprocal exchange of gifts and debts implied by (fake) gratitude is the death of democracy, for it transforms gratitude into an economic transaction that nurtures anger and resentment in those who are put in debt. Gratefulness is the emotional experience of being moved by thanksgiving

1. Whitman, "To a Common Prostitute," loc. 792.
2. Lakoff, *Political Mind*, 47.
3. Engels, *Art of Gratitude*, 39–40.

for existence. If progressives will add gratefulness to empathy, the foundation of a solid moral vision, an argument from pathos and ethos is thus prepared. Imagine gratefulness as the response to rage, anger, resentment, and violence and a door opens to new possibilities.

"The world does not look the same to someone who is angry and someone who is grateful."[4] Cultivating a different set of emotions offers us a new direction. This is about feelings. Our feelings are embodied. As Sara Ahmed makes clear, feelings are somatic and bodily. As we are affected by our five senses, we feel—contemporary scholars designate these feelings as "affect." This is what Ahmed calls "feminist cultural studies of emotion and affect, and Schaefer calls "the "phenomenological strain" of affect theory.[5]

Progressives, equipped with a moral vision, a deep ethos, also need to embrace the third of Aristotle's persuasive tropes: Pathos. Lawrence Grossberg writes that affect "encompasses a variety of ways in which we 'feel' the world in our experience, including moods, emotions, maps of what matters and of what one cares about, pleasures and desires, passions, sentiments, etc."[6] If we marshal affects along a different axis from Trump's political perversion, we set the stage for a more positive emotional commitment to democracy. Gunn suggests Trump's *perversion*—his contagious obsession with flouting conventions and transgressing taboos—is the motor that drives his rhetorical success. Gunn elaborates that Donald Trump seems to know that the offensive things he says and does are offensive, but he says and does them anyway. Trump knew his suggestion that Mitt Romney would have provided oral sex for his endorsement in 2012 was outrageous, but he said it anyway.[17] Trump knew bragging about the size of his penis during a Republican primary debate was juvenile, but he did it anyway.[18] Given the often sadistic (and sexual) character of Trump's rhetoric, it is more typical of *perversion*, a rhetoric typified by a deliberate and knowing deviation from assumed "norms." Trump's speech is best understood a textbook example of perverse rhetoric.[7]

Progressives, like General Motors trying to surpass Tesla in the production of electric cars, have to find an emotional message that doesn't desert ethos and logos. While Trump has managed to pleasurize the worst

4. Engels, "Kosmic Rhetoric," 64.
5. Ahmed, *Promise of Happiness*, 13; Schaefer, *Religious Affects*, 37.
6. Grossberg, *Under the Cover of Chaos*, 11.
7. Gunn, *Political Perversion*, 171.

habits of people, progressives have to reconnect with the most virtuous habits of people. Instead of producing shame, anxiety, narcissism, and alienation, progressives need a map for the opposite affects.

Instead of such negative, debilitating, hurtful affects, political life can be reframed as an experience of gratefulness. Life is good, in other words, and the woods are not full of monsters. As long as people are alive, they need not live in fear, for they can find meaning and purpose of living. No one is out to get them. The anchor institutions of democracy can be trusted. The system is not rigged.

Perhaps Whitman's full-throated songs of democracy should now fill our lungs, our minds, our hearts, indeed our bodies: "It seems to me that everything in the light and air ought to be happy; Whoever is not in his coffin and the dark grave, let him know he has enough. Gratefulness is an emotion of contentment . . . I exist as I am, that is enough, If no other in the world be aware I sit content, And if each and all be aware I sit content."[8]

In an African American Baptist church, a sister would now shout, "Sing it brother!" Whitman unleashes the second verse: "We thought our Union grand and our Constitution grand; I do not say that they are not grand and good—for they are, I am this day just as much in love with them as you, But I am eternally in love with you and with all my fellows upon the earth."[9]

On the third verse, the entire congregation rises as one to sing together Whitman's song: "I speak the pass-word primeval, I give the sign of democracy, By God! I will accept nothing which all cannot have their counterpart of on the same terms."[10]

Democracy is a politics of interaction, engagement, and relationship building. The impact of democracy as a good depends on people having more empathy, compassion, love, mutualism, mindfulness, and gratefulness. They will become accustomed to speaking to people as though they are divine and worthy of dignity. The conservative and evangelical attempt to demonize all Democrats is an anti-democratic rhetoric. We need to offer people reasons to deliberate rather than demonize.

8. Whitman, "Song of Myself," 211.
9. Whitman, *Leaves of Grass*, 113.
10. Whitman, "Song of Myself," 211.

"Democracy demands that people talk, laugh, argue, sing, and deliberate not only with their friends but also with strangers."[11]

My acceptance of Blight's challenge to "scream, sing, and fight" doesn't end here. In many ways it has only begun. I am determined to do everything possible to keep the contest and natural dissent of democracy from spiraling out of control. There's a tension here because I am still aware that I have pushed aside boundaries by declaring Donald Trump the embodiment of evil. I have tried to view him as merely mistaken, wrong, or even misguided, but that picture refuses to form in my mind.

I have reserved a space for dissent and offer this work as my ultimate dissent from the Age of Trump. There are plenty of reasons to meet my argument with a dose of skepticism and even accusations that I have gone too far, but I believe there is a danger to democracy in the character and rhetoric of Donald Trump that requires me to sound multiple alarms. The work of Robert L. Ivie on dissent in democracy has chastened me as I neared the completion of my work. Ivie argues that there is still a middle space in our political house that contains both opposition and agreement. He holds out the hope that there are still bridges to "generate constructive dialogue and deliberation."[12] Here the goal is a more equalitarian politics where consensus and dissent hold one another accountable. There is much to commend Ivie's approach.

Not taking that road was a decision made when I realized that Trump and the evangelicals deliberately demolished the middle space of deliberation with the overriding trope that "life is war." As Ivie puts it, "Dissent, in this context, is another word for strife. Like protest, it signals a schism—the estrangement of a house divided against itself. The vocabulary of war is readily applied to dissent of this kind, which is routinely framed . . . as contentious politics that is ridiculous, bizarre, and so dangerously out of step with the mainstream of society as not to warrant serious consideration of its radical ideas."[13]

My conclusion is that Donald Trump invaded democracy with a gang of religious zealots as surely as Putin and Russia invaded Ukraine. The invasion has placed democracy in a state of precarity. The response to the evil thus produced is not a debate about a middle space. It is a fight to save democracy. I was more persuaded by the words of historian David

11. Engels, "Kosmic Rhetoric," 67.
12. Ivie, "Enabling Democratic Dissent," 49.
13. Ivie, "Enabling Democratic Dissent," 47.

Blight: "Trumpism unleashed on 6 January, and every day before and since over a five-year period, a crusade to slowly poison the American democratic experiment with a movement to overturn decades of pluralism, increased racial and gender equality, and scientific knowledge. To what end? Establishing a hopeless white utopia for the rich and the aggrieved."[14] To this attempt at destroying democracy I became and remain a dissident in full-orbed dissent of Trump and his gangsters.

I have screamed: "This is evil." I have sung: "This is the good." Now, I will fight. I will not wield the sword like Simon Peter, the clumsy fisherman thinking he was a Roman warrior. I will fight nonviolently but fiercely. Blight says, "We are in a fight, and it needs to happen in politics."[15] I agree but I believe the battlefield must be expanded to a multitude of sites of dissent, communities, and ways of dissent that are contingent, unpredictable, but necessary. Among these sites, there must be the pulpits of the progressive churches.

I speak now as the pastor of a progressive congregation, as a Christian dissident. As a dissident in the Age of Trump, I end with a dissent offered on behalf of democracy. If possible, I would bring an entire orchestra with trumpet solos to blast out the dissent. Here, I believe I stand in solid democratic soil. "Dissent is a key word in the vocabulary of a democratic people. A healthy democracy encourages the rhetorical act of dissent as a right of free speech and an antidote to political repression. Dissent is the balancing point between stability and change, cleavage and consensus, politics and revolution, life and decay. It should be tolerated, not censured by authorities, punished by law, or otherwise suppressed." "When dissent is suppressed, especially in times of crisis, democracy itself is lost and the people are turned against themselves."[16]

Ivie argues that dissenters operate as tricksters by violating the norms and rules of decorum and deliberation to achieve their goals. Trump, in this sense, is the great trickster as he promises people dignity, power, and a greater America, but delivers the same old crony capitalism. A consensus, decades in the making, developed in ways that allowed Trump's dissenting voice to emerge. I am aware that I embraced the role of trickster in the attempt to expose what I consider Trump's evil. The norms, expectations, and restriction of rhetorical scholarship have been

---

14. Blight, "Trump Has Birthed a New 'Lost Cause' Myth."
15. Blight, "Trump Has Birthed a New 'Lost Cause' Myth."
16. Ivie, "Enabling Democratic Dissent," 46.

violated in certain ways by me. Since preachers are more prone to exaggeration than rhetorical scholars, perhaps you should blame the preacher in me that has made this audacious argument from Scripture, rhetoric, philosophy, and poetry.

The questions that linger for me are: Is there still a middle space of public life? Is there a possibility of consensus and dissent in the same arena? Dissent, in Ivie's proposal, "is understood as a hedge against fascism and a mode of argumentation for countering the discourse of endless war, which masquerades as a defense of democracy and represents the enemy as the embodiment of evil. Democracy exists only in the presence of dissent."[17] I am judged by Ivie's remarks because I have identified Donald Trump as the embodiment of evil. I am a proponent of dissent, in the senses proposed by Ivie, but first, Trump, the cancer on the body of democracy, must be removed. He is the right eye that offends the body politic, the right hand that offends democracy. Jesus insists, "If your right eye causes you to sin, tear it out and throw it away; it is better for you to lose one of your members than for your whole body to be thrown into hell. And if your right hand causes you to sin, cut it off and throw it away; it is better for you to lose one of your members than for your whole body to go into hell."[18] Trump threatens to send democracy to hell.

Having exorcised the demonic that threatens democracy, I now wish only to sing her praises. I stand on the shoulders of others who have imagined the same goal. Dale Smith investigates poetry as a rhetorical vehicle of dissent for shaping public consciousness.[19] Walter Brueggemann models the poet as the best way for preachers to proclaim the countercultural message of the gospel. "American public culture requires the social possibilities expressed through civil activism and dissent."[20] West says that the democratic tradition has been promoted by hip hop.[21] He insists that such poetry resides in the early work of hip hop poets. He says, "The prophetic and poetic voices of hip hop, like Chuck D or KRS-One, have built on the this [democratic] tradition, speaking more powerfully than any politicians or preachers of our day have been willing to do about

---

17. Ivie, "Enabling Democratic Dissent," 49.
18. Matt 5:29–30.
19. Smith, *Poets Beyond the Barricade*.
20. Brueggemann, *Finally Comes the Poet*.
21. West, *Democracy Matters*, 178.

the hypocrisies of both black and whites in American culture."[22] West points to Toni Morrison as the writer who offers "the most sophisticated exploration of this black enactment of dialogue, resistance, and hope ... The blues and jazz heritage speaks most profoundly in her literary works. She is the towering democratic artist and intellectual artist of our time. Texts embody and enact forms of deep democratic energies unparalleled in America's struggle with the dark side of its democracy."[23] Otis Moss III would respond that the poetry required for dissent is found in "blue note preaching."[24]

Morrison, speaking of the black community, explains: "Those people could not live without value. They had prices, but no value in the white world, so they made their own, and they decided what was valuable. It was usually eleemosynary [charitable], usually something they were doing for somebody else. Nobody in the novel, no adult black person, survives by self-regard, narcissism, selfishness. They took the sense of community for granted. It never occurred to them they could live outside of it."[25]

"The poet's role is not to oppose evil but to imagine it."[26] I have opposed and imagined. This has been a work of poetic and rhetorical imagination. Embedded in the overall fabric of the work is a biblical imagination that insists that the evil can be named, identified, and rebuked; the good can be named, identified, and lived.

That makes me a poet-dissident. Apply the term to all the people determined to live within the ethos of the good and within the truth. I have decided, as far as it lies within me, to reject what is evil and false in life and our democracy, those aspects of living with and within lies, of embracing and endorsing a power that is built on lies. In the place of the lies and the evil it embodies, I have chosen the good.

I am content at this juncture to be considered mad. After all, there are kinds of madness which are forms of inspiration. I'm neither a poet nor a prophet, but in the spirit of Amos and Whitman, I possess a kind of madness that cannot be silent in the face of the huge lies of our time. This aligns with the concept of "folly"—the foolishness that becomes the wisdom of God. "Mere sanity, which is of human origin, is inferior to that

---

22. West, *Democracy Matters*, 84.
23. West, *Democracy Matters*, 95.
24. Moss, *Blue Note Preaching*, 84, 93.
25. Quoted in West, *Democracy Matters*, 95.
26. Duncan, *Letters of Robert Duncan and Denise Levertov*, 669.

madness which is inspired by the gods and which is a condition for the highest kind of achievement."[27]

Part of my dissent is an attempt to reclaim the middle space of democratic deliberation by excising the evil that Trump embodies. Space has to be made for everyone even in the fiercest of disagreements. No one can be excluded. Here we can learn from Whitman who rejected none and permitted all—runaway slaves, prostitutes, farmers, mothers, children, dock workers, common workers, the deformed and sick, the poor and destitute—all with a place at the table. Here we can live out the vision of Jesus' promised "feast of enemies." At the Last Supper, Jesus and the twelve disciples gathered for a meal that intended to show that with all the party divisions among the twelve, the celebration of the messianic banquet would truly be a genuine feast of enemies. Here lies the religious thematic center of my work: the only politics that can save us now are the politics of Jesus—the politics of selfless, sacrificing, forgiving, reconciling good. Setting aside all philosophical and rhetorical misgivings, in Jesus we are shown and given the good that has the power to transform the worst of evil.

Like Whitman, we must gather the high and the low, rich with poor, men with women, gays with straights, black with white, North with South, East with West, urban with rural. I can think of no better way to place the final period than poetry from Whitman: "This is the meal pleasantly set . . . This is the meat and drink for natural hunger, It is for the wicked just the same as the righteous . . . I make appointments with all, I will not have a single person slighted or left away, The keptwoman and sponger and thief are hereby invited . . . The heavy lipped slave is invited . . . The venerealee is invited. There shall be no difference between them and the rest."[28] Amen.

---

27. Weaver, *Language Is Sermonic*, 68.
28. Whitman, *Leaves of Grass* (1855), 44.

Bibliography

Achter, Paul J. "Great Television: Trump and the Shadow Archetype." In *Faking the News: What Rhetoric Can Teach Us About Donald J. Trump*, edited by Ryan Skinnell, 115–29. Exeter: Imprint Academic, 2018.
Ahmed, Sara. *The Cultural Politics of Emotion*. New York: Routledge, 2013.
———. *The Promise of Happiness*. Durham, NC: Duke University Press, 2010.
Amatulli, Jennad. "Trump Says He's the Least Racist Person in this Room at Final Presidential Debate." *HuffPost*, October 22, 2020. https://www.huffpost.com/entry/trump-kristen-welker-least-racist_n_5f923e9dc5b686eaaa0fb460.
Anderson, Kevin. "Avoiding Dangerous Climate Change Demands De-Growth Strategies from Wealthier Nations." *kevinanderson.info*, November 25, 2013. https://kevinanderson.info/blog/avoding-dangerous-climate-change-demands-de-growth-strategies-from-wealthier-nations/.
Andrejevic, Mark. "The Jouissance of Trump." *Television & New Media* 17 (2016) 651–55.
Arendt, Hannah. *Eichmann in Jerusalem*. New York: Viking, 1964.
Ash, Timothy Garton. *The Uses of Adversity: Essays on the Fate of Central Europe*. New York: Random House, 1989.
Augustine. *Confessions and Enchiridion*, edited by Albert Cook Outler. Library of Christian Classics. Louisville: Westminster John Knox, 2006.
Aune, James Arnt. "Burke's Late Blooming: Trope, Defense, and Rhetoric." *Quarterly Journal of Speech* 69 (1983) 328–40.
Badiou, Alain. *Saint Paul: The Foundation of Universalism*. Translated by Ray Brassier. Stanford, CA: Stanford University Press, 2003.
Baker, Jean. "'Let's Talk Sense to the American People': Adlai Stevenson's Memorable 1952 Acceptance Speech." *History News Network*, 2008. https://historynewsnetwork.org/article/53682#:~:text=The%20shining%20exception%20remains%20Adlai%20Stevenson%E2%80%99s%20superb%20acceptance,before%20the%20speech%2C%20but%20after%20it%20they%20did.
Bakhtin, Mikhail. *Rabelais and His World*. Translated by Helene Iswolsky. Bloomington: Indiana University Press, 1984.
Bates, Katherine Lee. "America the Beautiful." *Hymns for the Living Church*. Carol Stream, IL: Hope, 1974. https://genius.com/Katharine-lee-bates-america-the-beautiful-lyrics.
Bawden, Tom. "Scientists '95 per cent certain' that climate change is man-made." *Independent*, August 21, 2013. https://www.independent.co.uk/climate-change/

news/scientists-95-per-cent-certain-that-climate-change-is-manmade-8778806.html.
Benen, Steven. "Even now, Trump continues to praise Putin's 'intelligence.'" *MSNBC*, April 4, 2022. https://www.msnbc.com/rachel-maddow-show/maddowblog/even-now-trump-continues-praise-putins-intelligence-rcna22866.
Berlant, Lauren. "Trump, or Political Emotions." *The New Inquiry*, August 5, 2016. https://thenewinquiry.com/trump-or-political-emotions/.
Betts, Doris. "This Is the Only Time I'll Tell It." In *The Christ-Haunted Landscape: Faith and Doubt in Southern Literature*, edited by Susan Ketchin, 232–37. Kindle ed. Jackson: University Press of Mississippi, 1994.
Beutler, Brian. "Why the Media Is Botching the Election." *New Republic*, September 13, 2016. https://newrepublic.com/article/136730/media-botching-election.
Black, Edwin. *Rhetorical Questions: Studies of Public Discourse*. Chicago: University of Chicago Press, 1992.
Blight, David. "Trump Has Birthed a New 'Lost Cause' Myth. We Must Fight It." *The Guardian*, January 8, 2022. https://www.theguardian.com/commentisfree/2022/jan/08/trump-has-birthed-a-dangerous-new-lost-cause-myth-we-must-fight-it.
Blumberg, Antonia. "Trump Saw A Military Parade In France And Now He Wants One Of His Very Own." *HuffPost*, February 6, 2018. https://www.huffpost.com/entry/trump-military-parade_n_5a7a3d9ae4b0d0ef3c0a716c.
Booth, Wayne. *The Rhetoric of Fiction*. Chicago: The University of Chicago Press, 1983.
Bort, Ryan. "Rep. Mo Brooks on Incendiary Jan. 6th Speech: Trump Made Me Do It," *Yahoo!News*, July 6, 2021. https://www.yahoo.com/entertainment/rep-mo-brooks-incendiary-jan-213657188.html.
Brague, Rémi. *The Wisdom of the World*. Chicago: University of Chicago Press, 2020.
Brewer, Edward. C. *Religious Rhetoric: Dividing a Nation or Building Community*. Lanham, MD: Lexington, 2019.
Brewer, Edward C., and Chrys Egan. "Clear and Present Danger Standard 100th Anniversary: Examining Donald J. Trump's 'Presidential' Rhetoric as a Clear and Present Danger." *First Amendment Studies* 55, no. 1. (2021) 44–58.
Britzky, Haley. "Everything Trump Says He Knows 'more about than anybody.'" *Axios*, January 5, 2019. https://www.axios.com/everything-trump-says-he-knows-more-about-than-anybody-b278b592-cff0-47dc-a75f-5767f42bcf1e.html.
Brown, Richard Harvey. *Society as Text: Essays on Rhetoric, Reason, and Reality*. Chicago: University of Chicago Press, 1987.
Brueggemann, Walter. *Finally Comes the Poet: Daring Speech for Proclamation*. Minneapolis: Fortress, 1989.
———. *Truth Speaks to Power: The Countercultural Nature of Scripture*. Louisville: Westminster John Knox, 2013.
Burke, Kenneth. "The Rhetoric of Hitler's 'Battle.'" *The Southern Review* 5 (1939) 1–21.
———. *A Rhetoric of Motives*. Oakland: University of California Press, 1969.
———. *The Rhetoric of Religion: Studies in Logology*. Vol. 188. Berkeley: University of California Press, 1970.
Burns, James MacGregor. *The Definitive FDR: Roosevelt: The Lion and the Fox (1882–1940) and Roosevelt: The Soldier of Freedom (1940–1945)*. Kindle ed. New York: Open Road Media, 2017.
Burnside, Tina, Zoe Sottile, and Nicole Chavez. "Florida rejects 41% of new math textbooks, citing critical race theory among its reasons." CNN, April 19, 2022.

BIBLIOGRAPHY

Business Insider. "Donald Trump's Ex-wife once Said Trump Kept a Book of Hitler's Speeches by His Bed." *Business Insider*, September 1, 2015. https://www.businessinsider.com/donald-trumps-ex-wife-once-said-he-kept-a-book-of-hitlers-speeches-by-his-bed-2015-8.

Butler, Judith. *Frames of War: When is Life Grievable?* New York: Verso, 2009.

Calvert, Clay. "Hate Speech and Its Harms: A Communication Theory Perspective." *Journal of Communication* (1997) 4–19.

Campbell, Will D. *Soul Among Lions: Musings of a Bootleg Preacher*. Louisville: Westminster John Knox, 1999.

Canney, Maurice A. "The Hebrew 'Melis.'" *American Journal of Semitic Languages*, vol. 40 (1923) 135–37.

Carlson, A. Cheree. "Gandhi and the Comic Frame: Ad Bellum Purificandum." *Quarterly Journal of Speech* 72 (November 1986) 446–55.

Cathey, Libby, and Meghan Keneally. "A Look Back at Trump Comments Perceived by Some as Inciting Violence." ABC News (go.com), May 30, 2020. https://abcnews.go.com/Politics/back-trump-comments-perceived-encouraging-violence/story?id=48415766.

Center for Disease Control and Prevention. "Vision Loss: A Public Health Problem. https://www.cdc.gov/visionhealth/basic_information/vision_loss.htm.

Chesterton, G. K. *Orthodoxy*. In *The Chesterton Reader: 21 Works in One Volume*. Kindle ed. London: Halcyon, 2009.

Chirindo, Kundai. "Precarious Publics." *Quarterly Journal of Speech* 107, no. 4 (2021) 430–34.

Chouraqui, Andre. "Introduction to the Psalms." *Liturgy O.C.S.O. Journal of Gethsemani Abbey*, vol. 13, no. 1 (1979) 3–29. https://cdm16259.contentdm.oclc.org/digital/collection/p15032coll3/id/56/rec/36.

Chua, Amy. *Political Tribes: Group Instinct and the Fate of Nations*. New York: Penguin, 2018.

Churchill, Winston S. *Blood, Toil, Tears, and Sweat*. Quoted in Steven Gregg Wittenberg, "Churchill Appraises Hitler: 1930–1939," unpublished thesis, College of Liberal Arts and Sciences University of Illinois Urbana, Illinois, 1992.

———. "We Take Our Stand for Freedom." House of Commons, London, October 5, 1938.

Coates, Ta-Nehisi. "The First White President." *The Atlantic* 320, no. 3 (2017) 74–87. https://www.theatlantic.com/magazine/archive/2017/10/the-first-white-president-ta-nehisi-coates/537909/.

Cone, James. *The Cross and the Lynching Tree*. Ossining, NY: Orbis, 2011.

Connor, Steven. *Dumbstruck: A Cultural History of Ventriloquism*. New York: Oxford University Press, 2000.

Craddock, Fred B. *The Cherry Log Sermons*. Louisville: Westminster John Knox, 2001.

Davis, Charles R. "Judge Calls Donald Trump a 'Charlatan' and Says 'Democracy Is in Trouble' after Trial of January 6 Defendant." *Business Insider*, April 14, 2022. https://www.msn.com/en-us/news/politics/judge-calls-donald-trump-a-charlatan-and-says-democracy-is-in-trouble-after-trial-of-january-6-defendant/ar-AAWez5d.

Davis, Ellen F., and Richard B. Hays, eds. *The Art of Reading Scripture*. Grand Rapids: Eerdmans, 2003.

Democracy Now! "Donald Trump Has Sued or Been Sued More Than 4,000 Times Since 1970." https://www.democracynow.org/2016/7/13/headlines/donald_trump_has_

sued_or_been_sued_3_500_times_since_1970#:~:text=According%20to%20 a%20USA%20Today%20investigation%2C%20Donald%20Trump,alleges%20 that%20Trump%20University%20has%20defrauded%20its%20students.

Desai, M. "Detractors Say that Global Warming Is Globaloney or Globalegook." In *Globalization, Growth and Sustainability*, edited by S. D. Gupta and N. K. Choudhry. Recent Economic Thought Series, vol. 58. Boston: Springer, 1997. https://doi.org/10.1007/978-1-4165-6203-0_11.

Dewey, John, and Melvin L. Rogers. *The Public and its Problems: An Essay in Political Inquiry*. University Park, PA: Penn State Press, 2012.

Dickerson, John. "Interview with Donald Trump." *CBS Face the Nation*, June 5, 2016. http://www.cbsnews.com/news/donald-trump-its-possible-muslim-judge-would-treat-me-unfairly.

Dow, Bonnie J. "Taking Trump Seriously: Persona and Presidential Politics in 2016." *Women's Studies in Communication* 40, no. 2 (2017) 136–39.

Duffy, Eamon. *The Stripping of the Altars: Traditional Religion in England, c. 1400–c. 1580*. New Haven: Yale University Press, 2005.

Duncan, Hugh Dalziel. "A Sociological Model of Social Interaction as Determined by Communication." *Critical Responses to Kenneth Burke, 1924–1966* (1924) 350–57.

Duncan, Robert Edward, Robert J. Bertholf, and Albert Gelpi. *The Letters of Robert Duncan and Denise Levertov*. Redwood City, CA: Stanford University Press, 2004.

EconoTimes. "Donald Trump Attacks Judges following dismissal of voter fraud claims." December 1, 2020. https://www.econotimes.com/Donald-Trump-attacks-judges-following-dismissal-of-voter-fraud-claims-1597535.

Edwards, Breanna. "NC Gun Shop Billboard Targeting 'The Squad' To Be Taken Down." *Essence*, August 2, 2019. https://www.essence.com/new/cherokee-guns-gun-shop-billboard.

Edwards, David. "Donald Trump Jr. Tells Young Conservatives: Following the Peaceful Part of the Bible Has 'Gotten Us Nothing'". *Raw Story*, December 19, 2021. https://www.rawstory.com/turning-point-usa-and-donald-trump-jr/?utm_source=ground.news&utm_medium=referral.

Eksil, Betul, and Elizabeth A. Wood. "Right-Wing Populism as Gendered Performance: Janus-faced Masculinity in the Leadership of Vladimir Putin and Recep T. Erdogan." *Theory and Society* 48 no. 5 (2019) 733–51.

Engels, Jeremy David. *The Art of Gratitude*. Albany, NY: State University of New York Press, 2018.

———. "Kosmic Rhetoric: Reading Democracy Alongside Walt Whitman and the Bhagavad Gita." *Quarterly Journal of Speech* 105, no. 1 (2019) 68–97.

Evans, Gillian Rosemary. *Augustine on Evil*. New York: Cambridge University Press, 1990.

Farley, Robert. "Fact Check: Trumps' Comments on Women." *USA Today*, August 12, 2015.

Falwell, Jerry. Sermon. Media Matters Staff, "Falwell dismissed scientific evidence on global warming, evangelical efforts to address issue." March 14, 2006. https://www.mediamatters.org/jerry-falwell-dismissed-scientific-evidence-global-warming-evangelical-efforts-address.

Farrell, Thomas B. *The Norms of Rhetorical Culture*. New Haven: Yale University Press, 1993.

Faulkner, William. *Requiem for a Nun*. New York: Vintage, 2011.

Feffer, John. *Splinterlands*. Chicago: Haymarket, 2016.
Fischer, Norman. *Opening to You: Zen-Inspired Translations of the Psalms*. London: Penguin, 2003.
Foss, Karen. "The Logic of Folly in the Political Campaigns of Harvey Milk." In *Queer Words, Queer Images: Communication and the Construction of Homosexuality*, 7–29. New York: New York University Press, 1994.
Foucault, Michel. "From *The Order of Discourse*." In *The Rhetorical Tradition: Readings from Classical Times to the Present*, 2nd ed., translated by Ian McLeod, edited by Patricia Bizzell and Bruce Herzberg. Digital ed. Boston: Bedford/St. Martin's, 2001.
———. *The Hermeneutics of the Subject: Lectures at the Collège de France 1981–1982*. Vol. 9. New York: Macmillan, 2005.
———. *Subjectivity and Truth: Lectures at the College de France, 1980–1981*. Basel, Switzerland: Springer, 2017.
Frank, David A. "The Prophetic Voice and the Face of the Other in Barack Obama's 'A More Perfect Union' Address." *Rhetoric and Public Affairs* (2009) 167–94.
Frank, David A., and Mark Lawrence McPhail. "Barack Obama's Address to the 2004 Democratic National Convention: Trauma, Compromise, Consilience, and the (Im)possibility of Racial Reconciliation." *Rhetoric & Public Affairs* 8, no. 4 (2005) 265–86. https://www.jstor.org/stable/41940015.
Freking, Kevin. "Staff Says Trump Is Joking, He Maintains US Doing too Good a Job on Testing." *Sentinel*, June 23, 2020. https://sentinelcolorado.com/news/nation-world/covid19/staff-says-trump-is-joking-he-maintains-us-doing-too-good-a-job-on-testing/.
Gamble, Joelle. "Populism Ascendant." *The Nation*, May 4, 2017. https://www.thenation.com/article/what-will-kill-neoliberalism/.
Gerson, Michael. "Trump's Harrisburg speech the most hate-filled speech in modern history." *PA Patriot News*, May 2, 2017. https://www.pennlive.com/opinion/2017/05/trumps_100th_day_speech_in_har.html.
Gibbon, Peter. "Martin Seligman and the Rise of Positive Psychology." *Humanities* 41 no. 3 (Summer 2020). https://www.neh.gov/article/martin-seligman-and-rise-positive-psychology.
Gilbert, Christopher J. "The Diapered Donald: Comic Infantilizations of a US American President." *Quarterly Journal of Speech* 107 no. 3 (2021) 328–53.
Gilbert, Martin. *Churchill: A Life*. New York: Rosetta, 2014.
Gilmore, Scott. "The Definitive List of Every Person Donald Trump Has Called a Loser." *Maclean's*, July 2015. https://www.macleans.ca/news/world/the-definitive-list-of-every-person-donald-trump-has-called-a-loser/.
Glaude, Eddie S., Jr. *Democracy in Black: How Race Still Enslaves the American Soul*. New York: Crown, 2017.
Golden, James L. *The Rhetoric of Western Thought: From the Mediterranean World to the Global Setting*. Dubuque, IA: Kendall Hunt, 2003.
Grassi, Ernesto. *Rhetoric as Philosophy: The Humanist Tradition*. Carbondale: Southern Illinois University Press, 2000.
Green House Think Tank. "Facing Up to Climate Reality." June 3, 2019. https://greenhousethinktank.org/tag/facing-up-to-climate-reality/.
Gregorian, Dareh. "Trump blasts McConnell as a 'hack' who lacks 'political insight.'" *NBC News*, February 16, 2021. https://www.nbcnews.com/politics/donald-trump/trump-blasts-mcconnell-hack-who-lacks-political-insight-n1258051.

Griffiths, Paul J. *Intellectual Appetite: A Theological Grammar.* Washington, DC: Catholic University of America Press, 2009.

Grossberg, Lawrence. *Under the Cover of Chaos: Trump and the Battle for the American Right.* London: Pluto, 2018.

Groundwater, Evin. "Review of: *Apocalypse Man: The Death Drive and the Rhetoric of White Masculine Victimhood.*" *Quarterly Journal of Speech* 107 no. 3 (2021) 365–68.

Gunn, Joshua. "Donald Trump's Perverse Political Rhetoric." In *Faking the News: What Rhetoric Can Teach Us About Donald J. Trump,* edited by Ryan Skinnell, 168–80. Exeter: Imprint Academic, 2018.

———. *Political Perversion.* Chicago: University of Chicago Press, 2020.

Haidt, Jonathan, and Tobias Rose-Stockwell. "The Dark Psychology of Social Networks." *The Atlantic,* December 2019. https://www.theatlantic.com/magazine/archive/2019/12/social-media-democracy/600763/.

———. "Why the Past 10 Years of American Life Have Been Uniquely Stupid." *The Atlantic,* April 11, 2022. https://www.theatlantic.com/magazine/archive/2022/05/social-media-democracy-trust-babel/629369/.

Hamer, Fannie Lou. "Testimony Before the Credentials Committee by Fannie Lou Hamer: Say It Plain." www.publicradio.org. https://americanradioworks.publicradio.org/features/sayitplain/flhamer.html.

Hannah, Barry. "Christ in the Room." *Oxford American* 48 Winter (2005) 74–75.

Hart, David Bentley. *The Doors of the Sea: Where Was God in the Tsunami?* Grand Rapids: Eerdmans, 2005.

Hart, Roderick P. *Trump and Us: What He Says and Why People Listen.* Cambridge: Cambridge University Press, 2020.

Hauerwas, Stanley. *In Good Company: The Church as Polis.* Notre Dame: University of Notre Dame Press, 1995.

———. *Unleashing the Scripture: Freeing the Bible from Captivity to America.* Nashville: Abingdon, 1998.

———. *Working with Words: On Learning to Speak Christian.* Eugene, OR: Cascade, 2011.

Hauerwas, Stanley, and Romand Coles. *Christianity, Democracy, and the Radical Ordinary: Conversations between a Radical Democrat and a Christian.* Eugene, OR: Cascade, 2008.

Havel, Vaclav. "Address by His Excellency Vaclav Havel, President of the Czechoslovak Socialist Republic." *Congressional Record* H392–95.

———. *Disturbing the Peace.* Translated by Paul Wilson. New York: Knopf, 1990.

———. "Message to the International Conference on Anti-Semitism in Post-totalitarian Europe." *The New York Times,* 1992, A15.

———. "On Kafka: An Address at the Hebrew University in Jerusalem." *The New York Review of Books,* April 26, 1990, 19.

———. "Politics, Morals, and Civility." In *Summer Meditations,* translated by Paul Wilson. New York: Knopf, 1992. file:///C:/Users/rwken/OneDrive/TFR-82-Politics-Morality-and-Civility%20Havel.pdf.

———. "The Postcommunist Nightmare." *The New York Review of Books,* May 27, 1993. https://www.nybooks.com/articles/1993/05.27/the-post-communist-nightmare/.

———. *The Power of the Powerless: Citizens Against the State in Central-Eastern Europe.* Oxfordshire: Routledge, 2009.

Hawhee, Debra. *Moving Bodies: Kenneth Burke at the Edges of Language*. Columbia: University of South Carolina Press, 2022.

Hearn, Alison. "Trump's 'Reality' Hustle." *Television and New Media* 17 (2016) 658.

Heath, Jim. "'It's Midnight in America'—Trump's Campaign Theme Is Dark and Destructive." *JimHeath.TV*, August 31, 2020. https://jimheath.tv/2020/08/its-midnight-in-america-trumps-campaign-theme-is-dark-destructive/.

Hedges, Chris. "Cornel West and the Fight to Save the Black Prophetic Tradition." *Truthout*, September 9, 2013. https://truthout.org/articles/cornel-west-and-the-fight-to-save-the-black-prophetic-tradition/#:~:text=%E2%80%9CThe%20black%20prophetic%20tradition%20has%20been%20the%20leaven-,Tubman%2C%20Sojourner%20Truth%2C%20Martin%20King%2C%20Fannie%20Lou%20Hamer.

Heer, Jeet. "Why Are Libertarians Mostly Dudes?" *The New Republic*, June 5, 2015. https://newrepublic.com/article/121974/cnn-poll-rand-paul-not-popular-republican-women.

Heschel, Abraham Joshua. *God in Search of Man: A Philosophy of Judaism*. New York: Farrar, Straus and Giroux, 1976.

Heiber, Helmut, and David M. Glantz, eds. *Hitler and His Generals: Military Conferences 1942–1945*. New York: Enigma, 2013.

Hesford, Wendy S., Adela C. Licona, and Christa Teston. *Precarious Rhetorics*. Columbus: The Ohio State University Press, 2018.

Holling, Michelle A., and Dreama G. Moon. "20/20 in 2020? Refractive vision, 45, and white supremacy." *Quarterly Journal of Speech* 107, no. 4 (2021) 435–42.

Huebner, Chris K. *A Precarious Peace: Yoderian Explorations on Theology, Knowledge, and Identity*. Kindle ed. Windsor, Ontario: Herald, 2006.

Hunt, Everett Lee. *Plato and Aristotle on Rhetoric and Rhetoricians*. New York: The Century Company, 1925.

Hunt, Lynn. *Inventing Human Rights: A History*. New York: W. W. Norton & Company, 2007.

Hurston, Zora Neale. *Jonah's Gourd Vine*. New York: Harper Collins, 2009.

Ivie, Robert L. "Enabling Democratic Dissent." *Quarterly Journal of Speech* 101, no. 1 (February 2015) 46–59.

———. "Rhetorical Aftershocks of Trump's Ascendency: Salvation by Demolition and Deal Making." *Res Rhetorica* 2 (2017) 61–79.

———. "Trump's Unwitting Prophecy." *Rhetoric & Public Affairs* 20, no. 4 (2017) 707–18.

Katyal, Neil K., and Thomas P. Schmidt. "Trump Is Threatening to Subvert the Constitution." *The Atlantic*, April 2020. https://historynewsnetwork.org/article/53682#:~:text=The%20shining%20exception%20remains%20Adlai%20Stevenson%E2%80%99s%20superb%20acceptance,before%20the%20speech%2C%20but%20after%20it%20they%20did.d.

Kaufman, Amanda. "McConnell on Trump: 'He's Always Setting Up Somebody to Blame It On.'" *Yahoo!News*, April 13, 2022.

Kelly, Casey Ryan. *Apocalypse Man: The Death Drive and the Rhetoric of White Masculine Victimhood*. Columbus, OH: The Ohio State University Press, 2020.

———. "Whiteness, Repressive Victimhood, and the Foil of the Intolerant Left." *First Amendment Studies* 59–76.55:1, 59–76.

Kennedy, Rodney. *The Creative Power of Metaphor*. Lanham, MD: University Press of America, 1993.

———. *The Immaculate Mistake: How Evangelicals Gave Birth to Donald Trump*. Eugene, OR: Cascade, 2021.

Kerr, Andrew. "Michael Flynn Promotes Petition Calling on Trump To Suspend The Constitution And Declare Martial Law." *Daily Caller*, October 2, 2020. https://dailycaller.com/2020/12/02/michael-flynn-petition-trump-martial-law/.

Ketchin, Susan. *The Christ-Haunted Landscape: Faith and Doubt in Southern Fiction*. Oxford, MS: University Press of Mississippi, 1994.

Kilander, Gustaf. "Tucker Carlson Doubles Down on Ukraine, Calling Support 'The Largest Political Flashmob in American History.'" *The Independent*, March 16, 2022. https://www.yahoo.com/lifestyle/tucker-carlson-doubles-down-ukraine-155341046.html.

Kierkegaard, Søren. *The Journal of Kierkegaard*. Translated by Alexander Dru. New York: Harper and Row, 1958.

Kirk, Chris, et al. "230 Things Donald Trump Has Said and Done That Make Him Unfit to Be President." *Slate*, November 7, 2016. http://www.slate.com/articles/news_and_politics/cover_story/2016/07/donald_trump_is_unfit_to_be_president_here_are_141_reasons_why.html.

Koonz, Claudia. *The Nazi Conscience*. Cambridge, MA: Belknap, 2003.

Krawczyk Kathryn. "Giuliani calls for 'trial by combat' at D.C. rally." *Yahoo!News*, January 6, 2021. https://news.yahoo.com/giuliani-calls-trial-combat-d-180408746.html.

Krois, John Michael. "Comments on Professor Grassi's Paper." In *Vico and Contemporary Thought*, edited by Giorgia Tagliacozzo et al., 185–87. Atlantic Highlands, NJ: Humanities, 1976.

Kumar, Anugrah. "Huckabee Says ISIS Beheadings Greater Threat Than Climate Change." *HuffPost*, June 21, 2015. https://www.huffpost.com/entry/mike-huckabee-climate-change_n_7632030.

Kuruvilla, Carol. "Trump Struggles with Basic Christian Teaching At National Prayer Breakfast." *HuffPost*, February 6, 2020. https://www.huffpost.com/entry/trump-prayer-breakfast-love-your-enemies_n_5e3c2d3bc5b6b70886fb8954.

Lachmann, Suzanne. "Why I Think Donald Trump Is Unfit to Be President: Instances Where Trump's Perspective, Insight, and Judgment Appear Impaired." *Psychology Today*, March 10, 2017. https://www.psychologytoday.com/gb/blog/me-we/201703/why-i-think-donald-trump-is-unfit-be-president.

Lakoff, George. *Don't Think of an Elephant: Progressive Values and the Framing Wars—A Progressive Guide to Action*. White River Junction, VT: Chelsea Green, 2004.

———. *The Political Mind: A Cognitive Scientist's Guide to Your Brain and Its Politics*. London: Penguin, 2008.

Levina, Marina. "Whiteness and the Joys of Cruelty." *Communication and Critical/Cultural Studies* 15 no. 1 (2018) 73–78.

Levine, Dan. "Trump Administration Calls U.S. Judge's Asylum Ruling 'Absurd.'" *Reuters*, November 20, 2018. https://www.reuters.com/article/us-usa-immigration-court-idUSKCN1NP242.

Levitsky, Steven, and Daniel Ziblatt. *How Democracies Die: What History Reveals about our Future*. New York: Crown, 2018.

Lincoln, Abraham. "First Inaugural Address." https://www.nps.gov/liho/learn/historyculture/firstinaugural.htm.

Linge, Mary Kay. "Violence Erupts at Trump Rally as Thousands Protest Election in DC." *New York Post*, April 4, 2022. https://nypost.com/2022/04/04/madonnas-unsettling-pre-grammy-tiktok-sparks-fan-concern/.

Lutz, Eric. "Trump Saw His Generals As 'Pussies': They Saw Him As Completely Unfit." *Vanity Fair*, September 10, 2020. https://www.vanityfair.com/news/2020/09/trump-saw-his-generals-as-pussies-they-saw-him-as-completely-unfit.

MacIntyre Alasdair. "A Partial Response to My Critics." In *After MacIntyre: Essays on the Recent Work of Alasdair MacIntyre*, edited by John Horton and Susan Mendus, 283–304. Notre Dame, IN: University of Notre Dame Press, 1994.

Mahler, Jonathan. "CNN Had a Problem. Donald Trump Solved It." *New York Times*, April 4, 2017. https://www.nytimes.com/2017/04/ 04/magazine/cnn-had-a-problem-donald-trump-solved-it.html.

Marche, Stephen. "Celebrity Warfare: Image and Politics in the Age of Trump." *Los Angeles Review of Books*, May 23, 2017. https://lareviewofbooks.org/article/celebrity-warfare-image-politics-age-trump/.

Marney, Carlyle. "Fundaments of Competent Ministry." Unpublished paper.

Marsh, John. *In Walt We Trust: How a Queer Socialist Poet Can Save America from Itself*. New York: New York University Press, 2015.

Marshall, Josh. "Full Transcript of Trump's 'Both Sides' Charlottesville Presser." *Talking Points Memo*, August 15, 2017. https://talkingpointsmemo.com/edblog/full-transcript-of-trumps-both-sides-charlottesville-presser.

Martin, Dan Desai. "The Wall Was Never Meant to Be a Literal Thing." *The American Independent*, January 7, 2019. https://americanindependent.com/trump-aide-border-wall-not-supposed-to-be-real/.

McClendon, James Wm. *Systematic theology: Ethics*. Nashville: Abingdon, 1986.

McCarthy, Craig. "11 Controversial Things Donald Trump Said During His Presidential Announcement." *NJ.com*, June 16, 2015. https://www.nj.com/news/2015/06/11_interesting_things_donald_trump_said_during_his_presidential_announcement.html.

McDonald, Scott. "Trump Says He's 'The Most Honest Human Being God Has Ever Created.'" *Newsweek*, April 9, 2022. https://www.newsweek.com/trump-says-hes-most-honest-human-being-god-has-ever-created-1696687.

McElvaine, Robert S. *The Great Depression: America, 1929–1941*. Portland, OR: Broadway, 1993.

McKane, William. *Proverbs: A New Approach*. Philadelphia: Westminster, 1970.

Medhurst, Martin. "Trump Tics: Making Hyperbole Great Again." *SBSNews*, August 17, 2016. https://www.sbs.com.au/news/article/trump-tics-making-hyperbole-great-again/zn5wxks4x.

Mencken, H. L. "As H. L. Sees It." *The Evening Sun*, September 18, 1926, 7, Column 2, Baltimore, MD. (*Newspapers.com*.)

Mercieca, Jennifer. "Afterword: Trump as Anarchist and Sun King." In *Faking the News: What Rhetoric Can Teach Us about Donald J. Trump*, edited by Ryan Skinnell, 182–87. Exeter: Imprint Academic, 2018.

———. "Dangerous Demagogues and Weaponized Communication." *Rhetoric Society Quarterly* 49 no. 3 (2019) 264–79.

———. *Demagogue for President: The Rhetorical Genius of Donald Trump*. Kindle ed. College Station, TX: Texas A&M University Press, 2020.

———. "The Greatest Story Ever Told About Hyperbole, Humbug, and P. T. Barnum!" *Zocalo Public Square*, October 27, 2017. https://www.zocalopublicsquare.org/2017/10/27/greatest-story-ever-told-hyperbole-humbug-p-t-barnum/ideas/essay/.

———. "How Donald Trump Gets Away with Saying Things Other Candidates Can't." *Washington Post*, March 9, 2016. https://newrepublic.com/article/131294/donald-trump-gets-away-saying-things-candidates-cant.

Middle East Monitor. "Trump to Muslim Congresswomen: Go Back to Your Own Countries." https://www.middleeastmonitor.com/20190715-trump-to-muslim-congresswomen-go-back-to-your-own-countries/.

Miller, James. *Can Democracy Work? A Short History of a Radical Idea, from Ancient Athens to Our World*. New York: Simon and Schuster, 2018.

Miller, Zeke, and Jill Colvin. "'Remember this day forever!' Trump says after Capitol violence." *Boston.com*, January 6, 2021. https://www.boston.com/news/politics/2021/01/06/trump-quote-capitol-violence/.

Moscow Times. "No Putin, No Russia." October 23, 2014. https://themoscowtimes.com/articles/no-putin-no-russia-says-kremlin-deputy-chief-of-staff-40702.

Moss, Otis, III. *Blue Note Preaching in a Post-Soul World: Finding Hope in an Age of Despair*. Louisville: Westminster John Knox Press, 2015.

Nakayama, T. K., and J. N. Martin. *Whiteness: The Communication of Social Identity*. Newbury Park, CA: Sage, 1999.

Nietzsche, Friedrich. "Lecture Notes on Rhetoric." *Philosophy & Rhetoric* 16 no. 2 (1983) 94–129.

———. "On Truth and Lying in a Non-Moral Sense." In *The Portable Nietzsche*, edited by Walter Kaufman, 42–46. London: Penguin, 1954.

Nunley, Vorris. "From the Harbor to Da Academic Hood: Hush Harbors and an African American Rhetorical Tradition." In *African American Rhetoric(s): Interdisciplinary Perspectives*, edited by Elaine B. Richardson and Ronald L. Jackson, 221–42. Carbondale: Southern Illinois University Press, 2004.

Obama, Barack. "More Perfect Union" Speech Transcript, March 18, 2008. https://www.rev.com/blog/transcripts/a-more-perfect-union-speech-transcript-barack-obama.

O'Connor, Flannery. *The Habit of Being: Letters of Flannery O'Connor*. New York: Macmillan, 1988.

———. *Mystery and Manners: Occasional Prose*. New York: Macmillan, 1969.

O'Neill, Onora. *A Question of Trust: The BBC Reith Lectures 2002*. London: Cambridge University Press, 2002.

Ott, Brian L., and Greg Dickinson. *The Twitter Presidency: Donald J. Trump and the Politics of White Rage*. Oxfordshire: Routledge, 2019.

Panetta, Grace. "Trump Says People Will Be 'Very Happy' with His 2024 Decision Because 'It's a Little Boring Now.'" *Yahoo!News*, April 7, 2022. https://news.yahoo.com/trump-says-people-very-happy-172154359.html.

Papenfuss, Mary. "Trump Attacks Kim Jong Un in Bizarre Twitter Rant." *HuffPost*, November 11, 2017. https://www.huffpost.com/entry/old-trump-twiiter-kimjong-un_n_5a07a7efe4b01d21c83ee7c4.

Pendleton, Karen. "Justice Roberts Says No Such Thing as 'Obama Judge,' But This One Raised $200k for Barack." *westernjournal.com*, November 25, 2018. https://www.

westernjournal.com/justice-roberts-says-no-obama-judge-one-raised-200k-barack/.

Perelman, Chaim, and Lucie Olbrechts-Tyteca. *The New Rhetoric: A Treatise on Argumentation*. Translated by John Wilkinson and Purcell Weaver. Notre Dame: University of Notre Dame Press, 1969.

Plato. *Apology*. Munich: BookRix, 2019.

———. *Gorgias*. Translated by Benjamin Jowett. Kindle ed. Public domain. Originally published 1892.

———. *Phaedrus*. Edited by Reginald Hackforth. Cambridge: Cambridge University Press, 1972.

Politico. "Donald Trump's 2016 RNC Draft Speech Transcript." July 21, 2016. https://www.politico.com/story/2016/07/full-transcript-donald-trump-nomination-acceptance-speech-at-rnc-225974.

Posner, Eric A. *The Demagogue's Playbook: The Battle for American Democracy from the Founders to Trump*. New York: All Points, 2020.

Price, Reynolds. *A Serious Way of Wondering: The Ethics of Jesus Imagined*. New York: Simon and Schuster, 2003.

Quintilian. *The Complete Works of Quintilian*. Kindle ed. Hastings, East Sussex, UK: Delphi Classics, 2015.

Radio Free Europe/Radio Liberty. "Russian Patriarch Says Gay Marriage 'Sign of Apocalypse.'" July 21, 2013. https://www.frerl.org/a/patriarch-russia-gay-apocalypse-kirill/25052758.html.

Rddad, Youssef. "Pastor Tony Spell returns to Central church to preach despite being on house arrest." *Baton Rouge Advocate*, April 26, 2020. https://www.theadvocate.com/baton_rouge/news/coronavirus/article_9723ecae-87d1-11ea-adac-e36fdc6742a9.html.

Read, Rupert. "Climate change is a white swan." *Medium*, February 20, 2017. https://medium.com/@GreenRupertRead/climate-change-is-a-white-swan.52ae656f5ba1.

———. "What Is New in Our Time, the Truth in 'Post-Truth': A Response to Finlayson." *Nordic Wittgenstein* Review Special Issue (2019) 81–96.

Reagan, Ronald. "Morning in America." www.ushistory.org.

———. "Address to Members of the British Parliament." June 8, 1982. *Ronald Reagan Presidential Library & Museum*. https://www.reaganlibrary.gov/archives/speech/address-members-british-parliament/.

Reilly, Katie. "Read Hillary Clinton's 'Basket of Deplorables' Remarks About Donald Trump Supporters." *Time*, September 10, 2016. https://time.com/4486502/hillary-clinton-basket-of-deplorables-transcript/.

Reisman, Sam. "Trump: 'Knock the Crap Out' of Protesters, I'll Pay Legal Fees." *Mediaite*, February 1, 2016. https://www.mediaite.com/online/trump-tells-crowd-to-knock-the-crap-out-of-protesters-offers-to-pay-legal-fees/.

Repucci, Sarah, and Amy Slipowitz. *Freedom in the World 2021: Democracy Under Siege*. New York: Freedom House, 2021. https://freedomhouse.org/sites/default/files/2021-02/FIW2021_World_02252021_FINAL-web-upload.pdf.

Reuters. "Putin Warns Against Pro-Western 'Traitors' and 'Scum.'" March 16, 2022. https://www.reuters.com/world/putin-warns-russian-against-pro-western-traitors-scum-2022-03-16/.

Richards, Ivor Armstrong, and John Constable. *The Philosophy of Rhetoric*. Oxfordshire: Routledge, 2018.

Ricoeur, Paul. *Freud and Philosophy: An Essay on Interpretation*. New Delhi, India: Motilal Banarsidass, 2008.

Roberts-Miller, Patricia. "Charisma Isn't Leadership, and Other Lessons We Can Learn from Trump the Businessman." In *Faking the News: What Rhetoric Can Teach Us About Donald J. Trump,* edited by Ryan Skinnell, 95–107. Exeter: Imprint Academic, 2018.

———. "Dissent as 'Aid and Comfort to the Enemy': The Rhetorical Power of Naïve Realism and Ingroup Identity." *Rhetoric Society Quarterly* 39 no. 2 (2009) 170–88.

———. "On Being Nice to Trump Supporters." https://www.patriciarobertsmiller.com/2020/04/27/on-being-nice-to-trump-supporters/.

———. "Rhetoric and Hitler: An Introduction." https://www.patriciarobertsmiller.com/category/hitler-and-rhetoric-fs-2018/.

———. "What Putin's Rhetoric Should Tell Us about Ours." https://www.patriciarobertsmiller.com/2022/03/23/what-putins-rhetoric-should-tell-us-about-ours/.

Roosevelt, Franklin D. "Annual Message to the Congress." January 3, 1934. *Public Papers* 3:8.

———. "Address at Denton, Maryland." September 5, 1938. *Public Papers* 7:513.

———. "Address at Notre Dame University." December 9, 1935. *Public Papers* 4:495–96.

———. "Inaugural Address." *Public Papers*, March 4, 1933, 2:14–15.

———. "Second Inaugural Address." *Public Papers*, January 20 1937.

Ross, Jamie. "Trump Says He's Unimpeachable Because He's the 'Greatest' 'Most Successful' President." *Daily Beast,* January 24 2019. https://www.thedailybeast.com/trump-says-hes-unimpeachable-because-hes-the-greatest-most-successful-president.

Runciman, David. "How Climate Scepticism Turned into Something More Dangerous." *The Guardian,* July 2017. https://www.theguardian.com/environment/2017/jul/07/climate-change-denial-scepticism-cynicism-politics.

Schaefer, Donovan O. *Religious Affects*. Durham, NC: Duke University Press, 2015.

———. "Whiteness and Civilization: Shame, Race, and the Rhetoric of Donald Trump," *Communication and Critical/Cultural Studies* 17 no. 1 (2020) 1–18.

Sedgwick, Eve Kosofsky. *Touching Feeling*. Durham, NC: Duke University Press. 2003.

Shaffer, Peter. *Amadeus: A Play by Peter Shaffer*. New York: Harper Perennial, 2001.

Shapiro, Gary. *Archaeologies of Vision: Foucault and Nietzsche on Seeing and Saying*. Chicago: University of Chicago Press, 2003.

Sharlet, Jeff. "He's the Chosen One to Run America: Inside the Cult of Trump, His Rallies Are Church and He Is the Gospel.*" Vanity Fair*, June 19, 2020. https://www.vanityfair.com/news/2020/06/inside-the-cult-of-trump-his-rallies-are-church-and-he-is-the-gospel.

Sharp, Carolyn J. *Irony and Meaning in the Hebrew Bible*. Bloomington: Indiana University Press, 2008.

Singletary, Kenneth. "Trump Says He Was Joking When He Said He Was the 'Chosen One.'" *Boston Globe,* August 24 2019. https://www.bostonglobe.com/news/politics/2019/08/24/trump-says-was-joking-when-said-was-chosen-one/Q6LcjcZScJqh5jv2ekzwTP/story.html.

Skinnell, Ryan. "What Passes for Truth in the Trump Era: Telling It Like It Isn't." In *Faking the News: What Rhetoric Can Teach Us About Donald J. Trump*, edited by Ryan Skinnell, 82–101. Exeter: Imprint Academic, 2018.

Slisco, Aila. "Marjorie Taylor Greene Says Bernie Sanders, Democrats 'Swore' College Oath to Communism." *Newsweek*, April 22, 2022. https://www.newsweek.com/marjorie-taylor-greene-says-bernie-sanders-democrats-swore-college-oath-communism-1638789.

Smith ,Craig R. " Ronald Reagan's Rhetorical Re-invention of Conservatism." *Quarterly Journal of Speech* 103 no. 1–2 (2017) 33–36.

Smith, Dale. *Poets Beyond the Barricade: Rhetoric, Citizenship, and Dissent after 1960*. Tuscaloosa, AL: University of Alabama Press, 2012.

Smith, David Livingstone. *Less than Human: Why We Demean, Enslave, and Exterminate Others*. New York: St. Martin's, 2011.

Sparrow, Stephen. "Walker Percy: Seer of the Self," Catholic Education Resource Center. 2003. https://www.catholiceducation.org/en/culture/art/walker-percy-seer-of-the-self.html.

Speer, Albert. *Inside the Third Reich*. New York: Simon & Schuster, 1997.

Steudeman, Michael J. "Demagoguery and the Donald's Duplicitous Victimhood." In *Faking the News: What Rhetoric Can Teach Us about Donald J. Trump*, edited by Ryan Skinnell, 7–19. Exeter: Imprint Academic, 2018.

Stevenson, Adlai. "Let's Talk Sense to the American People:" Adlai Stevenson's Memorable 1952 Acceptance Speech." *History News Network*. https://historynewsnetwork.org/article/53682.

Stuckey, Mary E. "FDR, the Rhetoric of Vision, and the Creation of a National Synoptic State." *Quarterly Journal of Speech* 98 no. 3 (2012) 127–49.

Strachan, Owen. *Christianity and Wokeness: How the Social Justice Movement Is Hijacking the Gospel—and the Way to Stop It*. New York: Simon and Schuster, 2021.

Susteren, Greta Van. "Trump Under Obama, We Don't Have Victories Anymore." *Fox News On the Record*, October 5, 2015. https://www.foxnews.com/transcript/trump-under-obama-we-dont-have-any-victories-anymore.

Taylor, Charles. *Sources of the Self: The Making of the Modern Identity*. Cambridge: Harvard University Press, 1992.

Terrill, Robert E. "Unity and Duality in Barack Obama's 'A More Perfect Union.'" *Quarterly Journal of Speech* 95 no. 4 (2009) 363–86.

TheDailyBeast.com. "Trump: 'Knock the Crap Out' of Protesters, I'll Pay Legal Fees." February 2, 2016. https://www.thedailybeast.com/cheats/2016/02/01/trump-i-ll-pay-for-protester-beatings.

Time. "Here's Donald Trump's Presidential Announcement Speech." June 16, 2015. http://time.com/3923128/donald-trump-announcement-speech/.

———. "Read the Sermon Donald Trump Heard." January 20, 2017. https://time.com/4641208/donald-trump-robert-jeffress-st-john-episcopal-inauguration/.

Tournier, Paul. *Guilt and Grace*. New York: Harper Collins, 1962.

Tracy, David. *The Analogical Imagination: Christian Theology and the Culture of Pluralism*. New York: Herder & Herder, 1998.

Trollinger, William Vance. *God's Empire: William Bell Riley and Midwestern Fundamentalism*. Madison: University of Wisconsin Press, 1990.

Trump, Donald J. (@realDonaldTrump) February 4, 2017.

———. (@realDonaldTrump) February 25, 2020 https://t.co/zHL01NL9Sb.

———. @realDonaldTrump. July 30, 2013. https://twitter.com/real donaldtrump/status/362218621428187137.

———. @realDonaldTrump. November 21, 2018.

———. "Donald Trump Speech 'Save America' Rally Transcript January 6 speech transcript." *Voice of USA Today*, January 11, 2021. https://voiceofusatoday.com/2021/01/11/donald-trump-speech-save-america-rally-transcript-january-6/.

———. "Statement by Donald J. Trump, 45th President of the United States of America." February 23, 2022. https://www.donaldjtrump.com/news/news-zu7hr2sngq1616.

United Nations. "Global Assessment Report on Biodiversity and Ecosystem Services." https://ipbes.net/global-assessment.

Wagner, Meg, Melissa Macaya, Mike Hayes, Melissa Mahtani, Veronica Rocha, and Fernando Alfonso III. "Congress Finalizes Biden's Win after Riot Disrupts Capitol." *CNN*, January 6, 2021. https://edition.cnn.com/politics/live-news/congress-electoral-college-vote-count-2021/h_1720eb971fab58eb2f141aacc9699b4b.

Wallace, Karl R. "The Substance of Rhetoric: Good Reasons." *Quarterly Journal of Speech* 49 no. 3 (1963) 239–49.

Weaver, Richard M. *The Ethics of Rhetoric*. Oxfordshire: Routledge, 1995.

———. *Language Is Sermonic: Richard M. Weaver on the Nature of Rhetoric*. Edited by Richard L. Johannesen and Rennard Strickland. Baton Rouge: LSU Press, 1985.

———. *Life Without Prejudice, and Other Essays*. Washington, DC: H. Regnery, 1966.

West, Cornel. *Democracy Matters: Winning the Fight against Imperialism*. London: Penguin, 2005.

Whitman, Walt. "By Blue Ontario's Shore." In *Leaves of Grass*, 479. Philadelphia: D. McKay, 1900.

———. *Democratic Vistas*. New York: JS Redfield, 1871.

———. "For You, O Democracy." In *Leaves of Grass: The First Edition 1855 + The Death Bed Edition of 1892*. Kindle ed. e-artnow, 2013.

———. *Leaves of Grass: The First Edition 1855 + The Death Bed Edition of 1892*. Kindle ed. e-artnow, 2013.

———. "Song of Myself." In *In Walt We Trust: How a Queer Socialist Poet Can Save America from Itself* by John Marsh, 211. New York: New York University Press, 2015.

———. "To a Common Prostitute." *Leaves of Grass, First Edition of 1855 + The Death Bed Edition of 1892*, Kindle ed., loc. 792. e-artnow, 2013.

Whyte, J. "Sorry, But You Are Not entitled to Your Opinion." *The Times*, August 9, 2004. https://www.thetimes/co.uk/article/sorry-but-you-are-not-entitled-to-your-opinion-gpbbnzjlspd.

Williams, Tennessee. *The Glass Menagerie*. New York: New Directions, 1999.

Wilson, Jeffrey Robert. *Shakespeare and Trump*. Philadelphia: Temple University Press, 2020.

Wingard, Jennifer. "Trump's Not Just One Bad Apple: He's the Product of a Spoiled Bunch." In *Faking the News: What Rhetoric Can Teach Us about Donald Trump*, edited by Ryan Skinnell, 33–47. Exeter: Imprint Academic, 2018.

Wingfield, Mark. "Donald Trump Jr. Tells Young Conservatives that Following Jesus' Command to 'Turn the Other Cheek' Has 'Gotten Us Nothing.'" *Baptist News* December, 2021. https://baptistnews.com/article/donald-trump-jr-tells-young-conservatives-that-following-jesus-command-to-turn-the-other-cheek-has-gotten-us-nothing/#.YeWeBHrMK3A.

Wittenberg, Steven Gregg. "Churchill Appraises Hitler: 1930–1939." Unpublished thesis, College of Liberal Arts and Sciences University of Illinois Urbana, 1992. https://www.ideals.illinois.edu/bitstream/handle/2142/93994/30112111736770_opt.pdf?sequence=1.

Wittreich, Joseph. *Feminist Milton*. Ithaca, NY: Cornell University Press, 2019.

———. Wikiquote. https://en.wikiquote.org/wiki/Talk:History.

Wyschogrod, Michael. *The Body of Faith: God and the People of Israel*. Lanham, MD: Jason Aronson. 1996.

Yoder, John Howard. *Original Revolution: Essays on Christian Pacifism*. Harrisonburg, VA: Menno Media, 2003.

———. The Politics of Jesus. Grand Rapids: Eerdmans, 1994.

Young, Anna. "Rhetorics of Fear and Loathing: Donald Trump's Populist Style." In *Faking the News: What Rhetoric Can Teach Us about Donald J. Trump*, edited by Ryan Skinnell, 23–41. Exeter: Imprint Academic, 2018.

Zagacki, Kenneth S. "Vaclav Havel and the Rhetoric of Folly." *Southern Journal of Communication* 62 no. 1 (1996) 17–30.

Zorn, Eric. "Donald Trump? Seriously? Yes, Seriously." *Chicago Tribune*, June 30. 2015. https://www.chicagotribune.com/nation-world/ct-donald-trump-republicans-primary-perpect-0701-20150630-column.html.

CPSIA information can be obtained
at www.ICGtesting.com
Printed in the USA
BVHW041024240523
664807BV00002B/9